Eastern European Journalism

Before, During and After Communism

Jerome Aumente
Rutgers University

Peter Gross
California State University-Chico

Ray Hiebert
University of Maryland

Owen V. Johnson
Indiana University

Dean Mills
University of Missouri

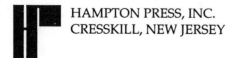

HAMPTON PRESS, INC.
CRESSKILL, NEW JERSEY

Printed in the United States of America

Library of Congress Cataloging-in-Publication Data

Eastern European journalism : before, during and after communism / Jerome Aumente . . . [et al.].
    p. cm. -- (The Hampton Press communication series)
    Includes bibliographic references and index.
    ISBN 1-57273-177-X. -- ISBN 1-57273-178-8 (pbk.)
    1. Journalism--Europe, Eastern--History. I. Series
PN5355.E852E19   1999
077--dc21   99-27158
                                         CIP

Cover photo: The Bucharest news room of Pro-TV, the leading commercial TV station in Romania. Pro-TV is a joint venture that brought together the largest Romanian media company, the Media Pro Group, and the Bermuda-based U.S. company, Central European Media Enterprises Group (CME). CME has invested in broadcast stations in almost every country in Eastern and Central Europe. 1997 photo by Fred Arn.

Hampton Press, Inc.
23 Broadway
Cresskill, NJ 07626

Eastern European Journalism

Before, During and After Communism

The Hampton Press Communication Series
Political Communication
David L. Paletz, Editor

Contents

About the Authors

Jerome Aumente is a distinguished Professor in the School of Communication, Information, and Library Studies at Rutgers, the State University of New Jersey. He was founding chair of the Department of Journalism and Mass Media, and is founding director of the Journalism Resources Institute in the school He has developed and administered over $2 million in grants to assist journalists and universities in Central and Eastern Europe, and has been to the region over 55 times since 1989. He works extensively in Poland where he established a Media Resources Center in Warsaw, and helped create the International School of Journalism at Jagiellonian University in Krakow where he is visiting professor and chairs its international advisory committee. He is codirecting a new partnership between Rutgers and the University of Sarajevo's Journalism Department. Aumente has done media work in Bosnia-Herzegovina, Serbia in Yugoslavia, Hungary, the Czech Republic, Slovakia, and Russia, in addition to Poland. He is a graduate of Rutgers University, the Columbia University Graduate School of Journalism, and was a Nieman Fellow at Harvard University. He was a print journalist for 10 years before joining Rutgers in 1969. He is the author of two other books, *New Electronic Pathways* and *Against Misinformation*.

Peter Gross is a professor at California State University-Chico in the Department of Journalism. Multilingual, he has worked and traveled extensively in Western and East/Central Europe. Since 1989, he has directed journalism workshops and lectured in a number of

East/Central European countries. Born in Romania, he was instrumental in establishing a new journalism program at the University of Timisoara, Romania, his native city. Gross has carried out training and assessment assignments since 1990 on behalf of the U.S. Information Agency and the Voice of America's International Training Program. He has also provided journalism training seminars at CSUC and/or in East/Central Europe for journalists and journalism students from Romania, Russia, and Albania. He is the author or co-author of five books, and dozens of articles and chapters published in American and European academic and professional journals, newspapers, and books. He also serves on the editorial board of *The Global Network* and *Dilema*.

Ray E. Hiebert has administered four journalism programs, as department chair at The American University, founding director of the Washington Journalism Center, founding dean of the College of Journalism at the University of Maryland, and founding director of the American Journalism Center in Budapest. He also helped establish the Voice of America's International Media Training Center and has worked extensively in Eastern Europe and Africa as a freelance journalist, lecturer, and visiting professor. He has been a Fulbright Fellow in Liberia and consultant to The Freedom Forum on journalism education in Eastern Europe. A graduate of Stanford University and the Columbia Graduate School of Journalism, he is author, co-author, editor, or co-editor of more than a dozen books on journalism, public relations, and mass communication.

Dean Mills is Professor and Dean of the Missouri School of Journalism. He received a B.A. from the University of Iowa in Journalism and Russian, an M.A. from the University of Michigan in Journalism, and the Ph.D. from the University of Illinois in Communications. He has also taught at Pennsylvania State University, where he was director of the School of Journalism; California State University-Fullerton, where he was coordinator of graduate studies; the University of Illinois and the University of Mississippi. Dr. Mills is a former Moscow and Washington correspondent for the *Baltimore Sun*. He covered the Soviet dissident movement, the Watergate scandal, the resignation of Vice President Spiro Agnew, and the Roe v. Wade Supreme Court decision. Mills does research on new media technologies, reporting techniques, and Soviet journalism.

Owen V. Johnson teaches journalism and history at Indiana University, where he has also served as director of the Russian and East European Institute. He is the author of *Slovakia 1918-1938: Education and the Making of a Nation*. His articles have appeared in *Journalism Quarterly, Journalism*

History, Studies in East European Social History, and in other journals and books. His professional journalism has been published in the *Christian Science Monitor* and broadcast on National Public Radio's "All Things Considered." He has served as president of the Slovak Studies Association, editor of the Czechoslovak History Conference Newsletter, and head of the History Division of the Association for Education in Journalism and Mass Communication. He is a recipient of the Stanley Pech Award for outstanding scholarship on Czechoslovak history.

Introduction

The ultimate outcome of the transition being played out in the old and new nation-states of East/Central European and in what used to be the Union of Soviet Socialist Republics (USSR) is still up in the air. Slow and uneven progress has been recorded in the two regions during 1990–1996. Ups and downs have frustrated their citizens, adding to the uncertainties of the transition's outcome and highlighting the renewed threat of right- or left-wing takeovers in these disparate nations whose common link is the now-rejected totalitarianism or authoritarianism justified on the still-born ideology of Marxism-Leninism.

The central role of the mass media in the post-1989 transition period has been averred by the rush to establish a multitude of new outlets, the struggles to again control or at least manipulate them, and by the emphasis placed on them in foreign aid programs carried out by Western governmental and nongovernmental institutions. Unfortunately, there have not been any models or theories to guide the systemic, contextual, and professional remaking of the mass media at the same time that they are expected to make various undefined, salutary contributions to remaking the societies in which they functioned. The pre-1989 studies of the Communist mass media did not consider the death of the Communist system and a transition from it. Therefore, a new era began without any practical or theoretical preparation for it in any area of human endeavor.

Communism's demise did not automatically establish democracy. In the mass media world of these former Communist countries, the liberation of journalists from the exigencies of Communist ideology and the control of its apparatus did not establish news media that are professional and capable of purposely, clearly, and directly contributing to the transition. The remaking of the mass media and their journalism in the regions under discussion as well as in the West was considered to be a task easily achievable by the injection of new technologies and training programs.

What was not appreciated was the difficulty of identifying new roles for the new media and journalism and, an even more burdensome task, gaining universal understanding and acceptance for them within the profession and the new political, business, and social/civic leadership. Furthermore, no one sufficiently focused on the human factor: how to change editors, producers, directors, and reporters' mentalities and habits, as well as those of media consumers, government and state officials, civic leaders of every stripe, and those who emerged as the first "captains of industry" in the now-privatizing economy. Even more important was the failure to foresee the enormous changeover from an essentially print media world to a television one and the change from a high-culture orientation to a popular, even low-culture orientation. In the context of education, specifically journalism education, a needed changeover from a theory-based education system to a practical-based one, or at least a reasonable mixture of the two, was also not anticipated and is proving a difficult process.

Additionally, both within and outside the regions under consideration, the context for remaking media and their journalism was forgotten:

- There was/is an absence of agreed on, shared societal values.
- New societal structures were or are still missing and need to solidify or be established; civil society needed to evolve in some countries and in others it needed to be established from scratch.
- The economic struggle is fierce and a continuing factor in media evolution, in their roles and professional development.
- Political struggles are at their most basic and a new political culture had to be or still has to be forged.

In most countries, the quick infusion of Western media products and technologies meant a news media that was/is still less professional in the context of opening and democratizing these former communist societies but was/is being produced with the latest or higher quality technology. The many training programs, colloquia, and seminars contributed much to the indigenous process of changing media and journalism but constitutes only part of the necessary ingredients for the remaking of the system and profession—a process that can ultimately only be carried out by the Czechs, Slovaks, Hungarians, Poles, Romanians, Albanians, Croats, Serbs, Russians, Ukrainians, Belarussians, and others who form the new nations of the former Yugoslavia and the Soviet Union.

For those of us who have focused our academic work on Soviet and East/Central European mass media even before the demise of the Communist systems, developments in the post-1989 period provide an exciting continuity to our study of historically unique types of totalitarian and authoritarian systems. Their present struggles in the transition from post-Communist, authoritarianism and in some cases (Romania and Albania) from Communist totalitarianism to post-Communist pluralism, offers a ready made laboratory for analysis and theory building in the area of mass media and journalism role(s) and effects in societal transition and development.

The bulk of work done on media and journalism evolution in East/Central Europe and the former Soviet Union has been country-specific. With benefit of hindsight, this book was conceptualized as a comparative study on five related themes, covering the pre-Communist, Communist, and post-Communist period:

1. the roots of journalism in East/Central Europe and the former Soviet Union
2. the role and effects of journalism leading up to the events of 1989
3. journalism in the transition period from 1989 to 1996
4. the contributions, trial, and tribulations of journalism in the transition period
5. the state of journalism education in the regions under consideration.

Journalism education was included because it provides a basis for understanding the degree of professionalism that was present in the news media in the pre-1989 period, at least in the context of the Marxist-Leninist role outlined for the media and the degree of "elbow room" provided. Even more importantly, it was included because it provides a measure of what the nature and extent of professionalism might be in the not-too-distant future of news media journalism in the post-1989 era.

The ultimate goal of this work is to identify patterns describing the official and unofficial media systems during the Communist period, the role(s) and effects of Communist and alternate or underground mass media and journalism (a) in the pre-1989 era and (b) in the demise of the Communist systems. More significantly, now that nearly seven years have passed since the momentous events of 1989, this work seeks to discern patterns in the role(s) and effects of new media and their journalism in the post-Communist transitions embarked on after 1989. As already mentioned, there was no model outlining the nature, processes, and affects of mass media in a post-Communist transition. The co-authors have attempted to fill that void.

Each of the co-authors has had extensive journalism training, consulting, and research experience and has written extensively on aspects of media and journalism in one or more countries in East/Central Europe and the former Soviet Republics. Each has contributed research findings, analysis, conclusions, and other thoughts to the six chapters.

The differences in style of presentation noticeable from chapter to chapter is due to the writing assignments drawn by each of the co-authors: Owen Johnson wrote Chapter 1—The Roots of Journalism in Central and Eastern Europe; Jerome Aumente wrote Chapter 2—The Role and Effects of Journalism and the Samizdat in Leading up to 1989; Ray Hiebert wrote Chapter 3—Transition: From the End of the Old Regime to 1996; Dean Mills wrote Chapter 4—Post 1989 Journalism in the Absence of Democratic Traditions; and Peter Gross wrote Chapter 5—Before, During, and After: Journalism Education. Chapter 6, the concluding chapter that seeks to outline a model of media and journalism in post-1989 transition, was jointly written.

There is no illusion about this work being the last word on mass media and journalism in the transition from Communist systems. Although this work covers the first phases of the transition, there will be a need to revisit the topic when all phases have been completed to reevaluate the model presented here for media and journalism in post-Communist transition.

Finally, the co-authors wish to thank all the institutions that have supported their various training, consulting, and research projects in East/Central Europe and the republics of the former Soviet Union and, ultimately, made this work possible: The Freedom Forum, The International Media Fund, The United States Information Agency, The Voice of America, Radio Free Europe/Radio Liberty, The International Research and Exchanges Board, The U.S.–Baltic Foundation, the Florence and John Schumann Foundation, and the U.S. Agency for International Development. The co-authors also thank photojournalist Fred Arn for allowing the use of his photograph of the Bucharest, Romania, news studio of Pro-TV on the cover of this book.

1

The Roots of Journalism in Central and Eastern Europe

Owen V. Johnson

This book about the journalism of Central and Eastern Europe defines the area following the Cold War geopolitical demarcation. After World War II the countries in this area were either part of or under the hegemony of the Soviet Union. As this chapter shows, however, the journalism and journalists in the countries of this region have widely varying historical heritages. The extent of the media's presence has been related to political freedom, economic growth, and sociocultural development. Even during the Communist period, the media's role ranged from repressed conformist to autonomous agent of change.

Despite the enormous diversity in the region, three major functions of the mass media can be identified: national, political, and economic. When national identity has been relatively unformed, as was the case in the majority of these countries in the 19th century, the media have articulated national ideas and have provided the institutions around which identities could be imagined. Without this cultural-psychological base, national political life could not succeed. When political life has been limited, the media have helped provide substitutes for political parties and parliaments. When the media have come to serve mass audiences, they have been important economic vehicles, either generating income to support political life or helping to support, through the advertising on their pages, economic growth, and development.

Given the long historical period this chapter covers—from the appearance of the first newspaper in the region in 1661 until the fall of Communism—and the broad geographic region in which the events took place, this chapter is more selective than the ones that follow. I divide the region into three general areas. The first is East Central Europe, made up today of the Czech Republic, Hungary, Poland, and Slovakia. Until 1918, most of this area was part of the Habsburg Empire and therefore very much a part of Europe. The second region is Southeastern Europe, including Albania, Bulgaria, Romania, and the former Yugoslavia. This region, built on complex national, linguistic, and imperial fault lines, was characterized by very backward development of the media. Not until communist rule after World War II did access to media become in any sense universal. The third region consists of the European parts of the former Soviet Union including the Baltic States, Ukraine, Belarus, and, of course, Russia. The authoritarian, centralized rule of the Russian Empire and later the USSR played a significant role in this region. The historical experience of each of these three regions will be divided into two or three periods. The first covers the long period from the beginnings of printing and journalism to the collapse of the old empires near or at the end of World War I.

The second period, relating to East Central and Southeastern Europe only, will incorporate the period of independence beginning in 1918 and continuing until the incorporation of the territory into the Soviet bloc. The final period will describe communist rule.

The goal of the chapter is to provide the texture of the historical background against which contemporary events take place, a significant advance over any study previously published in any language. Most research and writing on the history of this region has been focused on individual nations. Where that has not been the case there have been vast oversimplifications and generalizations. Because readers of this book are likely to be less familiar with the pre-communist media developments, this chapter provides more detail specific to each country on that period. This background also facilitates understanding the post-communist direction of media developments.

EARLY HISTORY

The local-language press of East Central Europe was developed by nations that were part of multinational empires, usually in subordinate positions. Newspapers therefore helped create modern nations and also reflected their growth. They also developed as national political institutions devoted to fostering national goals in politics, economics, and culture. These formative forays into the public sphere defined in some respects what place journalism would have in more recent times.[1]

The first Polish newspaper, *Merkuriusz Polski Ordynarjny*, edited by Jan Aleksander Gorczyn and Hieronim Pinocci, appeared in 1661, first in Krakow and then in Warsaw.[2] Hungary's first paper, published in Latin, was *Mercurius Hungaricus*, begun in 1705, although some Hungarians claim *Dracola Wajda*, begun in 1485, is the oldest publication in the world.[3] The first Hungarian-language publication, *Magyar Hirmondo*, was published in Bratislava, then a part of Hungary, 1780–88.[4] The first regularly published Czech paper was *Cesky postylion nebolizto noviny Ceske* (1719). The first Slovak paper was *Prespurske noviny*, published in the years 1783–1787. Until the 20th century, however, newspapers did not thrive in an area that, except for the Czech Lands, was primarily rural and agrarian.

Both the Czechs and Slovaks lived in the multinational Habsburg Empire, whose rulers developed an extensive system of newspaper censorship and control:

> Newspaper editors and publishers were harassed by numerous rules: only articles from the appropriate government bureaus might be published; those by private authors had to be approved. Only printers were allowed to see the censored proof-sheets; articles for the following day had to be submitted for censorship by noon the previous day. If an editor tried to oppose the censors, the forthcoming edition of his paper was threatened with a ban. Yet this was a weapon which had to be used very carefully, lest the next edition be too eagerly sought after. It was better, therefore, to threaten to remove the paper from the list of permitted publications altogether.[5]

As result, there were only 79 newspapers—the majority of them German—in the entire Habsburg empire before 1848. Only 19 of these could even discuss politics. The Czechs accounted for the largest number (13) of non-German newspapers in the empire in 1847. The collapse of centralized control during the "springtime of revolutions" in 1848 and the abolition of censorship in March of that year resulted in a quadrupling of the number of Czech newspapers.[6] Each newspaper gradually evolved a different political orientation, and came to represent a different political movement.[7] This period coincides with the emergence of Karel Havlicek, the "Father of Czech Journalism," whose three-times-a-week *Prazske noviny* was first delivered to 160 subscribers in January 1846.

From the mid-19th to the early 20th century, the Czech and Slovak press helped create a sense of Czech and Slovak national identity, even as some of the newspapers became increasingly politicized. There was little of the objective, fact-based, middle-class form of the press common in Western Europe. The first commitment of almost every newspaper was to the political party that sponsored it. In Bohemia alone, the number of political Czech newspapers grew from 10 in 1863 to 120 in 1895.[8] The most important paper during the entire period from 1861 until the outbreak of World War I was *Narodni listy*, which represented the national and liberal "Young Czech" perspective. The paper's goal was outlined by a leading Czech politician, F.L. Rieger:

> This paper aims to advance the political and public education of our nation in order that we may grow stronger in association with the other peoples of Austria and someday realize that constitutional independence which alone can guarantee the preservation of our nationality and the spiritual heritage of our past.[9]

In 1894, the paper's circulation of 14,100 made it the most widely read Czech paper. Readership was much wider, of course, because copies were readily available for perusal by patrons in cafes, bars, and reading rooms. It was the first Czech paper to use the telephone for reporting and to send regular correspondents abroad. It employed two of the best reporters of the era, Gustav Eim and Josef Penizek, and it was the Czech newspaper of record.[10]

Beginning around the turn of the century, some of the parties began to support urban, sensationalist, nonpolitical dailies. One of them was *Prazsky illustrovany kuryr*: "It was a fantastic newspaper, whose whole first page was always decorated with a drawing, preferably a hanging or some kind of bloodletting. Inside plenty of scandal and social gossip and bloody-sentimental novels, told in installments."[11]

Not only did these newspapers attract large numbers of readers to newspapers, but they helped finance the more limited-circulation political papers. They were staffed by dozens of anonymous journalists who hunted for daily happenings and court reports and prepared them for press. *Lidove noviny*, founded in Brno in 1893, became the most important Czech paper, and although not completely nonpartisan, it did develop into a very influential paper of the elite during the interwar period, even though at its peak it had only 32,000 subscribers and printed 44,000 copies daily.[12]

In Hungary the media were used in the 19th century to resurrect Hungarian national feeling and to help regain hegemony within the eastern half of the Habsburg Empire. A growing radical nationalist intelligentsia was the first to consciously employ the press to promote its cause. Lacking the money and patronage available to its more conservative aristocratic opponents, and holding a minority voice in reform Diets (parliaments) in the 1830s and 1840s, the radicals promoted their message through newspapers, pamphlets, and novels. The best example was *Pesti Hirlap*, a daily newspaper edited by Lajos Kossuth, the circulation of which reached 5,000 copies with an estimated readership of 100,000. The reach of the journal can best be understood by recalling that fewer than a million people in the country were literate and only 136,000 people could vote.[13]

Hungary offers the best evidence in pre-World War I East Central Europe of the way in which journalism overlapped with politics and literature. Many young Hungarian writers of this period made their living as newspaper journalists until they could make their mark (and living) as writers or politicians. As journalists, they could earn a living and reach the public. But, as Hungarian journalist Izidor Kalnoki observed, they did not fancy themselves as journalists:

> There are two things that matter in journalism: the knowledge of events, and the ability to comment on the events in such a way that it suits the political interests, the party affiliations, the financial wealth and the aims of the paper. . . . Thus, there is a moral and an immoral side to journalism: the first is for information and the second is for influencing the public. The first purpose is served by gray, nameless reporters, the other by great men and famous reporters.[14]

Young intellectuals on the make flooded Budapest—where half of Hungary's Hungarian-language publications were located—including 22 daily newspapers, hoping that they would not have to spend too much time in the mind-killing and ruthless profession of journalism. In this environment, older more literary and liberal newspapers such as *Pesti Naplo* and *Pesti Hirlap* began to lose their influence. In 1896, the city of Budapest permitted newsboys to hawk newspapers on the streets for the first time, the same year that the first penny newspaper, *Esti Ujsag*, was published. The Hungarian press was ethnocentric and heavily focused on domestic politics and economics. There was hardly any foreign news.[15]

Worth special mention is the birth of wired radio broadcasting in the Hungarian capital of Budapest in the late nineteenth century.

More than 6,000 subscribers listened to news broadcasts transmitted through copper wires and heard with earphones.[16]

Hungarian rule in Slovakia until 1918 made life difficult for the Slovak national press, which lacked an adequate economic base that would make possible broad circulation. In 1910, barely one-fifth of the population of Slovakia resided in towns or cities of more than 2,000 population. Perhaps 80% of the children did not attend school.[17] The only Slovak daily paper in the Hungarian kingdom before 1918 was *Slovensky dennik*, based in Budapest. There were no Slovak dailies in what is today Slovakia, although there were six Slovak daily newspapers in the United States! The Slovak press thus served to foster communication among the nation's political leaders and to help mobilize a nationally indifferent population.[18]

During much of the 18th century, the Polish king allowed only the Piarist religious order, to which he later added the Jesuits, the right of publishing newspapers. That monopoly did not come to an end until the desperate reform efforts begun in 1788 that failed to stave off the final partitions of Poland by Austria, Prussia, and Russia.[19] The 19th-century Polish press became an important national institution during the partitions. Because none of the partitioned parts had a meaningful level of self-government or local autonomy for any significant period of time, the press became the major national institution and political forum in each part of Poland. Dispersed in 120 cities, the press was a synonym for Poland, often the only organizer of Polish intellectual, social, cultural, and even sometimes political life. The Polish press was the most visible expression of Polish activities, ideas, and opinions. Polish periodicals were more likely to discuss common Polish affairs than they were to deal with issues of the respective empires in which Polish territory was found. The Polish press was an institution providing partial employment for national elites, especially the gentry. Only the church was more important than the press in preserving Polish identity. The Polish press could serve as a preserver of language and a source of employment for members of the elite. The Polish press, in contrast to the Czech, developed a greater sense of opposition to the regime. At the same time, the Polish press was even more political than the Czech or Slovak press. It was impossible to start a Polish political party without first starting a newspaper. Until Poland was reconstituted in 1918, the press served as a "parliament" by publishing the speeches of Polish members of the various imperial parliaments.[20]

The press in Austrian-occupied Poland had the strongest financial and commercial base thanks to the support of large publishing concerns in the Habsburg Empire. Subject to less political pressure, Polish journalists in Austria felt less inclined to treat politics as a cause. Prussia, in contrast, subjected the Poles in its territory both to Germanization and control by censors. Journalists either concentrated on educational and cultural development or emigrated, especially to the Russian part of Poland. Under Russia, conditions varied according to the changes in tsarist policy.

According to Jane Leftwich Curry, this experience of the partitions established many journalism traditions. These included the perception that journalists should be members of the intelligentsia who did not require special professional schooling, that committed professional journalists could also work in other professions without leaving journalism, and that strong ties should exist between journalism and politics.[21]

Early Baltic newspapers appeared under the strong influence of their German, Swedish, and Polish overlords. The history of Estonian and Latvian journalism until 1850 was closely connected with the development of the Baltic German community. Latvian press historians disagree whether the first paper in present-day Latvia was *Rigische Novellen* (1681) or *Rigische Montags (Donnertags) Ordinari Post Zeitung* (1680). The first regular newspaper in Estonia was *Revalsche Post-Zeitung* (1689–1710). Latvian and Estonian language papers came later, owing to the delayed development of a native-language intelligentsia. The first Estonian publication was *Tarto maarahwa Naddali-Leht*, founded in 1806. The first Latvian language paper was *Latviesu Avizes*, published in Jelgava beginning in 1822. The first newspaper in Lithuania was the Polish-language *Kurier Litewski* (1760–1763). Then came newspapers in French, German, Russia, and Yiddish. Apparently, the first regularly published Lithuanian weekly in Lithuania was *Lietuviskas Prietelis*, founded in 1849. Rising nationalism and renewed political activity released in the Baltics in the 1870s as part of Russian Tsar Alexander II's reforms contributed to the growth of the native-language press. The first national-oriented newspaper was *Ausra*, founded at Tilsit in 1883. In the two decades surrounding the turn of the century, other Lithuanian newspapers served as the organs of new political parties.[22] During the interwar period of Baltic independence, a party-oriented press thrived.

The political, social, and economic backwardness of Southeastern Europe delayed the development of the press. The appearance of the first newspapers and magazines was not just significant from an international standpoint but also because their mere existence gave evidence of a developing national consciousness and served to help further develop that consciousness, even if those papers were published in other than the nation's language. The first periodical publication in any of the South Slav languages, *Slaveno-Serbski Magazin*, first appeared in Venice in 1768. The first newspaper in the territory of the first Yugoslavia (and the first Slovenian newspaper), *Ljubljanske Novice*, was not founded until 1797. The Croatian press dates effectively from 1835 (*Narodna Novine*, published in Zagreb), but the most important Croatian paper in the 1848 revolution was *l'Avvenire*, published in Italian in Dubrovnik.[23] The domestic Serbian press began with *Novine Serbske* in 1834. The first Bulgarian and Romanian language papers appeared in the mid-19th century. The first newspaper to appear in a Romanian territory was the German-language *Temesvarer Nachrichten*, which began publication in April 1771. Newspapers in French and Hungarian followed during the next two decades. It was not until 1829 that the first Romanian language newspapers, *Curierul Romanesc* (Bucharest) and *Albina Romaneasca* (Iasi), were published. The first Romanian daily, *Romania*, appeared on the streets of Bucharest in 1838.[24] Even where the newspapers did exist in southeastern Europe their reach was very limited because of the rural agrarian society. *Gazeta de Transilvania*, a Romanian paper based in Blaj, Transylvania, had only 250 subscribers. It was the only Romanian-language newspaper serving the two million Romanian speakers in the province. Its readers constituted the Romanian elite in the Habsburg monarchy.[25] As had been the case with the Czech newspapers, the significance of these papers went beyond journalism:

> They gave journalistic life to the Romanian language, created a public forum for the discussion of Romanian problems, and developed and gave expression to a national consciousness. They also served as voices for the articulation of nationalistic sentiments and as catalysts for the unification and mobilization of public opinion in the struggle to achieve a united Romanian nation.[26]

The unification of the two main Romanian provinces, the recognition of the country's independence, and financial and commercial growth all helped increase the reach of the Romanian press. By the beginning of World War I, the circulation of some Romanian papers reached as high as 100,000. Newspaper staffs expanded as a result, and the first organizations of journalists were founded.[27]

In 1847, there were only one Slovene and five Croatian newspapers, numbers that only grew to six and eight during the following year of revolution.[28] Before World War I, a circulation of 10,000 copies for a Belgrade Serbian daily was unique.[29]

In Albania it was not until about 1910 that the first domestically produced newspaper was published, just two years before the country gained its independence. In the 1930s there were only three papers in Tirana, the Albanian capital, with the most important paper having a circulation of only 2,800. Communist rule would introduce the mass circulation press to Southeastern Europe.

PRECOMMUNIST RUSSIAN JOURNALISM

The precommunist history of the press of Russia and the newly independent states is one of development limited by authoritarianism or foreign
control. Even the arrival of the printing press in the 1560s failed to have
the revolutionary effect that it had in Western Europe. In a backward
cultural and social environment, the state was the driving force in the
development of printing.[30] One of the earliest forms of news periodicals
was the *kuranty*, a compilation of news and reports collected from
incoming newspapers and pamphlets received by the Diplomatic
Chancellery. Only two or three copies circulated among the Tsar and his
boyars.[31] As part of Peter the Great's effort to have the state take a more
active role in Russian life, he created *Vedomosti* (1702–1727) to make possible the public distribution of these reports. Long celebrated as the first
Russian newspaper, *Vedomosti* was more a perpetual celebration of governmental authority and military glory than a newspaper in any modern
sense.[32] It was almost only the gentry who read Russian journals for the
175 years after their first appearance.[33] Russian newspapers did not
begin to become influential until the "Great Reforms" of Alexander II,
who became tsar in 1855. Especially important was a significant easing
of censorship in 1865. Under the new law outspoken journalists thrived
on testing censorship's limits in open court, in full view of the public,
where the inconsistencies of Russian bureaucrats were readily evident.[34]
The tsar helped the development of the press in other ways, too, such as
permitting street sales, commercial advertisements and more foreign
news and courtroom coverage. During Alexander's reign the first rotary
presses arrived in Russia, greatly increasing the potential for large circulations.[35] Still, when the tsar was assassinated in 1881, only about 23,000
single issues of various periodicals were sold on Russian streets daily.

During the last three decades of rule by the Romanovs, the
printed word in Russia exploded, driven by rapid urbanization,
improvements in education, and an increasingly pluralist society. As
Jeffrey Brooks observes, "The growth of literacy, rising consumer
income, and improvements in technology facilitated a rapid expansion
of commercial publishing." Publishers began with popular fiction in the
form of single booklets, serialized novels published in cheap newspapers, short detective stories, and women's novels. Readers often con-
fused fact and fiction. According to Brooks the confusion was "sugges-
tive of the eagerness of lower class readers to accept everything that was
printed as true."[36]

It is perhaps surprising, therefore, that journalists for the mass
circulation press sought to find out and publish facts, to develop codes
of ethics, form a union, and organize schools of journalism. This may

have been done by the journalists to help set themselves apart from the intelligentsia who wrote long articles of interpretation and opinion for the "thick journals" and who disdained the popularity of the mass circulation press.

Gazeta kopeika, which promised the world each day for a kopeck, was a St. Petersburg tabloid aimed at the city's newly literate lower class. Founded in 1908, its circulation had reached 250,000 by the following year, with nearly half of each issue devoted to advertising. This paper and other tabloids, or what European journalism historians call "boulevard newspapers" reveled in apoliticism and, according to a Soviet historian, offered instead of news, "light reading, sensationalist rumors, incidents, vulgar jokes, patently indulging the prejudices of their subscribers."[37] According to a U.S. historian, however, these papers "made the news digestible for readers whose interest in politics may have been eager but not necessarily profound." She cites one of the best examples of the newspapers of this type, *Peterburgskii listok*, which "appealed to the diverse middle classes that were sorting themselves out in Russian cities at the end of the nineteenth century."[38] In most papers of this type there was a continual increase in the amount of space given to news of politics and government.[39]

Ivan Sytin, an entrepreneur as ambitious and energetic as Joseph Pulitzer or William Randolph Hearst, was the founder of the phenomenally successful *Russkoe slovo*, begun in 1895. In the early 1900s, Sytin put top priority on breaking news, giving fresh angles to older stories and making the paper graphically attractive. When war with Japan broke out in 1905, Sytin sent 20 correspondents to the combat zone. By the start of World War I, *Russkoe slovo's* circulation had reached half a million. One writer estimated that there were at least 10 readers for each copy. During the war, Sytin gave the paper a patriotic slant, and by the time the tsar was overthrown in 1917, circulation had skyrocketed to one million. Vladimir Lenin, leader of the Bolsheviks who seized power in November 1917, recognized the paper's influence when he observed that "by seizing power and taking over the banks, the factories, and Russkoe slovo, the Moscow Soviet would secure a strong foundation and enormous strength."[40]

Facilitating the growth of newspapers in late 19th-century Russia was the development of a series of news agencies, beginning with the Russian Telegraph Agency in 1866, followed by the International Telegraph Agency, the private cooperative Northern Telegraph Agency and Imperial Telegraph Agency, and the government Commercial Telegraph Agency and Petersburg Telegraph Agency. Not only did these agencies provide an additional source of news, but they also meant that Russian readers had access to foreign news, a commodity that was mostly absent in the past because of censorship.[41]

Although the Communists would later glorify the prerevolutionary impact of such political newspapers as *Pravda* and *Iskra*, they were in fact as insignificant at the time as were hundreds of other small political newspapers.

As a result of the first Russian revolution in 1905, the press won the complete withdrawal of preliminary censorship and the warning system, although tsarist officials continued to use administrative measures against leftist newspapers.

Because the Russian rulers disparaged a separate Ukrainian identity, it was difficult for Ukrainian media to develop under the tsars. From 1876 to 1917, the tsarist empire forbade the printing of books and newspapers in Ukrainian.[42] Greater progress was made in Galicia under Habsburg rule, in which the Ukrainian press came to life in 1848, then suffered a setback under the postrevolutionary crackdown. By 1875, there were 15 Ukrainian periodicals, with a triweekly being the most frequently published.[43] But real growth did not occur until the 1880s, when Ukrainian periodicals developed a mass audience for the first time. *Dilo*, an organ of the national populist movement, became the first daily in 1888. The limited Ukrainian presence in the cities was felt, however, in that, even by 1905, *Dilo's* daily circulation of 2,600 made it the largest Ukrainian daily in Lviv.[44] In Belarus, there was little significant media activity until the 20th century.

FROM INDEPENDENCE TO COMMUNISM

With the establishment of independent states in East Central and Southeastern Europe following the collapse of the Russian, Habsburg, and Ottoman Empires at the end of World War I, mass media's associations with national identity changed. Newspapers nearly everywhere were heavily engaged in domestic politics. In some countries large-circulation commercial newspapers made their presence felt.

The number of Czech and Slovak periodicals grew rapidly after the foundation of Czechoslovakia in 1918, rising from 2,060 in 1920 to 3,933 in 1931. More than 100 of these were daily papers, half of them published in Prague. Journalism was most important as a political force in the interwar period, but commercial functions grew increasingly important. Political parties were the chief financing agents for newspapers, and they kept prices low, which scared off commercial competitors. Political allegiance prevailed as a journalistic value over social responsibility. The unifying national function of journalism ceased to be important, because that role was taken over by the state's educational, scientific, and cultural institutions.

By far the most widely read Czech newspapers were the entertaining and mostly nonpolitical tabloid evening newspapers, sold largely by camelots, or news hawkers, which helped pay the bills for their dense political morning cousins. The most successful of the latter was *Vecerni Ceske slovo*, which printed up to 700,000 copies to serve a total Czech population of about seven million.[45]

The Nazi German occupation during World War II effectively eliminated national politics from the Czech press, although tabloid newspapers continued to be published. In semi-independent Slovakia, most of the newspapers served the interest of an authoritarian regime, although a few newspapers took a somewhat oppositional role. Ironically, the most open Slovak newspaper was published in Hungary.[46] Czech and Slovak journalism revived after the end of the war, although several of the leading newspapers of the interwar period were not allowed to reappear because the parties that they supported had been charged with collaborating with Nazi Germany. The communist party, the strongest in the country, tried to exert control on the press through the Ministry of Information by issuing a series of edicts and regulations and applications of old laws, but most of the time it was ignored.[47]

The press was an inseparable part of Polish politics during the interwar period. Several large publishing companies were established with modern equipment, most notably *Illustrowany Kurier Codzienny* in Cracow. These publications tended to be nonpolitical in outlook, but regional and social divisions were reflected in the slow development of the national press and in the development of a federal-style journalists' organization. A three-tier press developed: high-status, costly (and therefore with limited circulation) journals; middle-level political journals; and a money-making tabloid press in the cities. A newspaper was a vital part of a political party's activity. More than 40 daily newspapers were published in Warsaw at the end of 1935, including four by a single company, Dom Prasy. When Marshal Jozef Pilsudski seized power in 1926, one of his first steps was the establishment of a centralized system controlled by a small handful of political leaders to promote the government and its views. It employed more newspapers with higher press runs than any competitor, and it took over the Polish press agency. Threats, rewards, and financial backing were all employed to help bring the press into line. By 1936, the army was in charge of the press. The government press apparatus did not, however, reach as far as the Communist control later would, a reflection of the fragmented, specialized nature of the interwar government, with its rivalries among agencies and individuals. This preserved a diversity of thought and a basic freedom of expression until Nazi Germany invaded Poland in

September 1939. The occupation of Poland by Germany and the USSR put an end to the legal publication of the press. The vacuum was filled by several thousand underground titles.[48]

There was very limited freedom of the press in interwar Hungary, a reaction, in part, to the brief period of Communist rule at the end of World War I. Every paper needed a license to publish, and only half of the papers that applied received the license. In addition there were broad and arbitrary definitions of sedition; and discussion of foreign policy was off limits. The press in Hungary was different from that of any other East Central European country during World War II. When Germany invaded Poland at the beginning of the war, the Hungarian government instituted preventive censorship with a special committee, operating under the prime minister and the foreign minister, directed to read every published word. This was a positive step because journalists and editors were constantly able to test the limits, and even the Hungarian government sought to be as open as possible. Journalists developed a more convoluted writing style in an effort to get around censorship. This change, which required readers to learn to read between the lines, proved excellent preparation for the Communist system that would be instituted in 1947. The German occupation of the country in 1944 resulted in the closing of all left-wing papers and the replacement of all editors on progovernment newspapers.[49]

To the south, aided by modernization and new printing plants, the number of newspapers in Romania doubled during the interwar period. By 1936, there were 2,300 publications, including 118 daily papers. Most newspapers remained political vehicles, although the largest circulations, exceeding 100,000, were achieved by independent publications such as *Lupta, Timpul, Semnalul,* and *Jurnalul.* There was also an increase in the number of periodicals targeted at specific populations such as men, women, social groups, and generations. As Gross noted, "Journalism associations and unions also proliferated, testimony to the professionalization of journalism and the journalists' concerns for educational and journalistic standards, press freedoms, and journalists' rights." Their situation was made more difficult as the interwar period progressed, and Romanian government leaders, many under the influence of fascism, tightened their controls on the press. The government set up a Ministry of Propaganda to further its aims. A brief period of vigorous press life took place during the years 1944–47, aided by the almost complete abolition of press controls. The circulation of the Peasant Party newspaper *Curierul* reached 350,000. The seizure of control by the communist party in 1947 ended this brief period. The lively Romanian press would reappear only in 1990.[50]

In interwar Yugoslavia newspaper growth was limited by a population that was 70% illiterate and 85% agricultural. No newspaper could aspire to significant statewide circulation given the relatively underdeveloped transportation and communication system and the use of two alphabets. The largest paper in the country was the relatively independent Serb paper, *Politika* (80,000), followed by the more opinionated *Vreme* (40,000). There were also several smaller tabloids. The largest Croatian paper was *Novosti* (20,000).[51] During World War II, an estimated 3,500 papers were published in Yugoslavia, most of them by military units engaged either in civil war or fighting the Germans. Some of the journalists who worked on these papers became prominent postwar journalists.[52]

JOURNALISM IN THE SOVIET UNION

The picture most common in the west of Communist journalism was distorted. Except for the worst days of Stalinism, Soviet media were never as monolithic and uninformative as Western readers tended to describe them. Not only was the Cold War to blame for the misrepresentation, but also the Western philosophy of the media that has favored an objective, watchdog understanding of the role of the press.[53] Many Westerners doubted that a press whose mission was to serve the interests of a party could in any way be a somewhat independent force.

Yet Soviet journalists were a variegated group. Journalists in other countries ruled by Communist parties exhibited still greater diversity. Some tested the boundaries of the permissible and the possible. Some quietly advanced the interests of their patrons, who might reflect a perspective shared by a specific portion of the population such as urban dwellers, workers, collective farmers, or scientists. Soviet journalists found that the lessons they had learned during their training, whether in formal journalism education or within the collective at their place of work, conflicted with the reality of their jobs, and they sought through professionalism to resolve the conflicts. On each occasion when reform became possible, some journalists allied themselves with the reformers against the conservatives. The young men and women who supported Nikita Khrushchev's reform efforts in the late 1950s and early 1960s included many journalists. These *shestdesiatniki* (people of the sixties) retreated to more secluded positions in society when Leonid Brezhnev, scared by the reform movement of the "Prague Spring" in Czechoslovakia in 1968, tightened the reins. But they emerged again in the 1980s and were some of the leading agents of reform under Mikhail Gorbachev's *glasnost*.[54]

When the Bolsheviks came to power in 1917 as Russian tsarist power collapsed under both internal pressure and the impact of World War I, the overwhelming majority of the people that came to be included in the Soviet Union were out of reach of the mass media. Many were illiterate. A poorly developed infrastructure meant that distribution of newspapers was difficult. In the beginning the Soviet Union was primarily a rural society whose peasants saw little need for the media.

The type of paper envisioned by Lenin was a far cry from the commercial press that had been developing in the cities of Russia. In *What Is To Be Done?* Lenin explained how a national newspaper could serve as a coordinating center for a political movement in order to prevent the development of localism. But he was writing about an opposition movement; he gave far less thought to how to organize the press should the Bolsheviks gain power.

When the provisional government collapsed and Lenin and his comrades took over, they began by limiting the opposition press. The Council of People's Commissars, just two days after they took control, passed a resolution giving them the right to close down papers that advocated resistance or tried to sow disorder. But the shortage of paper, the cessation of advertisements, the nationalizing of printing facilities, and disrupted distribution were more effective in limiting the influence of the bourgeois press.

The new Soviet press did not fare much better, as Peter Kenez has pointed out:

> There was general agreement among the revolutionaries who concerned themselves with journalism that the press functioned poorly and could not carry out its assigned tasks. Observers criticized the content and format of the newspapers and also recognized their technical poverty. Worst of all, from the point of view of the Soviet leadership, their circulation remained low.[55]

In addition to the lack of paper, the Bolsheviks had few trained journalists, faced distribution difficulties, and had no desire or sense of how to make the press attractive. As Brooks noted, "The link between producers and consumers that the market had provided was cut, and Bolshevik publishers did not have to offer what consumers wished to read."[56] When journalists tried to intervene by taking control of the distribution of paper and information, the communist party resisted.

When the New Economic Policy (NEP) required that newspapers be self-supporting, there was a precipitous decline in circulation. *Bednota*, the first Soviet paper designed for the ordinary reader, saw its circulation drop from 800,000 to 35,000 when its readers were forced to pay for it.[57] By August 1922, total newspaper circulation in Russia had declined to 993,050, less than the number of copies that had been printed by *Russkoe slovo* alone in 1917. The solution was to restore advertising and to think about creating more attractive newspapers. The party also began to create newspapers to serve specialized audiences such as soldiers (*Krasnaia zvezda*) and peasants (*Krestianska gazeta*).[58] Still, the quantity of printed material in the USSR did not again reach prerevolutionary levels until the late 1920s.[59]

Kaltenborn referred to the Soviet Union of the 1920s as "Propaganda Land." "Nowhere else," he wrote, "does a government devote itself so religiously to the spreading of ideas. . . . If the Russian people were governed as well as they are propagandized, the Red regime would stand as a model."[60] Although it is true that the primary role of the Soviet press was propaganda, the media established for themselves already in the 1920s other important roles: They provided a basic summary of the most important national and international news; their solicitation of reader and correspondent letters were designed to correct societal wrongs; and they helped to generate and popularize the "new Soviet public culture."[61]

In the West, the popular understanding of these newspapers was that they were dull and gray. As historian Jeffrey Brooks observed, the truth was more complicated:

> The editors and journalists of the central press . . . produced an image of Soviet society that was accepted among a wide circle of friendly readers who had a stake in the system and were willing to believe in a public explanation that served their interests.[62]

From the early days of Soviet rule, *Pravda* was the preeminent authoritative voice. In the decade from 1918–28, official editorials, speeches, articles and announcements constituted roughly half the space in *Pravda* devoted to domestic affairs.[63] *Pravda's* combination of information, inspiration, and activity was a distinct change in the culture of journalism from *Russkoe slovo*. The result in the Soviet Union of the 1920s was a "gulf between the public values the Bolsheviks promoted and the values ordinary people actually held." The semi-educated, upwardly mobile read *Krest'ianskaia gazeta* and *Rabochaia gazeta*.[64]

Even in the darkest days of Stalinist repression in the 1930s, newspapers were hardly homogeneous:

> [Soviet central newspapers] did not all say the same thing, except on a few issues of particular political moment and delicacy. The newspapers had their own individual profiles, partly determined by their official focus and constituencies . . . and partly reflecting editorial judgment and the strengths and interests of their journalists.[65]

During the days of terror in the 1930s, papers like *Pravda* and *Izvestia* carried advertisements whose themes of conscious consumption would almost have fit in U.S. newspapers of the same decade. This is a far cry from the paper Vladimir Lenin had in mind when he founded *Pravda* in 1912 and who called on the media to serve as a collective propagandist, agitator, and organizer.

Although constrained by certain limits, the journalists had considerable autonomy:

> Editors and authors produced newspapers following party directives of varying distinctness but the result, even in *Pravda*, was a discourse derived as much from the staff's spontaneous, if politically constrained, reactions to Soviet life as from the leaders' wishes. The newspaper was therefore also the work of people who verbalized their own experiences, lexicons and observations in an effort to make the world around them intelligible within the official given limits.[66]

The journalists of the 1920s tended toward journalistic professionalism, whether they were ardent communists, apolitical, or ambitious. Some of this professionalism was rooted out at the end of the New Economic Plan in the late 1920s. It was replaced by the tight harnessing of the media to serve the purposes of Joseph Stalin, the man who had replaced Lenin as leader of the communist party:

> Journalists . . . were intimidated by the prevailing political atmosphere into relative ideological and stylistic uniformity. . . . [N]egative phenomena ceased to be reported, unless it was in the interests of Stalin's group to uncover economic "sabotage", political "deviations", or other "anti-social" manifestations which could be used to advantage in the inner-Party struggle.[67]

After the death of Stalin journalistic professionalism reemerged to influence strongly young journalists of the Khrushchev period, some of whom would in the glasnost period of Mikhail Gorbachev play leading roles as independent, muckraking journalists. It drew support from Khrushchev himself, from academically trained journalists, and from the rising educational level and urbanization of the Soviet population. Most significant, perhaps, was the decision by political leaders to preference a media of persuasion over the use of power and force.[68] Public relations replaced prison.

The new professionalism of the 1950s was reflected in the founding of the Union of Soviet Journalists and in the development of a system of journalism education at the university level. By 1970, there were nearly 50,000 professional journalists, or "workers of the pen, the television screen and the radio microphone."[69]

Radio was the first medium to gain an important role throughout Soviet society. Because there were so many areas of the Soviet Union beyond the reach of electricity, a system of wired networks was used. Receivers were placed in individual houses or apartments and broadcasts were distributed as well through a system of loudspeakers. The system was cheaper than over-the-air broadcasting and also helped to limit the access of the Soviet population to competing foreign broadcasts. Not until 1963 would the number of wave receivers in the Soviet Union exceed the number of wired receivers.[70]

It was not until the 1960s and 1970s that the printed Soviet word began to reach the broad range of people. Annual circulation of periodicals, which had peaked at 340 million in 1930, was still only 267 million in 1953. But by 1968 there were 2,362 billion copies.[71] Newspaper circulation, totaling only 44.2 million copies the year Stalin died, jumped to 125.5 million just 15 years later.[72] The Soviet journalists who wrote for these publications had multiple roles: ideological warrior, literary craftsman, publicist, investigative reporter, citizen's friend, and member of the collective. The most important newspapers were the all-Union papers such as *Pravda* and *Izvestia*, whose circulations climbed past 10 million. TASS played a particularly important role in the modern era, providing between a third and a half of all content for most newspapers.[73] Journalism was designed to serve the party through a complex system of appointments, rewards, party control, and censorship. Glavlit (the acronym stood for Main Directorate on Matters of Literature and Publishing) supervised the censorship.

The successors to party leader Nikita Khrushchev in the mid-1960s were nervous about the possibilities he had offered to the mass media for a more truthful representation of society. They replaced the editors of many journals with more cautious journalists who would be less likely to venture into unacceptable areas. Not until the Czechoslovak political reforms of 1968 (the "Prague Spring"), which Soviet leaders believed was instigated by the mass media, did they take a much more active role in directing the activities of the Soviet (and in some cases, other East European) media. The tighter control they instituted was counterproductive. It diminished the effectiveness of the media and diminished the attention and confidence of the population, particularly among the intelligentsia.[74] Professionalism was in crisis in Soviet journalism: Far fewer people were applying for journalism education; journalists—although only dimly aware of their readers—recognized the ineffectiveness of Soviet media policy; and journalists outside the major media institutions were overworked.[75]

By the last years of Leonid Brezhnev, the Soviet communist party leader who died in 1982, the picture painted in Soviet media about the country differed substantially from reality. Success stories in the media conflicted with the shortages and cramped quarters of daily lives. Even communist party officials of high rank were deceived by the propaganda of success.

A tiny number of dissidents who tried to tell a different story were largely unheard in their own country.[76] For disenchanted members of the intelligentsia, samizdat literature "undermined the entire moral legitimacy of the regime."[77] The circulation of these publications was largely in the cities. They rarely found their way into the countryside. How important foreign broadcasts were, such as those from Radio Liberty or the BBC, is a matter of dispute. Radio Liberty officials used arcane methods to measure what they claimed was a substantial listenership. But they had to massage so much of the data obtained from listeners who traveled abroad that they must be called into question. If the USSR was like the other communist countries of Central and Eastern Europe, polls were taken to gauge listenership, but the audience's lack of trust in the poll takers surely would also call their results into question. What does seem clear is that those who listened to foreign radios had already decided the Soviet system was dysfunctional, or they were regime officials who turned to foreign radio to access the domestic information unavailable from domestic sources that they found necessary to carry out their jobs.[78]

The most profound change in Soviet media under Leonid Brezhnev was the penetration of television into nearly every corner of the Soviet Union. Television was the most democratic of media because no matter what their economic, political, or educational status, all viewers saw the same programs. This was a distinct contrast to the printed press, whose audience was segmented. This was the most thorough penetration of any Soviet medium into the countryside. The people of the Soviet Union, although professing to be interested in TV news, tended to use television "primarily for entertainment and relaxation." Watching television increased the private sphere of people's lives, making them less accessible to organized political forces. Television was particularly welcomed by the population that was leaving the countryside and flooding into the cities. Torn from their rural roots, television became their new family. People watched TV news through a prism: They would ignore irrelevant or boring presentations, but would latch on instantly to any interesting story. This reception posed a challenge for Soviet TV managers who were charged with delivering a prescribed political message because they knew that without attractive packaging the audience would tune out.[79]

The preceding issues provided the challenge that faced Mikhail Gorbachev when in 1985 he replaced Konstantin Chernenko, the third successive ailing Soviet leader. Gorbachev had recognized for some time that undoctored facts and figures were necessary if party officials and the public were to be persuaded about the need for reform. He sought the transparency of public life. Given that he was a firm believer in the leading role of the communist party, he did not equate transparency with freedom of the press. Had the party leadership and its bureaucracy been more interested in making the communist system work rather than in preserving their power, the final outcome of glasnost might have been different. Glasnost went through three phases: supporter of economic reform, supporter of political reform within a one-party system, and advocacy of free speech.[80] At each stage, journalists and politicians differed on the wisdom of glasnost.

When Gorbachev first called for glasnost in 1985, only a few Soviet media institutions responded at first. Eventually, though, journalism helped to open up Soviet society by rewriting history, exposing corruption and inefficiency, and promoting debate and discussion. Glasnost meant more timeliness, an expansion in the news agenda, more factual information, more human interest, and more "moderately negative" stories. It also meant the use of more normal language.[81] Officially, *Pravda* was leading the media reform effort:

> We communist journalists working in different national conditions make no secret of our satisfaction when we say that *Pravda* is our friend. . . . The newspaper puts a public mirror to those who fail to match their words with deeds. It is an inspiration to the party and the society for fresh achievements. It has been developing a collective dialogue. Nothing is out of bounds for criticism. *Pravda* is campaigning for a radical restructuring of every sphere of life, and is itself doing the same thing in its content, structure and makeup. An imaginative effort is being made to give journalism a more effective edge.[82]

Glasnost certainly contributed to the end of the Soviet Union, but journalism and mass media could not have accomplished this on their own. Gorbachev and his advisers initiated glasnost. It gained strength with their blessing. Only a minority of journalists and media institutions were active proponents of glasnost. In many cases the media simply relayed the information received from political sources. The major accomplishment of the media may have been to confirm information such as about the string of prison camps called the *gulag* that people had previously known individually. Through the media this information became public. The inability of the Communist party to organize itself sufficiently for reform efforts in response to this new public knowledge demonstrated for all to see the party's bankruptcy.

The Soviet Union was a remarkably complex collection of nations, nationalities, and ethnic groups. The USSR was composed of 15 national republics with Russia by far the largest. Russian was the lingua franca of the country: All the central publications such as *Pravda* and *Izvestia* were in Russian; so was Soviet television. More than 70 languages were used in Soviet publications. Managing this ethnic complex was a challenge for the Soviet leadership. Policing and censoring the non-Russian media posed special problems. Policies regarding ethnic media varied over time.

When the Soviet Union was created in 1922, some nationalities did not have written languages, let alone a printed press. The establishment of ethnic and republic boundaries followed a general policy of divide and conquer. Ukraine was left with a significant Russian population. Belorussia (now called Belarus) had few Belarussian native speakers living in its cities.[83] The primary goal of the Soviet Union in its nationality policy was the maintenance of the unity of the country. Russian was promoted as the basic language of communication. Other languages were promoted to facilitate the sending of political messages to the entire population. Controls on the use of national languages were instituted to reduce the likelihood of national opposition.

This chapter would be considerably longer if the experience of each of the six former republics of the Soviet Union (outside of Russia) that are included in this book were discussed in its justified completeness.[84] Rather, by way of example, several particularly important developments are presented.

During the brief period of the independence of the Baltic states between 1918 and 1940, there was a significant growth in the circulation of newspapers. Latvia, for instance, ranked fourth in Europe in the number of newspapers and magazines per capita. *Jaunakas Zinas* printed 200,000 copies by 1938, making it the largest newspaper in the country's history. In fact, its circulation was more than all the country's other newspapers put together. One out of every 10 Latvians purchased the paper.[85] Circulation of the Baltic press dropped significantly after the USSR seized control of the three countries. Conditions improved not only there but in other Soviet republics as part of the Soviet reform period, the "Thaw" which started with Nikita Khrushchev's denunciation of Stalin at the 1956 communist party congress. This moderation ceased in the late 1960s after the Soviet leadership became aware of how the more open media in Czechoslovakia had an impact on western Ukraine. The politburo colleagues resolved that such developments would have to cease. By the mid-1970s, media serving the non-Russian population of the Soviet Union practically ceased to expand their reach. The leadership set about on a policy of promoting unrestricted growth of the Russian-language press and restricting publications in other languages.[86] Still, the republican languages fared better than those of the more minor language groups.[87] Soviet leaders feared the potential national republican movements gaining strength through the exercise of national media. There is evidence that this national media, combined with foreign radio broadcasts and word-of-mouth communication, strengthened national identity.[88]

The way in which national journalists and their media seized the initiative under Gorbachev provided strong evidence not only of the strength of national movements, but also in the way national media could be mobilized in support of national goals by providing a national perspective on events. By reporting on the successful outcome of national demonstrations, the media stimulated national activism.[89] In the Baltic countries, the media functioned as political party standins.[90] Their national strength was magnified because until political pluralism was allowed, no other organizing framework—other than occupational interest groups—was permitted.[91] Soviet leadership was optimistic that the new openness could be used in television as a powerful and responsive integrating force: they were wrong.[92]

Not all Soviet national-language media under glasnost became active in the national cause. In part it depended on the degree of success of Soviet nationality policy.[93] Near the end of Soviet rule, Belorussian media were still in a minority in Belorussia, whereas Russian remained the dominant language of the republican media. Local newspapers that had published before 1990 in both Russian and Belorussian were dropping the latter.[94] In Ukraine, political conservatism and heavy-handed censorship that was a response to national assertion two decades earlier limited the media role as a conveyor of national renewal. Vitalii Korotich, Ukraine's most famous reform journalist under *glasnost*, found success in the central Russian language magazine *Ogonek*. At the same time that central Soviet television was alive with exciting and enticing programs, "it was as if life at Ukrainian Television had died."[95]

Outside Moscow and in the non-Russian republics, the extent of openness in the press depended on the local party and government leadership. The Baltic republics used the opportunities to promote national patriotism.

COMMUNIST RULE IN EASTERN EUROPE

Despite outward similarities, there was an enormous difference in the roles and functions of the mass media in the various countries of East

Central and Southeastern Europe under Communism. Where they were more liberal, as in Poland, Hungary and Yugoslavia, there was a national subtext as well as a significant element of entertainment. The mass media were generally the most visible part of the liberalizing forces at play in Poland in 1956, and 1980–81, in Hungary in 1956 and in Czechoslovakia in 1968. That does not mean that journalism was necessarily a liberalizing force; rather, reformers used the media to convey their own liberal goals.

The Communist parties of the area were the dominant force in journalism, but the party presence in the media was not necessarily monolithic. Different publications served different parts of the population and represented in a modified way their goals. The main party organs were newspapers of record, providing official political roadmaps for party officials and other readers who needed to be informed. These newspapers, such as *Trybuna Ludu* in Poland, *Rude pravo* in Czechoslovakia, *Nepszabadsag* in Hungary, *Rabotnichesko delo* in Bulgaria, *Neues Deutschland* in Germany, *Scinteia* in Romania, and *Zeri i Popullit* in Albania, generally had the largest circulations in their respective countries. Newspapers aimed at young people, on the contrary, tended to be more open and to promote the aims of their readers as well as the party aims for young people. Furthermore, problems of particular concern to one audience were given considerable attention in the appropriate paper and less attention elsewhere. In 1982, when the specter of unemployment arose for some high school and college graduates in Czechoslovakia, there were articles about the subject in the Czech and Slovak youth newspapers, but little discussion of the subject in other media. This meant that a person who wanted to be broadly informed had to buy a variety of newspapers, and because of the low cost some people did.

The Communist regimes created a mass reading and viewing public, something that had not existed before. Nearly everyone read newspapers, and as television spread across the region in the 1950s and 1960s, its reach was nearly universal. A first TV channel was generally followed a decade or two later by more specialized fare on a second channel. Regimes viewed television as extremely important because it was the medium through which they could reach their entire populations. The messages they sent, however, were not always the messages the population received. A significant part of the population did not care to concern itself with the finer points of political rhetoric or found them irrelevant. In parts of Poland, East Germany, Czechoslovakia, Hungary, and Yugoslavia, citizens could watch Western television programs, and they did. What interested them in foreign television fare, however, was the entertainment, not the news. Only in East Germany, where language was not a barrier, was there some public interest in foreign television news.

In some of the East Central and Southeast European countries, the mass media provided a significant source of income for the ruling parties, just as they did in the Soviet Union.[96] In the sometimes peculiar cost-accounting plans, the costs of printed media doing their business did not equal the actual costs. News agency services, newsprint, printing, and distribution were available to newspapers very cheaply. Media owners passed back to the party a significant portion of their income, which in some cases, such as Poland, provided a significant part of the party's operating budgets. (This did not apply, of course, to broadcasting.)

Media played a significant role in political reform and revolution in all three Central European countries. The reforms of the Prague Spring of 1968 in Czechoslovakia were presaged in the Slovak press, given almost free rein by Alexander Dubcek after he became head of the Communist Party of Slovakia in 1963.[97] In 1968, the Czech press became particularly lively and independent. It was uncensored, informative, critical, and popular.[98] This was a matter of major concern to the Soviet overlords. Following the invasion by the Soviet Union and allied armies in 1968, control over the Czech and Slovak media was reestablished. Hundreds of journalists, mostly Czechs, lost their jobs. Even those who stayed would remain cautious right up to the end of Communist rule, fearful that if they tried to challenge the powers that be again, the result would be another invasion.

One of the most consistently open media systems under communist rule was found in Poland. Although the press and broadcasting were subject to various controls, many topics that were taboo elsewhere were vigorously discussed in the Polish media. Beginning as early as 1956, the behavior of Polish journalists was characterized by strong elements of professionalism. Reporters and editors were committed to stretching the limits of the possible in ongoing battles with censors. They used each of the crises of communist rule (1956, 1968, 1970, 1976, 1980–81) to argue that a more open media could help to alleviate tensions before they led to societal explosions. Many journalists became political leaders.

Given this relative journalistic freedom, it may seem surprising that changes in the press were one of the major demands of the rebellious Solidarity movement that first sprang to life in the shipyards of Gdansk in August 1980. Two factors were involved. One was that Polish journalists, for all of their freedom, were not sufficiently aware of the discontent of Polish society as they found out when they went to visit the striking shipyard workers. The other factor is that Solidarity was seeking its own access to the media, to break the Communist monopoly on communication channels. This would help the union to keep pressure on the regime to fulfill its promises. The emergence of the trade union

Solidarity speeded up the formation of a distinctly independent media that went underground after the declaration of martial law in 1981.[99]

The martial law declaration split Poland's journalists. The more militant journalists refused to work for most state and party publications. They either wrote for obscure official media such as a newspaper for the blind or wrote for the underground newspapers, whose total circulation reached as high as two million. Other journalists committed themselves to the martial law regime. Wieslaw Gornicki, for instance, became a speechwriter for President Wojciech Jaruzelski, whereas Jerzy Urban became the government's very visible press spokesman. Mieczyslaw Rakowski, once the editor of *Polityka*, the official opposition weekly, who had already become deputy prime minister in the reform government, eventually wound up as the Communist party's last leader. Even though he remained a loyal supporter of the Communist regime, he interceded where he could to assist fellow journalists who were in trouble with authorities. Some journalists, such as Nieman Fellow Andrzej Wroblewski, withdrew from active work in journalism for much of the 1980s.

What was particularly striking about the Polish media in the 1980s was the effort by the regime, having cracked down on the population on so many different occasions, to employ the media in an idealistic but doomed effort to win back the support of the populace. Urban held regular press conferences with the domestic and foreign media at which almost all topics could be discussed. These meetings were often televised, and their stenographic record was published in the government newspaper *Rzeczpospolita*. To distract the audience from political matters, television broadcast a popular Brazilian telenovella, "Isaura, the Slave Girl," which proved so popular that life in Poland virtually came to a standstill when the program came on the air. Polish radio took to presenting a weekly program of highlights from Radio Free Europe broadcasts.

The Polish media of the 1980s, although the most open media system in the communist bloc, demonstrated the failure of Communist media management. A Westerner whose only visit to a Communist country was to Poland would have noticed the censorship; would have been aware that some subjects were only discussed away from the prying ears of people and secret microphones; would have seen millions of Poles listening to broadcasts from the BBC, Voice of America, and Radio Free Europe; would have come across a wide range of underground publications (including postage stamps); and would have found some journalists in prison. It might have seemed to the visitor that everything bad that had been said about the Communist system was true. But if that same individual had visited other Communist countries, it would have been clear that the other systems were more repressive of their media systems, that journalists there were much more cautious and had far fewer opportunities to open up the system, and that the content of the media was more overtly political (Communist).

The primary function of Communist media, as propagandist and motivator, had demonstrated its failure over the course of several decades in Poland. "The press lies," a popular slogan in the heady days of 1980, provides the best evidence of this failure. The party's second approach, to coopt the media and through the media, the public, by treating them as allies in working together for the better future of Poland (a distinctly national, as opposed to Communist theme), had demonstrably failed with the crackdown on December 13, 1981. The final approach, allowing the most open media that the neighbor Soviet Union might permit, including lively discussion of many critical issues and broadcasting distinctly nonpolitical programs such as Kojak and Dallas, was designed to prevent the kinds of explosions that had broken out in the previous three decades. But the audience could no longer be seduced to support the communist system. There was nothing the communist party could do but yield its monopoly on politics. That is what happened in Spring 1989.

The Hungarian press and the intellectuals who wrote for it have traditionally been considered a major factor in the failed 1956 revolution. But after the Soviet invasion that spelled the end to that revolution, the regime's handling of the media provided a distinct contrast to the Czechoslovak experience. Within a few years, Hungarian journalists were welcome to write about a wide range of topics, with only a few subjects, including the 1956 revolution, off limits. The difference between the Czechoslovak and Hungarian experience can be explained by party leadership. Gustav Husak, who spent a decade in Communist prison in Czechoslovak, took over the leadership of the Communist Party of Czechoslovakia in April 1969. Although he was well aware of the price that could be exacted from those who stepped out of line in Stalinist days, he was unable to recognize that times had change and Stalinist rigidity was a thing of the past. Janos Kadar, installed by the Soviet invaders as head of the Hungarian Communist party, argued to his masters that in order to win back the support of the populace, goulash Communism was necessary, based on the slogan, "He who is not against us, is with us." The traditional leadership position of Hungarian intellectuals, exercised through journalism, could be maintained under this arrangement.

The media in Southeastern Europe had widely varying functions under communist rule. The media in Yugoslavia were among the freest in the communist bloc, and the Yugoslav News Agency Tanjug was a highly respected independent agency serving an international audience. Yugoslav media had the same degree of autonomy as did U.S. journalists. But the regional republic base of the media contained the roots of later destruction.[100] After the death of longtime leader Josip Broz Tito, however, the Yugoslav media increasingly were called into the service of national interests.

The role of Romania's media during Communist rule varied according to the style and politics of the party leadership. Gross outlines four stages:

1. 1947–1965: Closure of the old and attempts at stabilizing the newly established Communist regime.
2. 1965–1971: Attempts at softening the face of Communism, a degree of openness to some Western media, books, and the like.
3. 1971–1978: Romania's version of China's cultural revolution, with a highly nationalist theme and the push to create "the new socialist man."
4. 1978–1989: The dominance of an ever-increasing personality cult and Stalinist dictatorship.[101]

During the last period Romania was a "media black hole" with a press whose main task was to worship party and state leader Nicolae Ceausescu. It meant secret police involvement, the closure of overseas news bureaus, and extreme limits on travel. Severe restrictions on energy consumption drastically reduced television broadcast time to only a couple hours each evening.[102]

The Albanian Communist rulers may have controlled the press more tightly than Ceausescu, but the media reach was very limited until late in the Communist period. The sole continually published daily newspaper was *Zeri i Popullit*, whose circulation was estimated at 110,000, or about one copy for every 20 Albanians. The only other daily newspaper, *Bashkimi* (35,000 copies), also a four-page broadsheet, was published by a coalition of communist-led organizations. Most newspapers had no more than four columns per page.

The first television broadcasts in Albania took place in 1960, but unlike most other countries, broadcast day growth was very slow. As late as 1969, television was still on the air only three times a week for three hours each day. Two years later, the installation of a French-built transmitter resulted in daily transmissions of four and a half hours a day. As late as 1980, there were only 10,000 TV sets in the country.[103] Albanian TV's main claim to fame was that, in 1984, it had the highest percentage of national program production in Europe.[104] The adoption of color broadcasting in 1984 might have contributed to substantial growth of TV sets in the 1980s. But most people still had black-and-white sets because an Albanian-assembled color TV set cost 10 times a monthly salary, and in contrast to other East European countries, alternative sources of income that would make possible the accumulation of so much money did not exist.[105] In a poor country, with tight political control, mass media were a luxury. Instead, it seems likely that it was the availability of foreign television that led to the growth in TV sets. With the death of strongman Enver Hoxha, who had kept the watching of foreign programs a crime, television aerials were increasingly turned westward and southward. Those in the south could pick up signals from the Greek island of Corfu. To the north, where 75% of the TV sets were to be found, Italian television was dominant.[106] This process was speeded up when the Italian government monopoly on television was ended and the multiplicity of Italian TV stations destroyed the Albanian government's jamming efforts.

What happened in Albania under Communist rule was a late example of populations in Communist regimes seeking less politicized entertainment media. After Soviet Communist party leader Joseph Stalin's death in 1953, many of the countries under Communist rule created semi-tabloid evening papers that focused on the readers' ordinary world and featured a minimum of politics. A few of these papers had even begun earlier. The largest number were found in the Soviet Union, where they were a feature of the life of the capital city of each republic plus the largest cities in Russia. Outside the USSR, the largest number (14) was found in Poland, which featured a more decentralized system. These newspapers laid the groundwork for many of the post-Communist tabloids.[107]

CONCLUSION

The historical experience of the Central and East European area mass media does not define the present or future of that media, but it does limit the range of possibilities and helps to define the agenda of contemporary study. Four topics bear restating.

The growth of the audience has changed the media in this part of the world. Through most of the 19th century and sometimes well into the 20th century, Central and East European newspapers were read by a small fraction of the population representing national and political elites. They served often as substitutes for parliaments. Two forces helped change audiences. In the more western parts of the region, economic growth promoted the development of statewide distribution systems. This aided the development of the advertising that could support a mass circulation press. In the territories more to the east and south, mass audiences were developed by Communist rulers who sought to deliver their message to entire populations. Under Communist rule, mass media became universal nearly everywhere in Eastern Europe. The development of television in the region between the 1950s and 1970s extended the reach of media even further. Post-Communist economic and political elites would have to take account of the mass audience and its demands and expectations.

With the exception of Russia, mass media in Central and Eastern Europe have had at various times in their past some kind of association with national identity and/or national assertion. In the early days of the development of modern nations, newspapers served as a point of identity for their readers. In states where national issues remained unresolved, the national character of newspapers remained important. Under Communist rule, media were supposed to be national in form and socialist in content. When Communism collapsed, the national form remained for political and national leaders who wished to employ it. But the pre-Communist experience reminds us that the media much more often reflect the state or extent of national feeling, and rarely create it.

In the pre-Communist period, journalism often served as a substitute arena for politics. Political parties and leaders communicated with each other through the media. Newspapers that synthesized the debate and discussion or provided balanced and objective information were few. Most readers saw the world in partisan terms and preferred their newspapers to do likewise. With mass circulation and viewership a basic element in the post-Communist world, the relationship of media and democracy or of media and politics would have to be redefined in each country. Historians point out that in the United States, voter turnout increased during the Federalist-Anti-Federalist controversy in the 1790s and stayed high for a century. Decreasing voter turnout coincided with the shift of journalism away from a partisan outlook.

Far too little study has been made of the economic base of the mass media in Central and Eastern Europe. When technology was antiquated and political newspapers were published in only a few thousand copies, political parties could foot the bill as part of doing business. When newspapers developed large circulations, such as *Russkoe slovo* in the decades before the Bolshevik Revolution or *Vecerni Ceske slovo* in interwar Czechoslovakia, commercial principles applied. Under Communist rule, media costs were incorporated into central planning. Through some combination of subsidies and sales the media were paid for. In the post-Communist period, small-circulation political newspapers would no longer be viable, meaning that prospective newspaper publishers would have to develop sources of capital.

Governments and parties in Central and Eastern Europe have a long tradition of involvement in the operations of the mass media either by ownership or by law. Politicians, many of whom were once journalists, believed in powerful media effects and believed that media management was necessary in order to carry out their policies. With the development of the commercial imperatives, media control in the post-Communist era would become more complicated. The advent of cable and satellite television delivery posed a special set of problems, partly related to matters of control and partly related to a diffusion of audiences.

The profession of journalism in Central and Eastern Europe has a relatively limited history. In 1939 when Slovakia became independent under Nazi tutelage, there were only about 50 professional journalists, and a number of them immediately joined the new Slovak government. Except for Czechoslovakia, journalism education is a post-World War II phenomenon. This education almost always developed in literature departments at universities. Ruling communist parties soon required a greater political orientation so that journalism education became part skills training and part political instruction. Whether journalism education was a required element of being a journalism professional was an unanswered question when the Berlin Wall came tumbling down.These are some of the issues that the historical record has introduced. The way they are being addressed is the subject of the remainder of this book.

NOTES & REFERENCES

1. Stanley Z. Pech, for instance, concludes that "The attitudes of the Czech, Slovak, Slovene and Croatian newspapers of the 1848-1849 era appear to foreshadow, to a considerable extent, the dominant political attitudes of these four peoples as they evolved and crystallized in the ensuing decades." In "The Press of the Habsburg Slavs in 1848: A Contribution to a Political Profile," *Canadian Journal of History*, Vol. 10, No. 1, p. 48.

2. Tadeusz Butkiewicz, "Three Ages of the Polish Press," *Kwartalnik Prasoznawczy*, foreign language edition, No, 1, 1959, p. 10.

3. Anthony Smith, *The Newspaper: An International History*. London: Thames and Hudson, 1979, p. 9.

4. Miklos Vasarhelyi, ed., *A magyar sajto tortenete*, Vol. 1, 1705-1848. Budapest: Akademiai, 1979, p. 58. Vasarhelyi served during the 1956 Hungarian revolution as revolutionary leader Imre Nagy's press secretary. After serving a prison sentence, he was forced to limit himself to academic research on journalism and literary history until political conditions permitted his return to public life in the 1980s.

5. Alan Sked, *The Decline and Fall of the Habsburg Empire 1815-1918*. New York: Longman, 1989, pp. 47-48.

6. Jonathan Sperber, *The European Revolutions, 1848-1851*. New York: Cambridge University Press, 1994, p. 152.
7. Stanley Z. Pech, "The Press of the Habsburg Slavs in 1848: Contribution to a Political Profile," *Canadian Journal of History* , Vol. 10, No. 1, p. 39.
8. Frantisek Roubik, *Bibliografie casopisectva v Cechach z let 1863-1895*. Prague: Nakl. Ceske akademie Ved a umeni, 1936, pp. xiii ff.
9. Quoted in Bruce M. Garver, *The Young Czech Party 1874-1901 and the Emergence of a Multi-Party System*. New Haven, CT: Yale University Press, 1978, p. 102.
10. Garver, pp. 102–03.
11. Jiri Hronek, *Byl jsem pri tom, kdyz se hroutil svet*. Prague: Novinar, 1986, p. 14.
12. Jiri Pernes, *Svet Lidovych novin 1893-1993: Stoleta kapitola z dejin ceske zurnalistiky, kultury a politiky*. Prague: Lidove noviny, 1993, pp. 58-59.
13. Andrew C. Janos, *The Politics of Backwardness in Hungary 1825-1945*. Princeton, NJ: Princeton University Press, 1982, p. 74; and Geza Ballagi, *A nemzeti allamalkotas kora*. Budapest: Athenaeum, 1897, p. 57.
14. Sandor Szerdahelyi, ed., *A magyar bohemvilag: A Budapesti ujsagirok almanachja 1908-ra*. Budapest: A Budapesti Ujsagirok Egyesulete, 1908, pp. 63-64.
15. John Lukacs, *Budapest 1900: A Historical Portrait of a City and Its Culture*. New York: Weidenfeld and Nicolson, 1988, pp. 152–53.
16. Thomas S. Denison, "The Telephone Newspaper," *World's Work*, Vol. 1, No. 6, pp. 640-43.
17. Jan Havranek, "The Education of Czechs and Slovaks under Foreign Domination, 1850-1918," in Janusz J. Tomiak, Ed., *Schooling, Educational Policy & Ethnic Identity*. New York: New York University Press, 1991, pp. 250-253.
18. Owen V. Johnson, "Newspapers and Nation-Building: The Slovak Press in Pre-1918 Slovakia," in Hans Lemberg et al., eds., *Bildungsgeschichte, Bevolkerungsgeschichte, Gesellschaftsgeschichte in den Bohmischen Landern und in Europa*. Vienna: Verlag fur Geschichte und Politik, 1988, pp. 160–78.
19. Butkiewicz, pp. 10-11.
20. Sylwester Dziki, "Czy prasa dopomogla Polakom wybic sie na niepodleglosc," *Zeszyty Prasowznawcze*, Vol. 29, No. 4, 1988, pp. 5-20.
21. Jane Leftwich Curry, "The Partitions and the Polish Press," Conference on the Mass Media in Eastern Europe, Indiana University, October 1983.
22. Alfred R. Senn, *The Emergence of Modern Lithuania*. New York: Columbia University Press, 1959, p. 12.
23. Jonathan Sperber, *The European Revolutions, 1848-1851*. New York: Cambridge University Press, 1994.
24. Peter Gross, "Trials, Tribulations, and Contributions: A Brief History of the Romanian Press," *East European Quarterly*, Vol. 22, No. 1, p. 2.

25. Keith Hitchins, "The Sacred Cult of Nationality: Rumanian Intellectuals and the Church in Transylvania 1834-1869," in Stanley B. Winters and Joseph Held, eds., *Intellectual and Social Developments in the Habsburg Empire from Maria Theresa to World War I*. New York: Columbia University Press, pp. 155-156.
26. Gross, *Ibid.*
27. Gross, "Trials," pp. 9-10.
28. Sperber, p. 152.
29. J.N., "Journalism in Yugoslavia," *Central European Observer*, Vol. 4, No. 31, 1926, p. 545.
30. Gary Marker, *Publishing, Printing, and the Origins of Intellectual Life in Russia, 1700-1800*. Princeton, NJ: Princeton University Press, 1985.
31. Daniel C. Waugh, "The Publication of Muscovite *Kuranty*," *Kritika*, Vol. 9, No. 3, 1973, pp. 104-20.
32. Marker, p. 27.
33. See Gary Marker, "Russian Journals and their Readers in the Late Eighteenth Century," *Oxford Slavonic Papers*, Vol. 19, 1986, pp. 88-101.
34. Charles A. Ruud, *Fighting Words: Imperial Censorship and the Russian Press, 1804-1906*. Toronto: University of Toronto Press, 1982.
35. Charles A. Ruud, "The Printing Press as an Agent of Political Change in Early Twentieth-Century Russia," *Russian Review*, Vol. 40, No. 4, 1981, p. 379.
36. Jeffrey Brooks, *When Russia Learned to Read: Literacy and Popular Culture*. Princeton, NJ: Princeton University Press, 1985, pp. xv-xvii, 117.
37. Boris I. Esin, *Russkaia dorevoliutsionnaia gazeta, 1702-1917: Kratkii ocherk*. Moscow: Izd-vo Mosk. Univerzita, 1971, p. 47.
38. Joan Neuberger, "Stories of the Street: Hooliganism in the St. Petersburg Popular Press," *Slavic Review*, Vol. 48, No. 2, 1989, p. 180.
39. Louise McReynolds, *The News Under Russia's Old Regime: The Development of a Mass-Circulation Press*. Princeton, NJ: Princeton University Press, 1991, pp. 305-309, reports the results of a content analysis of eight important popular papers in early 20th-century Russia. She uses categories modified from Paul J. Deutschmann, *News-Page Content of Twelve Metropolitan Dailies*. New York: Scripps-Howard Research, 1959.
40. Quoted in Charles A. Ruud, *Russian Entrepreneur: Publisher Ivan Sytin of Moscow 1851-1934*. Montreal: McGill-Queen's University Press, 1990, p. 170.
41. Terhi Rantanen, *Foreign News in Imperial Russia: The Relationship Between International and Russian News Agencies, 1856-1914*. Helsinki: Suomalainen Tiedeakatemia, 1990.
42. Matthew Kaminski, "Ukraine's Schoolchildren Are Keystone to Building a Nation," *New York Times*, March 29, 1995, p. B8.
43. Varfolomii A. Ihnatiienko, *Bibliohrafiia ukrains'koi presy 1816-1916*, (Reprint.) State College, PA: University of Pennsylvania Press, 1968.
44. John-Paul Himka, *Galician Villagers and the Ukrainian National Movement in the Nineteenth Century*. New York: St. Martins Press, 1988, pp. 66-67.

45. Andrej Tuser, "Vecerniky v kontexte svetovej tlace," *Otazky zurnalistiky* Vol. 35, No. 1, 1992, p. 25; and Owen V. Johnson, *Slovakia 1918-1938: Education and the Making of a Nation*. Boulder, CO: East European Monographs, 1985, p. 81.

46. Zuzana Duhajova, "Legalna slovenska nel'udacka tlac v rokoch druhej svetovej vojny," *Zbornik Filozofickej fakulty Univerzity Komenskeho—Zurnalistika*, Vols. 17-18, 1991, pp. 97-107.

47. The Slovak situation is reviewed by L'ubos Sefcak, *Prehl'ad najnovsich dejin slovenskeho novinarstva od r. 1945*. Bratislava: SPN, 1968, pp. 139–168.

48. Andrzej Notkowski, *Prasa w systemie propagandy rzadowej w Polsce 1926-1939: Studium techniki wladzy*. Warsaw: PWN, 1987; see also Butkiewicz, pp. 27-31.

49. Miklos Vasarhelyi, "The Press in Hungary, 1919-1945," paper delivered at the conference, "The Role and Functions of the Media in Eastern Europe," Bloomington, IN, November 1983.

50. Gross, "Trials," pp. 12-16.

51. J.N., "Journalism in Yugoslavia," *Central European Observer*, Vol. 4, No. 31, 1926, p. 545.

52. Zoran Lakic, "Cultural Activity at Time of AVNOJ," *Socialist Thought and Practice*, Vol. 23, No. 12, 1983, p. 115.

53. In particular, Wilbur Schramm's "Soviet-Communist" theory, a product of the totalitarian model, was frozen like a boilerplate into nearly every mass communication and international communication book that came into being, despite its limited resemblance to reality. In Fred S. Siebert, Theodore Peterson, and Wilbur Schramm, *Four Theories of the Press: The Authoritarian, Libertarian, Social Responsibility and Soviet Communist Concepts of What the Press Should Be and Do*. Urbana: University of Illinois Press, 1956.

54. Although each has its limits, four books that discuss the communist period in the Soviet Union (and were largely or completely written in the pre-glasnost period) provide the most detailed background. They inform much of the discussion in this chapter. They include Thomas F. Remington, *The Truth of Authority: Ideology and Communication in the Soviet Union*. Pittsburgh: University of Pittsburgh Press, 1988; Mark W. Hopkins, *Mass Media in the Soviet Union*, 1970; Gayle Durham Hollander, *Soviet Political Indoctrination: Developments in Mass Media and Propaganda Since Stalin*. New York: Praeger, 1972; and Alex Inkeles, *Public Opinion in Soviet Russia: A Study in Mass Persuasion*, rev ed. Cambridge: Harvard University Press, 1958. Because of the immense specialized knowledge that is necessary, there is no single volume that does justice to the other countries that were ruled by communist parties in the Soviet orbit. The best effort was by Antony Buzek, *How the Communist Press Works*. New York: Praeger, 1964. There are excellent country studies on Poland and Yugoslavia (see later cites).

55. Peter Kenez, *The Birth of the Propaganda State: Soviet Methods of Mass Mobilization, 1917–1929*. New York: Cambridge University Press, 1985, p. 44.

56. Jeffrey Brooks, "Public and Private Values in the Soviet Press, 1921-1928," *Slavic Review*, Vol. 48, No. 1, 1989, p. 16.

57. Brooks, "Public and Private Values," p. 18.

58. Kenez, pp. 48, 225–232.

59. Brooks, "Public and Private Values," p. 17.

60. H.V. Kaltenborn, "Propaganda Land: Where Playing on the Mass-Mind is the Chief Business of Government," *Century Magazine*, Vol. 114, No. 6, 1927, p. 628.

61. Julie K. Mueller, "A New Kind of Newspaper: The Origins and Development of a Soviet Institution, 1921-1928," Ph.D., University of California, 1992; Jeffrey Brooks,"The Press and Its Message: Images of America in the 1920s and 1930s," in Sheila Fitzpatrick et al., eds., *Russia in the Era of NEP*. Bloomington: Indiana University Press, 1991, pp. 231–252.

62. Jeffrey Brooks, "Socialist Realism in Pr*avda:* Read All About It!" *Slavic Review*, Vol. 53, No. 4, 1994, p. 975

63. Jeffrey Brooks, "*Pravda* and the Language of Power in Soviet Russia, 1917-28," in Jeremy D. Popkin, ed., *Media and Revolution: Comparative Perspectives*. Lexington: University Press of Kentucky, 1995, p. 157.

64. Jeffrey Brooks, "Competing Modes of Popular Discourse: Individualism and Class Consciousness in the Russian Print Media 1880-1928," in Marc Ferro and Sheila Fitzpatrick, eds., *Culture et revolution*. Paris: l'Ecole des Hautes Etudes en Sciences sociales, 1989, p. 72.

65. Sheila Fitzpatrick, "Introduction," *Russian History/Histoire Russe* Vols. 2-4, 1985, pp. 135–136.

66. *Ibid.*

67. Brian McNair, *Glasnost, Perestroika and the Soviet Media*. New York: Routledge, 1991, p. 41.

68. Hopkins, p. 104.

69. Gayle D. Hollander, *Soviet Political Indoctrination: Developments in Mass Media and Propaganda Since Stalin*. New York: Praeger, 1972, pp. 34-36.

70. Alex Inkeles, *Public Opinion in Soviet Russia: A Study in Mass Persuasion*. Cambridge: Harvard University Press, 1958, pp. 234-253; and Hollander, pp. 100-102.

71. *Pechat SSSR za sorok let: 1917-1957*. Moscow Ministerstvo Kul'tury SSSR, 1957, pp. 107-108; and *Pechat SSSR v 1968 godu*, p. 56.

72. *Ibid.*, pp. 123 and 66, respectively.

73. Remington, *The Truth of Authority*, p. 109. For a detailed earlier study of TASS, see Theodore E. Kruglak, *The Two Faces of TASS*. Minneapolis: University of Minnesota Press, 1962.

74. Nils H. Wessell, "The Credibility, Impact and Effectiveness of the Soviet General Press: Analysis of Soviet Research on the Soviet Non-Specialized Newspaper," Ph.D., Columbia University, 1972.

75. Remington, *The Truth of Authority*, Chapter 6.

76. This is discussed by Heinz Brahm, "Glasnost—der Geist aus der Flasche," *Berichte des Bundesinstituts fur ostwissenschaftliche und internationale Studien* No. 58, 1990.
77. Michael Ignatieff, "Whispers from the Abyss," *New York Review of Books*, Vol. 43, No. 15, 1996, p. 4.
78. The variety of ways in which foreign information penetrated the Soviet information system is outlined in *Behind the Lines: The Private War Against Soviet Censorship*. New York: St. Martin's Press, 1985.
79. The best sources for broad review of Soviet television are William D. Parratt, "Soviet Television Broadcasting: Its Growth, Social Role, and Effects," Ph.D., Indiana University, 1975; Ellen P. Mickiewicz, *Media and the Russian Public*. New York: Praeger, 1981; and Mickiewicz, *Split Signals: Television and Politics in the Soviet Union*. New York: Oxford University Press, 1988.
80. David Wedgwood Benn, *From Glasnost to Freedom of Speech: Russian Openness and International Relations*. New York: Council on Foreign Relations Press, 1992, pp. 12-13.
81. John Murray, *The Russian Press from Brezhnev to Yeltsin: Behind the Paper Curtain* (Brookfield, VT: Edward Elgar, 1994), Chapters 4–5.
82. Zdenek Horeni, "The Standard Bearer of the Revolutionary Press: The 75th Anniversary of Lenin's *Pravda*," *World Marxist Review*, Vol. 30, No. 5, 1987 pp. 89-90.
83. Particularly useful for understanding the ethnic situation in the early years of Soviet history are Helene Carrere d'Encausse, *The Great Challenge: Nationalities and the Bolshevik State 1917-1930*. New York: Holmes & Meier, 1992; and Richard Pipes, *The Formation of the Soviet Union*, rev. ed. New York: Atheneum, 1968.
84. Extensive research and analysis of the mass media of most of the non-Russian former republics of the Soviet Union is needed. A valuable beginning on the Baltic countries is Svennik Hoyer, Epp Lauk, and Peeter Vihalemm, eds., *Towards a Civic Society: The Baltic Media's Long Road to Freedom-Perspectives on History, Ethnicity and Journalism*. Tartu, Estonia: Baltic Association for Media Research, 1993.
85. Inta Brikse, "Journalism in Independent Latvia during the 1920s and 1930s," in Hoyer et al. eds., p. 143.
86. Roman Szporluk, "Recent Trends in Soviet Policy Toward Printed Media in the Non-Russian Languages," *Radio Liberty Research Bulletin Supplement*, No. 2, 1984.
87. Rosemarie Rogers, "Language Policy and Language Power: The Case of Soviet Publishing," *Language Problems and Language Planning*, Vol. 11, No. 1, 1987, pp. 82-103.
88. Thomas F. Remington, "Federalism and Segmented Communication in the USSR," *Publius: The Journal of Federalism*, Vol. 15, No. 4, 1985, pp. 113-132.
89. Paul Goble, "Ethnic Politics in the USSR," *Problems of Communism*, Vol. 38, No. 4, 1989, p. 3.

90. Marju Lauristin and Peeter Vihalemm, "The Awakening (1987-1990)," in Hoyer et al., eds., p. 224.
91. This point is made indirectly by Thomas F. Remington, "Renegotiating Soviet Federalism: Glasnost and Regional Autonomy," *Publius: The Journal of Federalism*, Vol. 19, No. 3, 1989, p. 153.
92. The Soviet leadership's view is reflected in Ellen Mickiewicz, "Ethnic Differentiation and Political Communication," in T. Anthony Jones, Walter D. Connor, and David E. Powell, eds., *Soviet Social Problems*. Boulder, CO:Westview, 1991), pp. 24-38.
93. See Roman Szporluk, "West Ukraine and West Belorussia: Historical Tradition, Social Communication, and Linguistic Assimilation," *Soviet Studies*, Vol. 31, No. 1, 1979, pp. 76-98.
94. Kathleen Mihalisko, "Hard Times Ahead for the Belorussian Press?" *Report on the USSR*, Vol. 2, No. 48, 1990, pp. 15-17.
95. Bohdan Nahaylo, "Ukraine," *RFE/RL Research Report*, Vol. 1, No. 39, 1992, p. 10.
96. In the mid-1960s, sales from *Pravda*, *Kommunist*, and *Ekonomicheskaia Gazeta*, provided the Communist Party of the Soviet Union with 35% of its income. *Pravda*, March 10, 1966.
97. Jozef Weiser, "Zapas slovenskych novinarov o demokratizaciu a slobodu tlace (1956-1963)," *Zbornik Filozofickej Fakulty Univerzity Komenskeho*, Vols. 17-18, 1991, pp. 109-123.
98. Frank L. Kaplan, *Winter Into Spring: The Czechoslovak Press and the Reform Movement 1963-1968*. Boulder: East European Quarterly, 1977; and Dusan Havlicek, "The Mass Media in Czechoslovakia in 1956-1968," *Experience of the 1968 Prague Spring*, Working Study No. 16, November 1980-August 1981.
99. Jane Leftwich Curry, *Poland's Journalists: Professionalism and Politics*. New York: Cambridge University Press, 1990; and Madeleine K. Albright, *Poland: The Role of the Press in Political Change*. New York: Praeger, 1983.
100. Gertrude Joch Robinson, *Tito's Maverick Media: The Politics of Mass Communication in Yugoslavia*. Urbana: University of Illinois Press, 1977.
101. Peter Gross, *Mass Media in Revolution and National Development: The Romanian Laboratory*. Ames: Iowa State University Press, 1996, p. 9.
102. The phrase is from Dan Ionescu, "Tele-Revolution to Tele-Evolution in Romania," *Transition*, Vol. 2, No. 8, 1996, p. 42.
103. *Screen Digest*, March 1993, p. 62.
104. Tirana ATA in English, 0900 GMT, 24 July 1984, as recorded in Foreign Broadcast Information Service Daily Report Eastern Europe, July 26, 1984, p. B1.
105. Jacek Dyrlaga, "Prasa, radio i telewizja w Albanii," *Zeszyty i Prasoznawcze*, Vol. 29, No. 2, 1988, p. 102.
106. Piero Cappelli, "Albanians Deceived by Italian Media," *Media Development*, Vol. 39, No. 3, 1992, p. 41.
107. See Andrej Tuser, "Vecerniky v kontexte svetovej tlace," *Otazky zurnalistiky*, Vol. 35, No. 1, 1992, pp. 25-32, for a listing of many of these papers.

2

The Role and Effects of Journalism and *Samizdat* Leading up to 1989

Jerome Aumente

Society's need for accurate news and information and the individual yearning to express oneself freely and independently were severe casualties of the totalitarian regimes in the Soviet Union and the nations under its grip in Central and Eastern Europe.

However, just as it is impossible to hold back the natural flow of streams as they feed powerful rivers emptying into oceans, the revolutions that toppled Communist regimes in the region beginning in 1989 ultimately were propelled by an unstoppable flow of news and information—some of it in the official mass media; some from foreign broadcasts, and much of it from ingenious underground samizdat strategies dissidents devised to circumvent censorship and create alternative voices in print, broadcast, and clandestine audiovisual recordings.

After examining the topography of this informational warfare in Central and Eastern Europe, one finds varying degrees of resistance ranging from massive opposition in some countries to feeble, disorganized, and marginal efforts in others. In Poland, hundreds to thousands of underground samizdat publications blossomed during the period of martial law from 1981 after the suppression of Solidarity until 1989 when the dissident labor movement resurfaced, forcing the first free elections in the Soviet bloc. Poland initiated the chain reaction that shortly after 1989 hastened the breakup of the Soviet Union and brought freedom for its once captive Warsaw pact allies.

Thousands of journalists in Poland and elsewhere in Central and Eastern Europe in the decade or two before the changes of 1989 chose to leave the field rather than submit to further censorship and repression. Many hundreds of them were jailed, interned, or fired. Many more acquiesced to the powers that be, but chafed at the restraint of press freedoms. Others ardently supported a system that pampered and nurtured them as privileged *nomenklatura*, the party chosen elite, considered loyal and safe.

In the Soviet Union, even before Michail Gorbachev tentatively, and probably to his profound later regret, loosened the restraints of free expression with his policy of openness, or *glasnost*, in 1985, dissidents years earlier began testing the limits of censorship through the clandestine printed and broadcast word. Czechoslovakia produced its pantheon of outspoken leaders, many of them journalists and writers, who would not forget the brief sweet taste of freedom of the Prague Spring of 1968.

In some countries of the region, the years of resistance were a crucible that produced a new generation of young, avid journalists, many amateurs and untrained, who bravely wrote and edited the underground publications to surface later as seasoned journalistic leaders after 1989, the vanguard of an independent press.

Some who remained in the party-controlled establishment media did resist government from within, jabbing at the restraints of censorship or access to information. Others hesitated until the final weeks and days as public discontent boiled over in violent conflict in Russia or Romania, but finally used their print and broadcast outlets to chronicle the opposition, thus hastening the end of dictatorships.

Imagine the Central and Eastern European Communist countries as an extended ocean shorefront. In some of the countries a steady tide of news and information from the opposition eroded official beliefs, pounded and transformed the societal shoreline. In other countries, impregnable defenses of repressive control held stubbornly, and the changes came about without the media playing any significant role. Here we examine the dynamics of some of these experiences.

POLAND

Solidarity originated at a conference in Gdansk, Poland of independent labor unions chaired by Lech Walesa in September 1980. For 13 months it held sway, picking up 10 million members, propelled by previous years of resistance and periodic nurturing through underground publications. In December 1981, the Polish government, fearful of a possible Soviet invasion if it did not act, declared martial law, shutting down Solidarity and instituting repressive measures against the news media and the Polish Journalists Association, SDP, seizing the latter's resources and replacing it with an obedient, substitute organization subservient to the government.[1]

Solidarity went underground, and the resistance was supported by a national network of samizdat publications ranging from sophisticated large circulation newspapers to the flimsiest of typed and carbon copy publications.

When it surfaced again, Solidarity led the round table negotiations of 1989, which brought about the agreement for the first free elections in 1989 of any Communist country in the Soviet bloc. Demands for press freedom and a dismantling of a government-controlled print and broadcast press were prominent in the negotiations. A Polish government racked by strikes and economic unrest gave in to the demands for free elections, and in Spring 1989, the Communist Party was defeated.

Interestingly, the first non-Communist Prime Minister to emerge from this was Tadeusz Masowiecki, the former editor of the weekly newspaper, Solidarity. In the round table negotiations government, trade union reform, the judiciary, and the mass media were given high priority. At its first meetings, the opposition bluntly insisted that without media reform no major agreement was possible.

The opposition leadership for the media negotiations included Masowiecki; Krzyztof Kozlowski, later a senator and then deputy editor-in-chief of the Krakow Catholic weekly, *Tygodnik Powszechny*; and Adam Michnik, a leader of national prominence in the underground media and later an elected Parliamentarian, founder and editor of *Gazeta Wyborcza*, an election gazette that evolved after the 1989 elections into Poland's most successful national, independent newspaper.[2]

The government proposed an evolutionary approach, but the opposition demanded a more rapid easing of censorship, legalization of the underground press, free expression in newspapers, and an independent broadcasting entity. Kozlowski, chairman for the media negotiations, according to Tomasz Goban-Klas,[3] who sat with the government experts across the table, wanted a "new information order in Poland"—an end to state-controlled media, a free press, the right for anyone to own media, access to communication resources, an end to licensing, rehiring of journalists dismissed for political opposition, and a halt to customs seizure of foreign publications.

In the wake of subsequent revolutionary changes in other Soviet bloc countries, Poland's inclination toward gradualism and evolution as opposed to violent revolution might seem overly reticent. But it is important to remember the massive sea changes these demands represented during a dangerous period when a still seemingly impregnable Soviet Union held sway over the region.

Robert Downing in his *Radical Media*[4] describes a Poland with a history of lax censorship and a freer media, but then came an official clampdown in 1976 (only fanning an underground media wildfire that would continue throughout the 1980s). Censorship harshly forbade reporting of environmental threats, any negative reports of Polish history from 1939 onward, anything that would besmirch the image of the Communist Party (as, for instance, tracing the infamous Katyn massacre of Polish officers to Soviets and not the Nazis, as turned out to be the case).

In the face of censorship, Downing[5] found, papers such as *Gazeta Krakowska* in Krakow resisted, trusted by a public now skeptical of the media who were willing to pay up to 300 zlotys in Warsaw for a paper that officially sold for one zloty. Meanwhile, the police seized a million leaflets, silenced 11 radio transmitters, closed nearly 380 clandestine printing shops, and seized 500 typewriters.[6]

As it did through the 1980s, the Catholic press, a power in a country with over 90% of its population Roman Catholic, provided a haven for dissidents and alternative communication pathways. Poland had a history of resistance—rising up against the Nazis in World War II and paying the price of near total destruction of Warsaw, its capital.

Downing notes there were worker uprisings in Poland in 1956; students protests in 1968, protests in Gdansk in 1970 with many workers shot, and in 1976 worker strikes at the Radom and Ursus plants near Warsaw. And then came the famous shipyard strikes of Gdansk in 1980–81, which catapulted Solidarity and Lech Walesa to power and international recognition.

An important flowering of the dissident press that Downing and others trace came in 1976 with a new wave of underground media and signed "Communiques" put forward by KOR (a Polish acronym for the Committee for Workers Self Defense). Barely legible typed sheets, passed hand to hand, reported police abuse of workers and their families. Writers bravely used their names, and some were jailed.

More formal publications followed—*Information Bulletin* (named after a Warsaw uprising paper of 1944), *Glos* [Voice], *Robotnik* [Worker], and others.[7] Significantly, some KOR people emerged later as key advisors to Solidarity.

In a talk with Anna Husarska,[8] Adam Michnik fresh from the 1989 round table talks and editor-in-chief of *Gazeta Wyborcza* said the new paper would draw from many of the editorial board of the main underground weekly, *Tygodnik Mazowsze,* including Ernest Skalski and Helena Luczywo.

Michnik cautioned in 1989 that not all underground publications should abandon the clandestine network: "Let us wait for the censorship law to be liberalized. Underground publications in Poland were for the last seven and a half years the living symbol of the opposition's survival. They have established important new values, and we should avoid doing anything that could be interpreted as the liquidation of these values."[9]

In prison for 6 of the previous 20 years until 1989 for his dissenting views and subjected to 100 detentions, Michnik's caution could be understood. As a student he led demonstrations at Warsaw University in 1968, was expelled and later imprisoned; he joined KOR after the Radom strike in 1976 and edited the KOR "Communiques." He helped launch a clandestine educational university, the Flying University, and in 1980 became a main advisor to Solidarity. Thus was his journey from the underground press to the most prominent opposition daily in Poland after Communism's fall.

Clandestine publishing goes back centuries in Poland, and Ted Kaminski[10] notes that Austrian, Prussian, and Russian overlords severely curtailed free expression in partitions from 1795 to 1918. When Adam Mickiewicz, the poet, was banished to Russia, his work was smuggled back to Poland via France. Jozef Pilsudski, a young revolutionary, printed *Robotnik* while fleeing the Czarist police. Kaminski notes that KOR used its underground printing efforts in 1976 with 500 clandestine printing operations, and Solidarity in 1980 launched its own uncensored publications with the help of donated equipment from Western trade unions. Tygodnik Solidarnosc was a 500,000 weekly with presses in Gdansk, and the union even established its own press agency.

Kaminski[11] says Solidarity was caught off guard with the imposition of martial law in 1981 and thousands of books and equipment were destroyed or confiscated. The police tried to print bogus editions of the paper to infiltrate the distribution system but failed. By 1984, he estimates there were 500 clandestine publications with *Tygodnik Mazowsze* [Voice of Solidarity] the best known, and by 1986 about 930 publications having appeared, and 400 confirmed as then still in existence.

He estimates the state media by 1985 published 42 dailies with 8 million circulation and 8,000 titles. In contrast, uncensored literature was read by 3 million regularly, and 15% of the working class had access to the Solidarity press.

The criminal code of 1986 banning any activity "to create a public disorder" was used to arrest underground publication activists, Kaminski reports, with up to three year prison terms, long interrogation, and loss of jobs the punishment. There were amnesties in 1984 and 1986, with 70% of the estimated 225 prisoners freed. A new bill in 1986 reduced penalties to fines and confiscation of equipment, and detainees for three months were released without trial. Kaminski believes that 10,000 to 30,000 were involved in illegal press activities in 1986.

As in the rest of the Soviet bloc countries of the region, Poland's publishing, printing, and distribution resources and its sources of newsprint were strictly controlled by the Communist Party and its government appendages. Tadeusz Kowalski[12] said that "Robotnicza Spoldzienlnia Wydawnicza, 'Prasa-Ksiazka-Ruch," or RSW, was Poland's biggest publisher. Owned by the Polish United Workers Party (PUWP), the country's Communist Party, RSW controlled 86% of the daily newspapers, 76% of the weeklies, and 70% of circulation. It controlled book/press publication, printing, and distribution through an interconnected network of 80 units.

Again, as in other Communist countries of the region, the party controlled main editorial decisions and filled key posts with "nomenklatura," chosen and endorsed by the party. Other small parties in the nation controlled about 2% of the titles and circulation, and the Catholic Church had 2.7% of published titles and less than a single percentage point of total circulation.

Kowalksi[13] reports that in the 1970s Poland's press increasingly became more centralized and controlled and the reported reality more distorted as economic and personal conditions worsened. He describes the mass media as aloof from society's problems and seen as an untrustworthy mouthpiece for the ruling powers. It was in this environment that Solidarity met in Gdansk in 1980, where the shipyard workers demanded free speech and a free press, an easing of censorship, access to the religious media, and a plurality of voices in the media. Government pledged these rights and snatched them away with the declaration of martial law in 1981.

Karol Jakubowicz[14] traces Solidarity's later opposition roots as far back as 1969 and also to KOR in 1976, with an alliance of intellectuals and workers promoting clandestine publications. He notes that in the beginning, Solidarity not only published newspapers, but used point-to-point communications with teleprinters almost functioning as small printing presses. By 1981, Solidarity began with nine legitimate periodicals with a press run of over one million and had columns or pages in 45 other newspapers until martial law halted this short-lived above-ground experience.

It is little known, he writes, but just before martial law Solidarity also attempted to draft a new broadcasting law, with early drafts creating a public corporation under parliamentary supervision, with all major parties having access to broadcasting, and with listener and viewer associations to help influence content. Right of reply was to be guaranteed.

During the earlier repression of the 1970s, a flood of samizdat publications emerged, going from crudely typed and retyped carbon copies to more sophisticated printing technology and bringing tougher punishment and fines. Downing[15] reports that a central, illegal publishing group, NOWA, used five tons of paper a month, producing 200 different titles of pamphlets, journals, and books. He says that between 1977 to 1980 the underground publications were displayed more brashly on bookshelves and were read openly on buses and trains. It became chic.

All this helps explain why, as Solidarity emerged, a key demand in 1980 was an easing of censorship for the underground press. But the labor movement found its communication outlets steadily choked off and journalists supportive of Solidarity harassed; finally, in August 1981, Solidarity called a two-day strike of newspapers, winning concessions from government.

The people by now were accustomed to increasingly sophisticated underground papers. *Robotnik* in the 1970s went from typed carbon to a printing of up to 70,000 copies an issue. Other papers around the country took up investigative reporting and muckraking. Literary and political journals challenged everything from the command economy to the language and culture of a repressed society.

All the while came a steady chipping away at the credibility and authority of a government seeking to control news and information. Goban-Klas[16] says censorship was introduced in Poland with a "temporary" decree, left unchanged until 1981. Parliament in that year let journalists challenge censors in the courts, and Solidarity even won a case, but with martial law in 1981 liberalization ended. Despite this, the underground press of the 1980s flourished, with Goban-Klas estimating 500 periodicals publishing regularly and thousands of occasional, ephemeral papers and 10 major underground publishing houses.

Writing in *The New Leader*, Anna Husarska[17] reported that although it took state publishing six to eight years from date of manuscript to acceptance to publish a book, the underground press could get a mimeograph edition off the press in two or three months, with the first book in 1977. By 1986, she found a dozen major underground publishing houses turning out a book or two a month, listing 365 underground book titles, about 70% of the probable total. Two-thirds of the sentences for nonviolent crimes in 1985–86 were for publishing violations and 1,200 underground presses were seized from 1981-85.

By 1986, she counted 700 underground newspapers, bulletins, and newsletters in Poland with *Tygodnik Mazowsze*, a biweekly with a press run of 60,000 to 80,000 copies of four densely packed pages of type. Husarska found audiocassettes easy to copy and popular in the underground, with excerpts of banned books and internment camp songs recorded. There were about 350,000 videocassette recorders by 1986, she writes, with videos being swapped and rented, banned films copied, and underground video rent parties popular. Satellite dishes were restricted, but still could be found hidden among the clothes lines on roofs of dissidents. The foreign broadcasts of BBC, VOA, and RFE were popular, and Solidarity electronic wizards occasionally jammed Polish state broadcasting or broke in with their own messages during soccer games.[18]

In a study of video usage, Jerzy Pomorski[19] looked at the Communist bloc countries of the region and found the majority of VCRs were bought on the black or gray market, and that by 1987, Poland had an estimated 500,000 VCRs compared with 85,000 in the USSR. UNESCO placed the figure in Poland in 1985 at 700,000, and Radio Free Europe estimated the total as high as a million. Pomorski estimates that in 1987, 32% of Poles watched videos at public screenings. Besides the rentals of above ground video outlets from about 100 rental stores, privately recorded videos were estimated at 5 to 7 million a year and increasing by a million more each year by 1987. All this provided a tremendous window that the authorities found impossible to close, despite various attempts to do so.

Karol Jakubowicz[20] reports that Poland by 1986 had a population of 37.4 million, over 15 million radios, and nearly 10 million television sets. The country counted 45 dailies, 51 nondaily papers, and 2,178 other periodicals. The Catholic Church had about 50 newspapers and periodicals and a daily newspaper. For many banned journalists, the Catholic press was an important outlet.

Writing in *Media, Culture and Society*, Jakubowicz[21] estimates some 1,200 journalists connected with Solidarity were purged from the official media during the 1982 bloodletting, and during this time many migrated to church publications. The history of Polish underground journalism, he notes in the same article, stretches back to the period of 1944 to 1948, when about 300 publications appeared in opposition to Communism. During the Nazi occupation of World War II in Poland, he estimates the resistance published 2,000 periodicals and 1,500 books, aside from dozens of books and periodicals that appeared in territories incorporated into the Soviet Union.

Jakubowicz estimates that the opposition press from 1976 to 1981 generated 1,000 Solidarity periodical titles from mass circulation national and weekly papers to factory and college bulletins. When Solidarity was banned in 1981 during martial law, he estimates a total of 2,077 underground periodicals, with circulation varying from 50,000 to 80,000 publications to single-sheet ephemerals. In 1989, about 600 periodicals were regularly being published in 46 of Poland's 49 provinces.

Rounding out these voices of opposition, according to Jakubowicz, were clandestine publishers who brought out 4,500 book titles from 1977 to 1989, with book runs of 1,000 to 7,000 copies featuring 60% political and social issues, 25% historical content, 15% novels, and 20% translations. The streets were messaged with graffiti, and Jakubovicz notes the emergence of 10- to 30-minute broadcasts from clandestine stations on radio and television.

As a sign of its openness, Jakubovicz[22] cites a 1979 UNESCO study that showed Poland's broadcast news almost equally divided between news of the West and the Eastern bloc, greater than other Soviet bloc countries. By 1987, in advance of the changes two years later, state television featured a daily news show, "Panorama," with excerpts from CNN, and by 1989, Polish radio began a 15-minute show with excerpts from VOA, RFE, BBC, and Radio France. (This perhaps to make amends for the martial law era of the 1980s he describes when television executives were severely condemned by the people as tools of propaganda and without credibility.)

By 1990, the Central Office for Control of Press, Publications and Public Performances in Poland was abolished, according to Peter Kaufman.[23] Uncensored books already were being snapped up on the day of availability in 1989, and Poland's underground publishing house NOWA emerged above ground after 13 years and created a nonprofit foundation to preserve its assets.

Gordon Skilling[24] looked at underground press activities across the region and declared, "the phenomenon of independent communications in Poland was unequalled elsewhere in the communist world, both in quantity and variety of form and content" but experienced significant change in the successive periods around and after Solidarity. In the five years before Solidarity, underground editors carried out their work with a relative openness. At the same time, the official media seemed to benefit from this opening and moved toward less censorship. The underground titles almost seemed less needed as the 1970s came to a close. But the brief hope and flowering of openness in 1980 with the rise of Solidarity was abruptly halted with martial law in 1981. Once again the flow of underground media went from a moderate stream to a renewed deluge of samidzat publications.

In her comprehensive review of journalism in Poland from World War II until the changes of 1989, Jane Curry[25] estimates that one third of the working journalists (about 2,000) were fired or refused to work when martial law was imposed in 1981. They were among the first in the professions to resist. Many of them went to alternative or underground publications. The Polish Journalists Association, SDP, had 643 members in 1951, and when it was peremptorily shut down by martial law in 1981—its records and physical assets seized and turned over to a government-controlled replacement, the Polish Journalists Association of the Polish Republic, or SDPRL—it had 9,000 members, with a little less than half of them party members.

Curry found that many left journalism. Membership in the imposed substitute organization of SDPRL, or alternate refusal to join, was a political statement. By May 1983, it had 5,375 members, about 65% of them Communist party members. Curry estimates that 70% of these were formerly in SDP, many young, uncommitted to SDP, and eager for the jobs that opened up with the repression.

Over the years SDP had been perceived as more focused on pensions, aid, and physical comfort for its journalistic membership. But with its ban in 1981, the association went underground and its leadership, in support of Solidarity, were seen as important elements, even heroic, in the dissident movement. Stefan Bratkowski became a national and international example of a top SDP leader who resisted. Maciej Ilowiecki was another among many who also gained such prominence.

With martial law in 1981, the increasing censorship of the year or so of Solidarity's free period ended. SDP's assets were seized, journalists were arrested or went underground. The entire crew of Wroclaw TV, for instance, went into hiding. The Communist regime allowed only three national papers to function; military TV and radio were allowed to continue.

But the harassed journalists regrouped, meeting in churches and underground meetings, and soon the complex panoply of underground media kicked into full gear. The official attempts to block off unofficial news and information were futile. The flow merely went underground and surfaced in the 1989 round tables and victories that ended Communist rule after more than four decades.

RUSSIA AND THE FORMER SOVIET UNION

The well-spring for the Communist mass media ideology that spread throughout the entire Soviet bloc nations in Europe came from the beliefs of Lenin that the press must play the role of propagandist, agitator, and collective organizer. Rilla Dean Mills[26] notes the Soviet concept of the mass communications and the press as an essential means of ideological, political, and economic education, a potent tool to organize the masses.

As editor of *Iskra*, [The Spark] the predecessor to Pravda, Lenin envisioned the paper as an enormous set of bellows with which to fan the sparks of class struggle and ignite popular indignation. The journalist was perceived as a revolutionary allowed, indeed expected and encouraged, to mix opinion with "factual" reporting to achieve the Communist ideals. Objectivity in the sense of being nonpartisan was an enemy of "truth" as the Communists perceived it, a concept that seems an anathema to Western standards of ethical reporting.

Yet this journalistic sword of Lenin is two-edged, and many see it as a catalyst in the downfall of the Soviet Union and Communist rule. Although the sporadic and uncertain outbursts of press dissidence in the Soviet Union might seem minuscule, even unimportant by Western measure, Mills cautions that it was not so simple nor insignificant.

Those Communist leaders with a sense of history knew that the Soviet press itself evolved from a few revolutionary sheets into a massive system with 63,000 journalists, 7,985 newspapers in 56 different languages, and a far-reaching multichannel broadcasting network that covered the vast expanse of the Soviet Union.

For this reason, Mills underscores the concern that the Soviets and their counterparts in the bloc countries saw in the rise in status of journalists and their impatience with restraints and censorship and, most troubling, the appearance of an underground press. The revolts in Hungary in 1956, in Czechoslovakia in 1968, and in Poland in 1981 were sparks to be stamped out without delay.

In Russia, Mills found dissident journalists operating illegally during the 1960s and 1970s in the Soviet Union, publishing and occasionally broadcasting versions of events at odds with the official position. Although Westerners might scoff at a few hundred dissidents publishing smudged carbon copies, he writes, the Soviets remember how similar innocuous tinder fired major conflagrations. Thus the underground press opposition in the Soviet context was important, with more than 400 dissidents imprisoned in the mid-1970s and their activities restricted. From 1979 to June 1980 alone, 71 dissidents were convicted and 86 arrested.

Mills notes *The Chronicle of Current Events* first appeared in 1968 and became an important Soviet underground newspaper. It dryly reported news events in a U.S.-type of reporting, in its painstaking typescript, but it also gave Russians a sense of what they were not getting from their own censored press—for example, news of the arrest of dissidents or religious persecution of Jews and Baptists.

Although small in number, the dissidents hoped, and were proven right in believing, that the resistance, even though just a whisper, would be amplified by reports in the foreign press and broadcasting beamed back into the country. Thus, as in other countries of the region, there was a steady prying away of the censored control of free expression just as the steady, repetitive motion on a decaying painful tooth will eventually loosen it from the socket.

The challenge to the official viewpoint, the monolithic view of the regime, was steady and appeared in samizdat publications ranging from feminist journals to publications challenging the arrest of "psychiatric internees," or the harassment of religious or the handicapped.

Remember that the term *samizdat* which became the common catchword for underground press throughout the Communist countries of Central/Eastern Europe comes from the Russian *samo* or self, and *izdat*, or publishing, and was coined as a wry putdown of the compound names of official Soviet publishing companies.[27]

A sense of earlier samizdat activities in the Soviet Union is important for another reason. It is counterpoint to the argument that all serious opposition and loosening of press restraints can be traced back to the days of "glasnost" in 1985, the year that Soviet premier Michail Gorbachev declared this policy of open and frank discussion of economic and political realities. Gorbachev saw the media as an ally in his twin goal of "perestroika," reforming the system without replacing it. Unquestionably, he aimed the country in a new direction of self-exploration and expression, but he had unwittingly pushed it to the edge of a precipice. Once it began zooming down the icy slope of change there was no way to stop the momentum. It ended with the crashing dissolution of Communist control over the Soviet Union and its East/Central European allies.

Elena Adrounas[28] believes the mass media in the Soviet Union "were instrumental in the radical change that shook the country. They roused the people and generated wide popular support for the democratic movement that overpowered the ruling mechanism of the Communist party." It was a process of logical example: By freeing themselves, the media created a concomitant hunger in the people generally for more freedom and free expression, she feels.

In her insightful analysis of the Soviet media in transition, she notes that before perestroika the media were seldom criticized or reviewed, and that state television went unchallenged. Just as in other countries like Poland, once opposition and multiple voices were unleashed, the demands for alternative print and broadcast channels increased. Gorbachev tried to brake this impulse even while he trumpeted glasnost, or openness, but she says he did not understand press freedom in the Western sense. Ironically, he was most impatient with those publications closest to his own aims, *Moscow News*, *Argumenti i facti* or *Ogonyok*. By 1990, *Argumenti* saw its circulation balloon to 33 million, giving it a certain built-in immunity. "Glasnost was by no means an equivalent of press freedom but paved the road for it," she believes.[29]

"The Law of the Press and Other Mass Media" was adopted by the Soviet Legislature in June 1990, and Adrounas says it was the first legal document in the history of the Soviet Union regulating the media. Press freedom was given lip service in the Soviet Union Constitution, but as with its allies, the Soviets controlled the press by putting publishing, printing, distribution, and newsprint access under party control; establishing a state controlled broadcasting network; and enforcing party selection of key editors.

Now a new law opened press freedom debate in 1990, and the democrats fought for more rights—the right for citizens or groups to own publications, a reduction of censorship, demands that were familiar in Poland, Hungary, and Czechoslovakia years earlier. It did appear as if totalitarian control of the press might be easing, and new publications surfaced in the Baltics and throughout the country even before the law was approved, Adrounas notes. She found that by March 1991, 1,773 All-union publications were registered, half of them new, with 803 founded by state institutions, 291 by public associations, 27 by parties, 19 by religious associations, and 241 by private individuals.[30]

With perestroika there was some pressure to create collectives and give journalists more power in running the publications, an impulse Adrounas found echoing the acquisitive Bolshevik times of 1917, when the cry was to "rob what has been robbed." Still censorship existed; the military forbade any muckraking of its troubles or abuses by declaring such stories "state secrets," and economic and publishing/printing/distribution restraints kept the opposition press from going full throttle.

Gorbachev even tried to suspend press law and impose censorship when he did not like the way his role was interpreted in the invasion of Lithuania. Official television remained silent on support the Baltics got from the other republics during the growing secession movement, and Gorbachev wanted to suspend the Law of the Press he had previously approved. Androunas notes that Estonia's attempt at independence, for instance, was blacked out by broadcasting restrictions.

The Ukraine and Georgia complained bitterly of press restraints and seizure of printing equipment or lack of access to television during debates on nationalism or independence referenda. Thus she sees the glasnost era as a process of progress and retreat, forward and backward, as free press and free expression were supported only to be undercut when they became too threatening or inconvenient. All the while, journalists conditioned to support the powers that be, regardless of power struggles and leadership changes, also put expediency over conviction, further restraining a robust, free press from blossoming.

It is impossible to put an entire nation on the psychiatrist's couch and identify which impulses here, which influences and pressures there, accounted for later actions. But it seems clear that the steady liberalization of the mass media and freeing up of the press, and the ever-present demands from dissidents for more freedom and open expression, amplified by their samizdat voices or foreign broadcast media, impacted on some of those journalists. They stepped out of the shadows of their state-controlled news media jobs and ultimately gave accurate reports of the uprisings that swept the countries between 1989–1991, bringing an end to Communist control of the region. They did this sometimes with bravery and at great personal or professional danger.

Television played a particularly crucial role in the Soviet Union's dismantling during the August 1991 unsuccessful coup by hardline Communists hoping to reverse the liberalizing trends of glasnost and perestroika and halt Gorbachev's move toward a new confederation of independent states. We discuss later Romania's and Czechoslovakia's similar spontaneous and unforeseeable roles by television in the chaotic period of uprisings, coups, and countercoups in 1989 helped accelerate democratic change and destroy Communist control.

In the Soviet Union, on August 19, 1991, the State Committee on the State of Emergency tried to seize power, arresting Gorbachev and clamping down on the press, television, and radio. Moscow, Leningrad, and the Baltic States were prime targets. News was strictly controlled or censored. Victoria Bonnell and Gregory Freidin[31] note that from Glasnost in 1985 until the aborted coup of 1991, Soviets saw television becoming more of an open forum for ideas.

Leningrad, a maverick in state television, with a potential viewing audience of 45 million, produced probing programs such as "600 Seconds," "The Fifth Wheel," and "Alternative." There were attempts to stifle such free press impulses, but these were resisted.

Suddenly came the August 19th coup and television was reduced to emergency announcements appealing for Soviet patriotism in ponderous pre-glasnost voices. Dead air time was filled with ballet and opera to mask the absence of news. But there were seeds of opposition in the controlled media, and when the emergency committee went on live television with a press conference to defend the coup, state television producers and camera people deliberately focused on the nervous, trembling hands and runny nose of one of the coup leaders. Orders to edit this out in later broadcasts, along with the derisive laughter and disrespectful questions of skeptical reporters at the press conference, went unheeded. It was said the televised spectacle influenced other officials to distance themselves from the coup.

Even more significantly, Bonnell and Freidin[32] note, on August 20, Sergei Medvedev, a television reporter in Moscow for "Vremia," showed the tanks rolling into Moscow, reporting in a breathless battlefield voice. The camera and the report then switched to a towering Boris Yeltsin, standing on a tank and reading a statement demanding a new Russia and an end to Communism. There were scenes of people being interviewed who came to support the democrats because they said they had learned the lesson of Vilnius or their hearts simply told them to do so.

In analyzing the tapes, the authors say that actually the crowd was small around Yeltsin and the tank, and a long shot not taken would have easily shown the sparseness of the crowd and diminished the impact of the resistance. Back at the studio, Medvedev did last-minute editing up to air time, fooled his supervisors into thinking he had harmless tape, and went on the air. The coup leaders were furious and he was demoted and banned from the air. His report became a signal telling people where to go to defend the White House. Subsequent reports on "Vremia" showed people sitting on tanks, fraternizing with soldiers, cadets refusing to fight, and the sum total to viewers was that of a coup deflating from lack of support and growing opposition.

By August 21, the coup was declared over; Yeltsin fired the TV head and put broadcasting under Russian government control. The plotters were arrested. A film of three citizens killed in street resistance galvanized the country. Emotional funerals for the three was televised, and while a freed Gorbachev tried to downplay any sense of a coup, the publicity war was won by Yeltsin who pictured it as a near successful coup that only Russia resisted. The authors feel this set the stage for Gorbachev's exit and the downfall of the USSR. Thus state television, however belatedly in the history of events, played a crucial role in reshaping the nation and bringing an end to the Communism that so long controlled broadcasting.

In December 1991, five months after the failed coup, Gorbachev resigned and Yeltsin took power with the disintegration of the Soviet Union and the emergence of the confederation of independent states. But a disappointed Adrounas describes state television grovelling over Yeltsin, just as in August it had briefly lapped up the directives of the coup leaders and before that toadied to Gorbachev when his power seemed unchallenged.

Throughout the subsequent years leading up to 1995, there were disappointing incidents of new press restraints and repression, attempts at censorship and control. But the move away from previous days of totalitarian control, the absence of a multiplicity of media voices, and a people willing to be fed only censored scraps of news and information seemed gone forever, at least for the time being.

THE BALTIC STATES

Protest in the Baltic states came in various ways from individual acts of defiance to resistance through the underground press. Ray Hiebert[33] marks Lithuania's road to independence with the death of a 19-year-old student who burned himself to death in the public gardens of Kaunas to protest Soviet oppression.

It was also a time of "doublethink" and "double-talk," when one said one thing but meant another, and the entire population became astute at reading between the media lines for the true meaning.

In Estonia, journalism professors created their own "double-think." If party hacks constantly quoted Marx or Lenin, Hiebert writes, then the journalism professors would get across their true feelings by quoting a young Marx, who in his early years as a journalist supported liberal concepts of the press, including independent newspapers outside of government and free of censorship.

The underground press in the Baltics, Hiebert says, resulted in a samizdat outpouring of books, almanacs, magazines, and more than 30 regularly published underground newspapers between 1972 and 1988. These were produced under difficult and dangerous conditions, with the KGB following and searching suspects, meting out punishment and convictions. In Lithuania, with a particularly strong samizdat, one of the leading newspaper contributors, Algirdas Statkevicius, was arrested and imprisoned in a psychiatric ward for many years.

Hiebert reports that the most significant underground publication in Lithuania was *Lietuvos Kataliku Baznycios* [Chronicle of the Lithuanian Catholic Church], produced from 1972 to 1988 by Roman Catholic priests, usually in editions of 60 to 80 typewritten pages and primarily recording cases of religious persecution. Despite threats, harassments, and arrests, the Chronicle was the first and longest running regular samdidzat effort. It lasted until its mission no longer seemed needed in 1988.

Latvia was strictly controlled by the Soviet Union and the Communist party until 1985, when glasnost brought about some relaxation of media with differing opinions appearing in the press and unauthorized publications openly sold. A truly adversarial press emerged in 1988, especially with the publications of the Latvian Popular Front, the leading anti-Communist dissidents. By early 1990, Hiebert reports, this media activity led to the election of Popular Front candidates to parliament and the beginning of changes in government. Journalists were active in politics, and many were elected to parliament or became active in government.

Estonian mass media was under the control of the Communist party in 1988, but became agents of change, joining forces with the

Popular Front during the "singing revolution" period from spring of 1988 to the fall of 1989. Journalists already had achieved some independence from the Communist Party but then became advocates of the Popular Front against the regime.

Meanwhile, in 1988, the journalism department at Tartu University became independent and established its own curriculum without Moscow's control. The emphasis on Communist studies was reduced and student electives given greater choice.

The Baltics were more or less independent by end of 1990, although still technically a part of the Soviet Union. In 1991, Lithuanian television began to act as if it were truly free from Soviet domination. Moscow sent troops to Vilnius to restore Soviet authority. Troops surrounded the TV tower in Vilnius on January 13, 1991. In the assault, 14 unarmed civilians were killed, but the more grievous wounds were suffered by the Gorbachev regime in the worldwide condemnation that followed. By the end of the year, the Soviet Union would be no more, and the Baltic States were well on their way to true independence.

ROMANIA

When Nicolae Ceausescu came to power in Romania in 1965, there was a token attempt to loosen press constraints and end a jamming of foreign broadcasts, but this quickly ended as he came back from jaunts to China. He immersed himself in all points of control of the media, and in the 1980s, as he saw rapid changes in the countries around him in Eastern Europe, his nervous grip on the media became more severe.

His final days in 1989, ironically, would be hastened by a televised portrait album of horrors that speeded his own fall, captured ultimately with televised images of the bodies of his wife and himself shown after their summary trial and immediate execution.

In his fine analysis of the Romanian media and journalism, Peter Gross[34] concludes that an underground dissident press, with some rare exceptions, did not exist in Romania. This coupled with a majority of journalists who were supplicants to totalitarian regime—"a defiled profession" as one emigre observer labeled them—greatly impeded any transition to democracy up until 1989, when the country exploded with a long-suppressed anger.

In its final days, state-controlled television did uncap its lens and played a significant role informing the populace of the uprising. Television certainly affected the direction of events, just as we saw in the abortive coup of 1991 in Russia, which was influenced by television coverage. But for decades journalists in Romania were expected to further

communism, avoid any attacks on the socialist order, respect party leaders—thus protecting their license to practice, their advancements and
foreign travel perks. Many journalists simply dropped out; some turned
to radio, which for some reason was less scrutinized and seen as a less
important medium.

Gross notes that by the end of the 1980s, the number of dailies in
Romania fell to 36, a mere 9 national and regional radio stations were on
the air, and Romanians had 1 national television channel broadcasting a
sparse three hours daily. Journalism as a profession all but disappeared
by the 1970s. Romania's foreign correspondents were recalled in 1977
because of defections. Foreign papers were banned and contacts with
Western journalists forbidden. Censorship appeared at the micro level in
papers, and even when officially ended in 1977, a form of collegial self-
censorship was even more stifling with stories ground to dust as they
were passed from nervous hand to hand, with as many as six separate
reviews. Gross laments the tampering of photos, the twisting of information to fit the party line, and a wooden language that stultified.

Only sports reports, obituaries, and foreign stories that fit in
with the regime's policy seemed untouched. Gross found some rare
exceptions to the censorship—some student publications such as
Bucharest's *Viata Studenteasca* with its publication of forbidden poems,
or other efforts such as *Dialog*.

For the most part, the regime stifled any kind of underground
press opposition by criminalizing it. The Securitate enforced it, and the
means of public and private communication were strangled. Even the
right to own a typewriter was strictly regulated beginning in 1977. Gross
reports that an individual needed permission from the militia to have
one, samples of the script from all typewriters were kept on file, and
annual renewable permits were required.

With prison, beatings, or house arrest a real possibility for
samizdat efforts, some dissidents sought to sublimate their protest in
novels or simply opted out of the national dialogue. There was no alternative media, and freelance dissenting journalism evaporated. Gross
found that the Hungarian minority in Romania did create an underground press of sorts, and from 1981–83, 10 issues of *Ellempotok* were circulated and from 1983 to 1986, *Hungarian Press of Transylvania* did record
the oppression of Hungarians and the problems of Romania.

Despite the later claims of journalists after 1989 that they had
contacts with the opposition, Gross flatly says, "no Romanian underground press was established." One might count the leaflets stuffed in
mailboxes by a dissident, or a one-page newspaper on Bucharest streets
a year before the revolution produced by the later editor-in-chief of
Romanian Libera, who was arrested for denouncing the regime and held

in solitary confinement until released during the revolution of December 1989. He went directly back to his newspaper and was chosen to lead it.

Yet there was no real opposition press that could develop its own style or approach, no environment to deprogram the mind from the dull proselytizing of the controlled media. Gross feels that this left the country without a dissident movement to foment public opposition or give voice to alternatives or collective anger. He concludes that the newly freed Romanian media in 1989 were a cathartic outlet for pent-up rage but failed to provide constructive discussion as to alternatives.

With the reviled tyrant fled then dead, journalists could abandon communism but not the codes and languages long ingrained in themselves, and few journalists with credibility could step forward. Add to this the general distrust the public had of most media after decades of official, controlled propaganda (a feeling incidentally almost universal throughout the former Soviet bloc).

However, once the volcano of Romanian anger erupted, its heated flow was channeled over the airwaves by a series of unplanned events and some deliberate acts of courage. The revolt began in Timisoara on December 15, 1989. Ceausescu and his wife fled, and combat between the army and the Securitate battling in the street of Bucharest and in other towns held the nation's as well as the world's attention.

The spark was a dissident Protestant minister who resisted transfer. Gross notes that it was not the Romanian press but Radio Free Europe's Romanian service and Hungarian Radio and TV that reported the incident. People came to the church, clashed with police, and it erupted into a larger anti-Communist demonstration with the revolt spreading throughout the city. The Romanian media were silent but sent signals that could be read by the population. Foreign word-of-mouth reports sent the issue cascading around the country.

Official radio and television sought to play down the uprising, but the TV pictures of a weakened Ceausescu on his balcony and a sense for a real overthrow of the government suddenly sent the dictator and his wife fleeing, with a major revolt erupting on December 22.

Gross writes there were unverifiable reports that Romanian radio played a 19th century song, "Lion Cubs," on December 21 to signal a national uprising among clandestine free trade union movement, and a newspaper published a column with supposed signals for the uprising. Yet Gross finds no evidence the Romanian media even partially informed their audience of the events of December 15 or immediately thereafter, only that people used to reading between the lines sensed something major was happening.

With the army and the Securitate fighting in the streets, people moved to take over and protect the precious TV tower. On December 22, dissidents captured television and announced the creation of a National Salvation Front. People were urged to come and defend the station, and demands for free thought, free expression, and free elections were announced.

Television became the showcase to parade the captured son, Nicu Ceausescu, showing lavish gold objects in the dictator's palace and steak-fed dogs. A star anchor went on television and said that Romanian television had lied for 25 years and now must tell the truth. Gross describes the sight in the next two weeks as anyone was invited to the studio, and many came, to speak freely and vent their anger at the dictatorship. It became a nationwide community forum, with the people as witnesses of the upheaval.

Finally, on December 26, Romanians saw the bodies of the executed Nicolae Ceausescu and his wife Elena slumped against a wall. A scene of the firing squad was later suspected as staged, but there was no question about the summary trial and immediate execution that did take place.

Gross said that although Romanian television was too untrained and inept to report all the events, the simple act of turning the cameras in the right direction and vividly showing the fighting of the army and the hated Securitate was enough. A new independent TV station appeared, however briefly, in Timisoara with equipment and tapes loaned by Yugoslavian TV stations. "Free Timisoara TV" showed the fighting, the mass graves being opened, and although amateur, was an instant success.

On the newspaper side, the Romanian Communist Party paper *Scinteia* [The Spark] printed as usual on December 22 at 9 a.m., but then the staff decided to prepare a "real newspaper" called *Scinteia Poporului* [The People's Spark]. It lacked much news, Gross reports, but the headlines praised the people, spoke of the army's and people's uprising, and the foreign response. The symbolism was important and two days later the paper changed its name to *Adevarul* [The Truth].

As in other countries after the fall of Communism, the novelty of unfettered newspapers caused a boomlet of circulation, with the paper selling 2 million copies a day and *Romania Libera* 1.2 million. Although publications in the aftermath of the revolution quadrupled from 495 to 1,994, and the party press shrunk, the bubble burst, and by 1994, *Adevarul* went from 2 million to 90,000 and *Romania Libera* to 150,000 from 1.2 million.

Gross describes the outpouring as newspapers changed their names and affiliations from Communist Party control to independent, Communist journalists who days before praised Ceausescu suddenly had a conversion to democracy and tried to align themselves with the dissidents, usually not successfully.

Anti-Communist papers appeared and old staffs were fired or marginalized. Once banned writings reappeared, untrained but eager young journalists surfaced, older journalists wrote ponderously, but Gross laments the absence of factual reporting and the emphasis on violence and recriminations.

In the aftermath of all this, Romania faces the problems of high costs of production, shrinking audiences, and a broadcasting market that went independent quickly. But some time must elapse before the 100 radio station licenses issued in 37 cities can actually get studios up and running, although Gross predicted 75 stations on the air by 1995.

The brief euphoria with Free Romanian TV lasted only a few months, and Romanian state television continued to dominate, although racked with dissension. Attempts were made by Parliament in 1991 to include press freedom in a new constitution, but a better trained judicial system and a sharpening of press rights and access to information still awaits the reality that only time and good will can deliver. In the meantime, an estimated 20,000 full- and part-time journalists, 5,000 listed in four associations, need training and support to raise their levels of professionalism to be able to play a creative role in restructuring the nation democratically.

THE CZECH LAND AND THE SLOVAK REPUBLICS

Czechoslovakia became the Czech and Slovak Republics. The two grew more distant and finally separated after 1989 into distinct and separate entities and now constitute the Czech land and the Slovak Republic. There were four revolutionary periods in the history of Czechoslovakia, but in none did the mass media play a dominant role, although in each the media did find the events reshaping their structure, according to Owen Johnson.[35] Communication played a role in the 1989 revolution by delegitimizing the old regime—not by overt opposition, he contends, but by failing to persuade its audience and by simply mirroring events of the Velvet Revolution of November 1989.

Johnson dates the modern Czech press back to the 1860s and the modern Slovak press to the turn of the 20th century. The publications helped to foster a national identity. Some of the first papers were, interestingly enough, fact-based and objective but owed their allegiance to political parties. Gradually some Czech papers found an audience by becoming urban and nonpolitical, if sensationalist.

Johnson found that the press turned gray and boring under Communist control, and it was only after the death of Stalin and the riots in Plzen in 1953 that the press became more liberal, but still modestly so in comparison with Poland or Hungary.

Although a tangible element of the Prague Spring of 1968, the short-lived revolution that ended with an invasion of Soviet bloc countries was the visibility given reformers in print and broadcast coverage, journalists played a far lesser role in the events. Johnson says it was a revolution largely from below, with people using media channels to function as revolutionaries and the papers and radio the main source for political statements on the fragile democracy (television reached only half the population at that time).

From 1963 on, journalists in Czechoslovakia did demand liberalization and press freedom and were severely repressed following the Warsaw pact countries invasion in 1968. Hundreds perhaps thousands, lost their jobs. As in counterpart countries of the region, the Czech regime saw press freedom as a weakening of party and government authority and severely resisted any loss of control. Johnson sees a linkage between the events of 1968 and the revolution of 1989 and its aftermath. Although the Czech and Slovak countries were joined as one country, the media of each tended to reflect a more inwardly focused nationalistic set of concerns. In Slovakia there was little availability of Czech papers and an absence of Slovak papers in the Czech lands.

Johnson writes that after 1968 young journalists joined the system, attracted by the lure of pay and perks, whereas older journalists were expelled or decided to leave the field. It created a vacuum of leadership in which there were no leaders for the nascent reform movement, mostly an inexperienced generation focused more on professional opportunities.

In an unpublished manuscript, Johnson[36] writes that after the 1968 events journalism education increased as young people admitted to programs were conditioned to play it safe, joined the Communist Party, and "for the most part they carefully avoided challenges within their own institution and within the media at large." Today, he says, that approach is no longer viable as interest remains high in journalism education at Charles University, with 350 applications in 1991 and 10% admitted.

Charter 77, a human rights declaration issued in 1977, became a focal point for dissent in Czechoslovakia, and Skilling[37] says it stimulated a veritable explosion of typewritten materials that surpassed anything before it in the country. There were sanctioned Charter 77 documents cleared by a review board of members and a host of others prepared by individuals. Interestingly, Skilling notes that unlike the trend in Poland for massive duplication and mass distribution, Charter 77 documents were painstakingly typed in carbons. These were distributed to foreign broadcasters, the media, and policymakers as a way to influence thought on the key issues of reform and also evade the laws that seemed to sharply prohibit mass distribution while being tolerant of the cottage industry's typing reproduction for a limited audience.

However, there were also instances of clandestine publishing houses of Catholic orientation publishing books using offset techniques. A large number of periodicals did appear regularly from 1977 on, but again in typewritten form from Prague or Brno. Among the other typewritten "publishing" houses Skilling includes *Expedice*, edited by later President Vaclav Havel, the playwright, with 250 titles issued by 1987.

Yet even the Communist Party felt increasing pressure after 1985 for a more open and informative mass media, better reporting of societal problems, and more information on the reforms that were sweeping the rest of East/Central Europe. Still, any spilloff from the greater openness of glasnost after 1985 was limited. Critical dissent of society seemed to find more expression in fiction than the press. Newspaper reading and television watching did increase, but people remained deeply skeptical of the official party line.

Although the underground or samizdat press was another source, it was very limited in the 1980s. Foreign broadcasts from abroad were welcomed, and through them the dissidents knew they were being noticed. Johnson[38] dryly states: "In the late 1980s there was no need for dissidents or anyone else to conduct propaganda to persuade the Czechs and Slovaks that the Communist system was bankrupt and should be replaced."

Thus the interplay of a liberalizing media and a steady diet of foreign broadcasts that eroded the official party line did help delegitimize the governing regime, he contends, and the media acted as weather vanes for the impending changes. There were numerous clandestine meetings behind closed doors. But the pace of resistance, to foreign observers, seemed slower than in Hungary or Poland because journalists did not take full advantage of the 1980s potential for liberalization, even by 1989. The fear and memory of the 1968 crackdown remained and with it came a temerity for which some journalists paid dearly after the events of 1989, Johnson says.

There were journalists who contributed to the underground publication, *Lidove Noviny*, beginning in 1987, including Vaclav Havel, Rita Klimova, and Vaclav Klaus. For them, samizdat journalism was a waystation until they could assume roles of public leadership, and in this they mirrored trends in countries such as Poland. Later the publication sought to become a newspaper of record and thought but suffered a reputation as a spokesperson for the regime of President Vaclav Havel and saw a steady decline in circulation.[39]

The Velvet Revolution of November 1989 erupted when demonstrators were clubbed by police while commemorating the 50th anniversary of Nazi closure of Czech universities. Johnson says the media played little role in this event, and the crucial factor was not coverage but word- of-mouth and some foreign broadcasts that spread the word. CNN, German, and Hungarian TV provided coverage. Then too the exodus of East Germans seeking to escape by clamoring for passports in Prague also had a significant effect.

Actually, students began demonstrating in 1988 to recall the Prague Spring and kept returning to the streets through 1989. Word of mouth, theater presentations, hand bills, posters, and slogans were the people's channel, not the mass media, and the culmination of the uprising was the demonstrations in Wenceslaus Square in November 1989. This time the demonstrators demanded live broadcast coverage, and Czechoslovak TV finally did so on November 20, Johnson says. Within five days the demonstrations were being shown in their entirety.

The newspapers stepped in with *Svobodne Slovo* issuing a joint statement of the party leadership and the editors on November 20 criticizing the Communist Party for not talking with the demonstrators, but authorities shut down the presses after only a 1,000 papers were printed. Nearly 400 journalists publicly demanded press freedom on November 20. With the change in government also came the expulsion of many older party-approved journalists from the media.

Johnson says the new leadership in government felt the media were influential because they themselves were heavy media consumers. But after 50 years of restricted media the people were distrustful of most news media and consumption sharply dropped. Sensationalist tabloids did increase to the dismay of dissidents who had fought for press freedom. In Slovakia the media focused more on the nationalism that would culminate a short while later with a complete break from the Czech Republic.

The East/Central European region in countries such as Poland, the Czech and Slovak Republics, and Hungary have a long tradition of diversity of information as heirs to the pluralist press traditions of the Habsburg Empire before 1918, with all of them independent countries between the first and second world wars, Johnson notes.[40] The region was the world's largest consumer of newspapers at one point.

In looking at trends after 1989 in other parts of the region, Johnson found Albania had laws to fine and imprison journalists for publishing state secrets and did so in 1993, as well as jail terms for anyone criticizing the president. Bulgaria taxed media to exert economic and political control, and journalists struck in protest. Croatia cracked down on critical voices in the press. Slovenia found its young journalists influenced by the Western European neighbors trying to resist press freedom pressures. Serbia was harassing its independent press sources.

Even in Russia, Johnson found Yeltsin acting with great contra-diction after fighting for more press freedoms in 1991. When Yeltsin used tanks to oust the Parliament in 1993, he sent censors to all of Moscow's main printing houses and shut down Pravda and other papers for a time. While issuing decrees in 1994 for more government access to information, he also announced other decrees calling for government oversight of press performance as to accuracy and objectivity—obvious contradictions to a free and unfettered press.

Governments in all the newly independent NIS states retained government control of press production and distribution, and Johnson reports press censorship and restrictions in Turkmenistan and Uzbekistan just as severe as days of old.[41]

ALBANIA

Cathy Packer[42] conducted extensive interviews with Albanian journalists in 1993 and found them identical on several points—the party exerted strict control over the country's newspapers, meting out strict punishment for violations, and there was little opposition until the government loosened its grip in the mid-1980s. Albania kept its press on a tight leash, with censors calling in editors for the most minute "violations."

Journalists talked of their amazement as some visited other countries in the bloc or read an interview with a Western editor to see the differences under which they labored. Even in recent years, after the toppling of the Communist regime, Albanian journalists still struggled with censorship by newer political parties, physical threats, beatings, and attempts to introduce repressive press laws.

HUNGARY

Hungary in 1976 marks a year when dramatic opposition was under-scored by the appearance of the first samizdat publication according to Ray Hiebert.[43] He cites Miklod Sukosd,[44] who labels the 1976–1988 period in Hungary as a time for the "double media system" when a growing number of illegal, independent sources, and channels of social communications competed with the official media.

Intellectuals networked typewritten and mimeographed reports among themselves, and by the early 1980s illegal publishing houses appeared. There was a flourishing underground market for computers, printers, and VCRs to further these samizdat efforts. By the mid-1980s, the legalized production of antenna dishes gave Hungarians international television news reports.

Hungary thus presented a twofold media face, according to Sukosd, with the official media controlled, subsidized, and censored by the state and the illegal media private, communally owned, uncensored, and market-driven. Hiebert cites such leading samizdat publications at the time as *Beszelo* [The Speaker], founded in 1981; *Hirmondo* [The Newsletter]; *Demokrata*, and *Armlat* [Currents]. Illegal publishing houses including AB Konyvkiado and Magyar Oktober Konyviado (The Hungarian October Publishing House) turned out books, periodicals, and leaflets.

In the beginning, underground editors and writers used pseudonyms, but by the 1980s switched to their real names, even listing their home addresses. Hiebert cites among them Miklos Haraszti, later a member of Parliament in 1990–1994 and a leading total press freedom advocate, and other underground journalists like Janos Kis, Ferenc Koszeg, Ottilia Solt, and Laszlo Rajk, who all became leaders of the country's strongest opposition party in 1990–1994, the Free Democratic Party.

Skilling[45] feels the movement of Charter 77 in Czechoslovakia also stimulated interest in samizdat efforts in Hungary, with 34 of Hungary's intelligentsia signing a letter of solidarity with their Czech colleagues. Skilling said the Hungarians published several important volumes in 1977–78, one the results of a survey of attitudes toward Marxism with negative reactions and a radical demand for reforms, called *Marx in the Fourth Decade*, and a second volume, *Profile*, consisting of essays by 34 non-Marxist authors whose work was rejected by official journals.

Other highlights of the Hungarian samizdat effort in the late 1970s and later included the opening of a "book store" for samizdat literature in the apartment of Laszlo Rajk, son of a former Foreign Minister who was executed in 1949. Then appeared *Beszelo* [News from the Inside or the Talker], with issues of 1,000 copies and 120 pages, and *Kisugo* [The Outformer], with more radical dissent. But Skilling[46] says that in comparison with Poland or even Czechoslovakia, the samizdat efforts in Hungary were small, numbering no more than 50 or 60 activists, several hundred active supporters, and several thousand readers.

The police subjected the samizdat journalists to intense surveillance, phone taps, raids, fines, and threats in the late 1970s. But over time the official media could not ignore the underground media, at first reporting on the existence of the samizdat and the government's inability to eliminate it. Gradually, the lower ranks of official media such as specialized journals increasingly reflected, even if informally, the illegal media.

This metamorphosis continued into the mid-1980s, when main official newspapers openly commented on or quoted the underground publications, until toward the end of the decade the banned publications were legalized. This pattern occurred in other Soviet bloc countries. In Hungary, for example, *Beszelo* became a registered, legal weekly newspaper in 1989, a dramatic symbol of this remarkable transformation.

It is important to note that Hungary was undergoing fundamental changes in other ways during this era. A 1983 electoral law required at least two candidates for each political office. Even though it was still a one-party system, the door opened to debate and differences. With different factions emerging because of the law, the four national morning newspapers began to choose sides and support different political viewpoints. But Hiebert[47] believes that perhaps the most important change in this period was the 1986 new press law that stripped away the exclusive right of the Socialists (HSWP) to control media content. Each publication was now responsible for its own content, and journalists were given the right to gather information. Soon newspapers displayed differing viewpoints and journalists became more assertive.

This set the stage for a public viewing of internal political differences ordinarily not found in the controlled party press of the region. In 1987, Janos Kadar as both prime minister and party secretary saw age and party differences depleting his power. Karoly Grosz was named prime minister and Kadar remained party chief. The newspapers became pawns in the political battle, Hiebert says, with Grosz using the government newspaper, *Magyar Hirlap*, for his podium and Kadar supported by the newspaper, *Nepszabadsag*.

Then on September 27, 1987, Democratic Forum, the first powerful non-Communist Party was formed. One of its leaders was Imre Pozsgay, a former Socialist Party regional chief and general secretary of the Patriotic People's Front National Council (a Socialist Party organization).

Pozsgay and the Democratic Forum drafted a proposal critical of the Socialist Party's handling of the socioeconomic crisis and suggested democratic alternatives for Hungary. On November 14, 1987, *Magyar Nemzet*, one of the four main national newspapers printed a full-page interview with Pozsgay.

It was the first time an official Hungarian newspaper published information in opposition to the ruling party.The paper sold out instantly, and for the next two years the paper reflected the views of Democratic Forum. Gabor Toth, one of the paper's editors, told Johnston M. Mitchell[48] his paper sold out everyday for two years and could have doubled circulation if allowed more newsprint.

By May of 1988, there was a palace revolt that pushed out Kadar. Grosz took over the party and prime ministry and made Pozsgay a state minister in a conciliatory move toward Democratic Forum. The national newspapers became increasingly divided partisan forums for the various political factions, again reflecting the remarkable press diversity that was now in play.

Miklos Nemeth, a liberal protege of Grosz, became prime minister, and on April 24,1989, he used his powers over the broadcast media, calling in during a live news broadcast about the controversial building of the Gabcikovo-Nagymaros dam to denounce party secretary Grosz's position on the dam. Mitchell writes that for the first time ever the government had struck down the party line, a prime minister had rebuked a party leader, and the entire nation watched through the news media.

Two months later, an extraordinary act took place when the body of Imre Nagy, the prime minister during the 1956 uprising who was executed by the communists for his role, was given a hero's reburial in Budapest. He was a hero to the people and a villain to the party's hardliners. Yet the four national newspapers gave extensive coverage to the reburial, much to the consternation of the hardliners. Andras Banki, deputy editor of *Magyar Hirlap*, which gave 6 of its 12 pages to the reburial story, called the coverage "the true beginning of the free press and a pluralistic society in Hungary."[49]

Hiebert[50] traces the final days of Communist control in Hungary and the impact on the media: In September 1989, the Grosz government broke its accord with East Germany, and opened the border to Austria, letting a flood of East Germans who gathered in the West German Embassy in Budapest to escape. This major breach in the Iron Curtain could never be closed again by the Communists.

In October, the Hungarian Socialist Workers Party disbanded, parliament rewrote the constitution allowing a multiparty system and free elections in 1990. The Hungarians held discussions with the Soviet Union in 1990 for withdrawal of its troops from Hungary. In March 1990, two days before the first free election, *Nepszabadsag's* newspaper staff voted to become independent of the Socialist Party. The Communists were soundly defeated in the general election.

Hiebert notes that with party decline and the severe national economic plunge, the print media in Hungary saw a major reduction in state subsidies. Previously, journalists balanced their own journalistic instincts against the needs of the state. Now they had to concentrate on making a profit by providing a product the people would buy.

He cites the Soviet model of controlling the print media by isolating each element—publishing, writing–editing, printing, and distribution. The components lacked coordination and were often hostile or indifferent each other. This worked in an era of state-subsidized publications, when cross-financing let successful publications carry the money losers, but not in the new era of market-driven competition.

Printing was still dominated by three huge state printing houses—Kossuth, Szikra, and Atheneum—and they had long-term contracts, could inflate prices, do sloppy work, delay production, or miss deadlines at the whim of the party. These tactics were used as control, even punishment, but they continued even after the party was out of power.

Hiebert also notes the national postal service, Magyar Posta, had a total monopoly on distribution of newspapers and magazines since the 1940s. Like printing, it was used as a control factor by the party and continued even after the political changes of 1989. U.S. Ambassador to Hungary Mark Palmer[51] wrote in 1989 a series of postal increases "were intended not just to soak the newspapers, but actually to discourage them from signing up new subscribers." Distribution costs alone were 30% to 35% of a newspaper's newsstand price, an extremely high ratio.

Palmer also noted that another obstacle was the attitude of the journalists themselves. He said that just when state censorship was fading, a new emphasis on turning a profit left many Hungarian journalists surprised and resentful. Now they had to follow the dictates of business managers, not what the state wants. They must fundamentally change the approach to their work, Palmer wrote, and "Hungary's editors, journalists and publishers must concentrate on what the public wants."

Hiebert[52] believes that whereas journalism and government from 1990 to 1994 struggled with these obstacles, they were not truly successful in overcoming them and the challenges continue. In this, Hungary mirrors the experience of many of its former Communist counterpart countries in the East Central European region, which struggled with the many impediments to achieving a free press, devised tools of underground samidzat opposition, reshaped political and party configurations, fought censorship, and emerged in the 1989 sunlight only to find the journey to a viable, economically secure press was just beginning.

CONCLUSION

Unquestionably, news and information played a major role in the events leading up to 1989 and the dismantling of the East/European Communist bloc of nations and the Soviet Union. The Marxist–Leninist movement saw mass communications as an essential component in bringing about a Communist world order, and in each country of the East/Central European region we see a depressing repetition of the same patterns of repression.

All means of print and broadcast communications were in the hands of centralized party or government control. Publishing houses, printing, all editorial functions, distribution, newsprint, and book paper supplies were carefully controlled. In broadcasting, the channels of radio and television, the means of transmission, and production were all under state control. The journalists and key management personnel in this elaborate network of print and broadcast were strictly regulated. Their education, selection, and employment were used as means of control, reward, or punishment.

It is hard to believe, but the most innocuous tools of private communication from paper, ink, carbon paper, and typewriters to more complex means of print reproduction, from mimeograph machines to computers, were strictly regulated. The means of reception—radios and television sets, rooftop and satellite antennas, cable connections; the recording and playback equipment from simple tape recorders to elaborate multiunit devices for high-speed copying—were restricted. Telephones, when one could get them and when they worked, were carefully monitored.

Yet despite all the elaborate precautions, despite the Byzantine censorship requirements that piled higher and higher in paranoiac fear as totalitarian regimes felt their grip slipping, despite the demands for loyalty, despite internments, arrests, firings, economic punishment, or exile, despite all this, dissidents found a way to speak out.

Although there were many commonalities in the official policy of the Soviet bloc nations to discourage a free press or open dissent, we can also observe significant differences in severity and approach to how these controls were imposed in the USSR, and the Central and Eastern European nations.

Poland faced nearly a decade of martial law during the 1980s after a brief experiment with press freedom and open expression. Still, that nation of 40 million in a largely homogenous population with a single dominant language (despite some ethnic minorities) was able to disseminate opposition positions nationally in the underground press without confronting the complexity of the USSR with 56 languages in its various republics.

In contrast to many of the Soviet bloc countries, Poland also had a strongly entrenched Roman Catholic Church in a country of over 90% Catholics, many fervent adherents. The Church publications and its various meeting places provided a haven for dissident journalists who were barred from nonsectarian media.

Much of the political and journalistic leadership found sustenance in overt or subtle support from the church. Journalists in the USSR could not fall back on such assistance, in which religion was more assiduously opposed by the regime. However, in the Baltic states, Lithuania saw its underground press in the 1970s and 1980s being helped by Catholic priests who produced their own samidzat publications.

A review of the Soviet bloc region also shows that the degree of resistance by working journalists or underground dissidents to press restrictions also varied greatly. It was stronger in countries such as Poland and Czechoslovakia, perhaps less so in Hungary and minuscule in Romania, Albania, or Bulgaria.

The crackdown on journalistic dissidents was also more pronounced in the Soviet Union, although the period of glasnost did produce a visible thawing. Yet this was offset by the country's strongly held traditions from Lenin onward that the press was a tool of propaganda with fact and opinion liberally mixed and the adherence to party policy and the absence of criticism of the government a matter of dogma.

In Poland, and in Hungary and Czechoslovakia (later the Czech and Slovak republics), with a longer history of diverse media expression, the adherence to the Lenin dogma of the media control was less severe. Hungary had a twofold press, one controlled and the other illegal, private, and more open going back to the 1980s, although not as robust as in Poland during Solidarity's opposition to martial law.

Through its Charter 77 human rights activists in Czechoslovakia, declarations of opposition were disseminated to a wider audience by feeding the statements to the Western press and wire services and having these loop back into the country via the broadcast channels of VOA, BBC, RFE, and the like. This dependence on foreign broadcasts to get their dissident messages heard within their own country, in fact, became a common tactic in many of the Warsaw pact nations before 1989.

In common, all the Communist governments in the Central/East European region resisted to the very end giving any real degree of freedom to journalists. Censorship, overt or by vague rules of self-censorship, was rampant in every country. The degree of repression and the tendency to jail dissident journalists rather than simply fire them, however, did vary from country to country.

The impact of television on the toppling of Communist governments also varied greatly by country. In Poland, the round table discussions and the Solidary victory at the election polls in 1989 were key elements of change. The active underground press rototilled the soil for this, but television was strictly controlled by the state, with only small and tentative experiments with liberalization before 1989.

However, in the Soviet Union, television showing the resistance to hardliners by Boris Yeltsin in 1991, when he famously stood on the tank to defy his opponents, is considered a pivotal element in rallying support for the democratic forces. In Czechoslvakia, word-of-mouth and televised reports from Hungarian and German television and CNN (Cable News Network) were considered essential elements in the Velvet Revolution in 1989.

In Romania, the television reports of the steady erosion of Nicolae Ceausescu's regime and the vivid pictorial reports of his and his wife's execution fueled that country's change of government. In the Baltics, the dramatic reports of the resistance in Vilnius against Russian troops, and the killing of unharmed civilians, grievously undermined the Soviet Gorbachev regime and contributed to revolutionary change.

We have seen dramatic examples of individuals who risked their lives and freedom to create and operate elaborate alternative news and information resources through the underground or samizdat press. Others, those above ground, resisted the censorship laws and tested the outer boundaries of what information they could gather, edit, and report. All the while foreign broadcasts kept up a steady stream of news reports that, in some cases, were key factors in the subsequent revolutionary movements of the 1960s, 1970s, and into the important two decades leading up to 1989 and beyond. Western journalists supported their colleagues in the East with sympathy and resources.

The lessons we are learning from this long assault on free expression and press freedom are still being compiled. One of the strongest is the dangerous consequences when governments meddle in free press principles and twist the channels of communication to their own ends. Another is the resilience that people, individually or in organized networks, show in dissenting from this and finding ways to get around the blocked channels of communication and create alternative ones to open the floodgates of news and information.

A final lesson is in the danger of complacency. The years after 1989–91, when the major political changes occur, show us that the hold on democratic principles as it relates to a free print and broadcast media, and the ability of people to use these resources, can easily slip away. Even those who fought for press freedoms and who gained power in democratic elections sometimes develop amnesia and find themselves repressing the very free press principles they fought to achieve. Sometimes it is masked under the rubric of public good, or bureaucratic convenience, but it has the same dank smell of repression.

It will take years to gather all the stories of individual bravery and to properly collect, index, and make available the rich legacy of printed and audiovisual outpourings from the samizdat era of the underground resistance. But even half-told, the story is one of great courage and resilience and the inevitability of the human spirit to speak out, aside from the simplicity or complexity of the technology, in whatever formal and informal means of communication are available. This is the message and the lesson of East Central Europe over these last many decades.

END NOTE

Even in 1997, the impact of the underground or samizdat press, eight years after the political changes of the the Central and Eastern European region, can only be partially measured. In Poland, for example, there is a distinct tendency on the part of some young people to forget about the past and move on.

In discussions with younger journalists and students preparing for future media careers, there is a reluctance, almost an unwillingness, to look at the brave work done by their predecessors less than a decade before.

This is partially due to the desire to simply forget the unpleasant years of repression. Those who were leaders in the underground press share this reluctance, at times perhaps fearful of boring their younger colleagues with what now may appear to be old war stories.

Some, including university archivists at places such as Jagiellonian University, wish to preserve the underground publications, as fragile and ephemeral as they are, before they disappear from both Poland's physical landscape and the psychic consciousness of the population.

During martial law, there were incidents of librarians who at some danger to themselves hid away copies of the publications for future preservation.

It is hoped that through a more formal gathering of such materials within the context of a national archive initiative, the complex history of the resistance will be preserved. But there is no guarantee of this without special funding and Polish institutions willing to take a leadership role. At the same time, it is important to launch an oral history project in which the key players could be systematically interviewed and their contributions recorded and codified for future scholarship.

Just in random interviews, this author has found any number of stories either spontaneously presented or, more often, offered reluctantly after some prodding, once trust has been established.

I recall a seasoned senior print journalist in Krakow, who nonchalantly described her experiences in helping smuggle in an offset printing machine so that her underground paper could be produced. An elaborate clandestine drop was devised, with an auto trip from Warsaw to Krakow employing switched cars and taxis. Even her own pregnant condition was used as a diversion to throw off the secret police. In the end, they were followed, discovered, arrested, and imprisoned by the police.

Young student journalists in Poznan shortly after 1989 described to me their own experiences in preparing and distributing a university underground resistance paper, and proudly calling themselves members of "The Flying University," modeled after previous underground universities that appeared throughout the oppressive decades of the Communist regime.

There was a respected radio journalist in Warsaw who casually described the experience of having her family visit her in jail, being imprisoned for months for simply trying to report the truth of what was happening in the shipyards of Gdansk, or a journalist, a good friend, and colleague, who one day during our travels casually pointed out the jail where he was imprisoned after publicly marching in the streets of Krakow to protest martial law. He chose to work as an orderly in a mental institution until the day came that he could return to free and independent journalism after 1989.

At one of the numerous workshops we conducted around Poland for media professionals and students, a participant once gave me copies of small books, fitting in the palm of one's hand, that he had published during martial law. One I examine now and treasure is a once banned history of the life of one of Poland's heros, Jozef Pilsudski. It is painstakingly and minutely printed on typed pages, photo-reduced to tens of thousands of words in a condensed format to use every bit of precious paper, hand stapled, and marked with the stamp "Libertas."

As outsiders, we are rightfully reluctant to get too deeply involved in the internal debates of what ought to be done to preserve this past. Ultimately the initiatives must come from the Poles themselves—the journalistic practitioners who were at the center of the activities and the trained researchers and archivists who can properly gather the material. It requires a collective will of the people to then utilize the materials in their educational institutions and discuss them in public forums.

Scholars in Poland are gathering these materials, and it is essential that they become part of the textbooks and curriculum of journalism and media studies programs, and add to the rich tapestry of this poignant part of the country's history.

One night in a Warsaw apartment, a few years after the end of martial law, we looked at the rough cut on video of what was to be a future television documentary of the events surrounding the resistance that spread nationwide from the shipyard workers of Gdansk in the 1980s. The filmmaker, our host, was piecing the documentary together from segments of film he had carefully hidden throughout various parts of Poland so that they would not be confiscated and destroyed by the secret police during the darkness of martial law.

Poland, like many of the other countries of Central and Eastern Europe, is in a time of slow and fragile healing. The reluctance to dwell too much in the past influences the desire for reconciliation rather than revenge. It is this mood that has underlined the reluctance to open up previous secret police files and identify previous agents, collaborators, and supporters of the regimes, whether in the media or elsewhere.

Still, years later, journalists who were expelled from their publications find it difficult to forget. In our workshops, especially in the first years after the end of martial law in 1989, there were vigorous debates over the reluctance of the newer journalists to work, even sit, alongside those who they considered, if not collaborators with the old regime, at least pliant participants by their silent acquiescence.

Editors still tell us of the difficulty of getting some of the former underground reporters to break away from the one-note reporting of opposition to the former totalitarian regime, and to adopt the professional standards of general, nonpartisan, well-rounded reporters able to report all sides of a story, fully and fairly.

At times, in the workshops, we had to vigorously insist that reporters in their coverage of, for example, local and regional elections cover both the democratically minded candidates they personally supported and the members of the former regimes they despised but who were now legal candidates entitled to fair and full press coverage in a new independent Poland.

How can I report the name and candidacy of someone who formerly played a role in my being jailed? one journalist asked. As unpleasant as this might be, it had to be done if the longer term trust and respect for a free press is to be preserved was our response.

Another, speaking of a broadcaster who had reported the official statements of the enforcers of martial law while dressed in a military uniform, said to me one day that when he hears his voice, even on the radio, it is as if he "sees the voice dressed in a military uniform."

Many former underground journalists have made an admirable transition to the general reporting and editing roles that today underpin the most respected publications. Numerous top editors and staff of *Gazeta Wyborcza*, one of Poland's leading daily newspapers that grew out of opposition and underground impulses, are examples of this successful transition.

Then, there are others who relished the heady, exciting days of underground press opposition, but could not make the transformation to a nonpartisan press and have moved on to other careers, or simply disappeared into the population.

All these contrasting views in the prism of underground, resistance media need to be studied carefully, the artifacts of the movement in print and audiovisual form preserved, and the lessons of history learned.

NOTES & REFERENCES

1. Arthur Banks *Political Handbook of the World: 1989*. New York: SCP Publications, 1989, p. 494.
2. Tomasz Goban-Klas, "Making Media Policy in Poland," *Journal of Communication*, Winter 1990, pp. 50ff.
3. *Ibid.*
4. Robert Downing, *Radical Media*. New York: South End Press, 1984, pp. 322-345.
5. *Ibid.*
6. *Ibid*, p. 327.
7. *Ibid*, p. 330.
8. Anna Husarska, "After the Round Table: A Talk with Adam Michnik," *The New Leader*, April 3, 1989, pp. 8ff.
9. *Ibid*, p. 10.
10. Ted Kaminski, "Underground Publishing in Poland," *Orbis*, Fall, 1987, pp. 313-ff.
11. *Ibid*
12. Tadeusz Kowalski, "Evolution after Revolution: The Polish System in Transition," *Media, Culture and Society*, 1988, pp. 183-196.
13. *Ibid.*
14. Karol Jakubowicz, "Solidarity and Media Reform in Europe," *European Journal of Communication*, 1990, pp. 333-353.
15. Downing, *op. cit.*
16. Goban-Klas, *op. cit.*
17. Anna Husarska, "Voices from the Underground: Publishing in Poland," *The New Leader*, December 15–16, 1986, pp. 86-ff.
18. *Ibid.*
19. Jerzy Pomorski, "The Use of Video and East-West Flow," in Jorge Becker & Tamas Szecssko (Eds.), *Europe Speaks to Europe*. London: Pergamon Press, 1989, pp. 166-181.
20. Karol Jakubowicz, "Poland: Media Systems in Transition, " *Intermedia*, June –July, 1989 pp. 25-28.
21. Karol Jakubowicz, "Political and Economic Dimensions of Television Programme Exchange Between Poland and Western Europe," *Democracy and the Mass Media*. London: Cambridge University Press, 1990, pp. 138-ff.
22. *Ibid.*
23. Peter Kaufman, "Coming Up for Air," *Publishers' Weekly*, September 7, 1990, pp. 14-22.
24. H. Gordon Skilling, *Samizdat and an Independent Society in Central and Eastern Europe*. Columbus: Ohio State University Press, 1989.
25. Jane Curry, *Poland's Journalists: Professionalism and Politics*. New York: Cambridge University Press, 1990.
26. Rilla Dean Mills, "In the Communist World," in L. John Martin and Anju Grover Chaudhary, (Eds.), *Comparative Mass Media Systems*. New York: Longman, 1983, pp. 167-186.

27. *Random House Webster's College Dictionary*, New York: Random House, 1990, p. 1187.
28. Elena Adrounas, *Soviet Media in Transition*. Westport, CT: Praeger, 1993.
29. *Ibid*, p. 4.
30. *Ibid*, p. 43.
31. Victoria Bonnell and Gregory Freidin, "Televorot: The Role of Television Coverage in Russia's August 1991 Coup," *Slavic Review*, Winter 1993, pp. 811-839.
32. *Ibid*.
33. Ray Hiebert, Unpublished manuscript notes to the author, 1995.
34. Peter Gross, *Mass Media in Revolution and National Development. The Romanian Laboratory*. Ames: Iowa State University Press, 1996.
35. Owen V. Johnson, "Czechs and Balances: Mass Media and the Velvet Revolution," in Jeremy Popkin, ed., *Media and Revolution*. Lexington: University of Kentucky, 1995.
36. Owen V. Johnson, "Media," unpublished manuscript to the author, 1992.
37. Skilling, *op. cit.*
38. Johnson, 1995, *op. cit.*
39. Johnson, 1992, *op. cit.*
40. Johnson, *ibid.*
41. Owen V. Johnson, "East Central and Southeastern Europe, Russia and the Newly Independent States", Chapter 10, in John C. Merrill, editor, *Global Journalism: Survey of International Communication*. White Plains, New York: Longman, 1995, pp. 155-171.
42. Cathy Packer, "The Emergence of the Free Press in Albania," in Al Hester and Kristina White, eds., *Creating a Free Press in Eastern Europe*. Athens, GA: The James M. Cox, Jr., Center for International Mass Communication Training and Research, The University of Georgia, 1993, pp. 83ff.
43. Hiebert, *op. cit.*
44. Hiebert, *op. cit.*: "For this analysis, I am indebted to Miklos Sukosd and his unpublished (as of 1994) manuscript, *Hungarian Politics: The Mass Media from Stalinism to Post-Communist Democracy in East Central Europe*. Sukosd is an assistant professor of sociology at the Central European University in Budapest.
45. Skilling, *op. cit.*
46. *Ibid*, p. 35.
47. Hiebert, *op. cit.*
48. Johnston M. Mitchell, "*The Evolution for Freedom: The Mass Media in Eastern and Central Europe*", edited by Al Hester and L. Earle Reybold. Athens: University of Georgia, 1991, pp. 136-137.
49. *Ibid*, p. 139.
50. Hiebert, *op. cit.*
51. Mark Palmer "Printing with Red Ink—Newspaper and Magazine Publishing in Hungary," unclassified U. S. Information Agency cable (April 25, 1989) in Ray Hiebert notes and unpublished manuscript, 1995.
52. Hiebert, *op. cit.*

3

Transition:
From the End of the Old
Regime to 1996

Ray Hiebert

When Communist governments began to collapse in East/Central Europe in 1989, optimism prevailed about the quick movement toward democracy, the rise of press and mass media freedom, and the development of a free market economy.

To be sure, the mass media had played a significant role in bringing about the post-Communist era. As Teresa Sasinska-Klas, professor of journalism at Jagiellonian University in Krakow, properly points out, the media played an important role "in the reconstruction of Polish society towards democracy and a free market economy" and was "the catalyst of these changes, even though [the media were] undergoing a fundamental transformation" themselves.[1] This can be said about the media in other countries of the region as well. However, the road to reconstruction, democracy, and a free market economy was neither straight nor smooth.

Even after new governments were elected, they often resorted to old totalitarian methods in their eagerness to retaliate against former totalitarians, including control of the press to further political interests.

In some countries political power fragmented into dozens of different parties and ideologies. Countries formerly supported by the old Soviet Union found themselves cut off from their old patronage, and without the necessary new infrastructure of a free market, their economies stagnated. Foreign capital needed to jump-start a new system, especially in the media sphere, was slow in coming to some parts of the region.

Old forms, especially in media, remained largely in place. It was difficult to get agreement on new media laws. It was hard to replace a generation of journalists, conditioned over decades to supporting the party line, with a new generation who had fact-based reporting skills and investigative zeal. It was simply too expensive, without enormous foreign capital investment, to purchase new private printing presses and construct broadcast studios and transmitters; all this expensive technology had been "publicly" owned and therefore controlled by the party and the government. That condition continued through much of this transitional period. So too did centralized distribution of print media. For years the party had been able to control the press partly by controlling its circulation, and there was no quick dissolution of this infrastructure after the 1989 revolution.

Even as late as the fall of 1996, as this was being written, experts on the subject such as Karol Jakubowicz, chief adviser to Poland's National Radio and Television Council, chairman of the supervisory board of Polish Television, and a lecturer at the University of Warsaw's Institute of Journalism, wrote that: "Throughout the [region], governments continue to finance the press; control newsprint, printing plants, and distribution; and, often, control broadcast-transmission networks."[2]

It is important to recognize that in many of these countries, as Jerome Aumente, professor of journalism at Rutgers University, points out about Poland, the changes in journalism were usually incremental rather than sudden and revolutionary.[3] The changes were often based on cultures and social patterns that had existed before, and those that were changing did so fairly slowly.

In Russia itself, the pattern was typically atypical. As Alena Androunas writes about with authority in one of the most complete and penetrating analyses of the Soviet and Russian media's transition, the Communist Party leadership was itself responsible for breaking its monopoly on the media. President Mikhail Gorbachev introduced the concept of *glasnost*, or increased openness, as a way of strengthening his hand against other communist leaders who opposed his reforms of the party and the economic system. But *glasnost*, which Gorbachev intended to be a process controlled by the party leadership, quickly took on a life of its own, and the party lost control of the mass media. Power over the media passed at first to the Soviet government, as codified in a new press law approved in 1990. Then, when the Communisty Party and the entire Soviet government were discredited by the aborted putsch of December 1991, power passed to the reform government of Boris Yeltsin.[4] Since then, as Dean Mills writes in another chapter in this book, the Yeltsin government has tried, with decreasing success, to impose its own will on the media.

New forms of journalism and mass media did rise, but they were forms that did not often further the goals of an informed electorate needed to build a strong democratic society. Much news reporting was marked by partisan advocacy rather than objectivity. Many new media, including pornographic, artistic, religious, and alternative forms, were developed to relieve pent-up frustrations from decades of repression. Much was done simply to make a profit in a new marketplace, regardless of ethical concerns, and sensationalizing media content was often the easiest way to make money. The new entrepreneurs of East/Central European journalism sometimes seemed to be more similar to the robber barons of the 19th-century United States than to socially responsible professionals in a 20th-century democracy.

It was a mistake to expect U.S. media experience to translate easily to East/Central Europe. For one thing, not all democracies shared the United States' absolutist ("no law") philosophy about press freedom. In trying to forge a transition from communism to democracy, many East/Central Europeans felt they had a right to look at other models of democracy, not just that of the United States.

In addition, countries and cultures of East/Central Europe did not have much of a democratic tradition (except in Czechoslovakia), causing the process of democracy-building to be slower than Americans anticipated. Also, these countries had less affinity with U.S.-style "objective" journalism and more with Western European partisanship and advocacy, in which media align themselves with particular political ideologies, and media of the party in power become more or less "official" media.

In some countries the old journalists who worked under communism were regarded as enemies of the new democracy, especially by right-wing nationalists. In some countries, the press and mass media reverted to older cultural patterns and roles. This was exemplified most clearly when Czechoslovakia split into two different countries because of their traditionally separate cultures. The Slovak media returned to their old nationalistic traditions characteristic of Slovak culture, whereas the Czech media were "torn between an individual, serve-the-public ethic and an aphilosophical bottom-line ethic," attitudes characteristic of the more cosmopolitan Czechs.[5]

It should be pointed out that there were different phases of the transition for the media. Sasinska-Klas divides the transition in Poland into three periods: (a) the phase of "lively enthusiasm and obligatory transformation" (from mid-1989 to mid-1991), (b) the phase of "apparent stabilization and fundamental transformation" (mid-1991 to the end of 1992), and (c) the phase of the "fight for the market" (from the beginning of 1993 to the present [1996]).[6] Not all countries fit easily into this construct, but all experienced definite phases of change and development.

Finally, and perhaps most important, the economies of East/Central Europe in the first five years of post-Communism were not yet strong enough to support independent media completely across the full media spectrum. It would take a long time before newspapers could get two thirds of their financial support, or radio and television 100% of their revenues, from advertising, as is the case in the U.S. Conspicuous and wasteful consumption, which is both the cause and result of U.S. advertising, was a new phenomenon even in Western Europe and had never been a tradition in East/Central Europe. So it could be a fairly long time before media could be sufficiently supported by advertising to become completely independent of government subsidies, foreign investments, or the influence of political ideologies and vested interests.

GOVERNMENT AND PRESS: MEDIA WARS

It should not be surprising that in the first years of post-Communism, the pendulum of politics swung back and forth between extremes of left and right, nationalist or conservative and liberal or radical, capitalist and communist or socialist. In many countries voters in their first free and multiparty elections swept the old Communists out of power, only to bring them back (albeit in new clothing) when the second wave of elections came around.

The first regimes voted into power after the "velvet revolution" were often composed of the most strident anti-Communists, or, as in the case of Boris Yeltsin, old Communists who had reformed. People who had spent time in prison as dissidents were sometimes the new heroes elected to public office, whether they had any talent for leadership or not. Many were right-wing nationalists, less interested in promoting free speech and press than in furthering a nationalistic cause. In many instances they became almost as repressive about the press as the former Communist party bosses had been.

Ironically, in a number of countries journalists became part of the new governments. In Poland, Aumente points out, the first new prime minister was a journalist, Tadeusz Mazowiecki, who had been editor of the Solidarity newspaper and before that editor of a Catholic opposition newspaper. The editor of the successful new daily *Gazeta Wyborcza*, Adam

Michnik, was elected to the first post-Communist Parliament. Aumente says that "people like Michnik and Mazowiecki played key roles as advisors to the fledgling Solidarity movement and were close to Lech Walesa, until later political differences drove them apart."[7]

With the defeat of Communism, press freedom had begun to flower. This meant, of course, that the press was now free at last to criticize the new governments. But when the press engaged in such criticism, the new government leaders felt betrayed; after all, they said, they had been democratically elected, and a free and democratic press ought to support a freely elected government. The new government leaders were often highly critical of the press because most of the journalists were the same people who had worked for the Communists. In addition, new leaders frequently had little idea how a free press works or how good press relations could be used to work with a free press in order to achieve at least some understanding of each other. One after another, the new government leaders—Vaclav Havel in the Czech Republic, Josef Antall in Hungary, Boris Yeltsin in Russia, Lech Walesa in Poland, Zhelyu Zhelev in Bulgaria, among others—felt the stings from critical journalists and lashed out against a free press.

It has been said that "since 1989, Hungary has enjoyed a press that is among the freest and most competitive in the former communist bloc as a result of the country's smoothly negotiated transition to democracy."[8] Yet the new Hungarian government's reaction to press freedom was fairly typical. The first post-Communist government (a coalition led by the conservative party, Magyar Democratic Forum, MDF) claimed the media had "declared war," and it fought back with all its might, a situation that became known as the "media wars." The MDF government threatened critical publications and journalists. It used its control of the monopoly in printing and distribution to reward supportive publications and punish those which were critical. It established a new daily newspaper (*Uj Magyarorsag*) and a new magazine (*Magyar Forum*) to carry the government line, and it surreptitiously provided financial support for several weak newspapers, which in turn gave comfort to the government. These newspapers would have gone out of business without that support.

Variations on this theme marked the relationship between new governments and the mass media in much of post-Communist East/Central Europe. Lech Walesa in Poland, dissatisfied with the National Broadcasting Council, forced its head to resign. Communists were returned to power in the Parliament in the second fully free post-Communist elections in September 1993.

In Slovakia, prime minister Vladimir Meciar tried to control the press by placing limits on access to information, delaying foreign investment in media companies, and intervening in appointments to state broadcasting.[9] In 1992, Meciar stopped the privatization of Danubiaprint, the plant that printed all the country's newspapers, and control of the printing press allowed government to pressure journalists at will. Most of the media remained state-owned, giving government authority to fire journalists who were not cooperative. In November 1994, the ruling party was able to dismiss all but one of the 18 members of the state radio and television supervisory councils for political reasons.

Early in its post-Communist period, during the May 1990 election, the interim Romanian government decreased newsprint allocations and press time for opposition party publications. It allocated 50% of television time to the 80 opposition parties and took the other 50% for itself. The government ran a "continuous campaign" to discredit the opposition press, writes Peter Gross, "accusing it of being a destabilizing factor, of being supported by foreign powers, and wanting to 'sell the nation.'" Often it was the ex-Communists in government who were most skillful at manipulating the media and gaining or regaining power because they had the most experience. Eugen Serbanescu of *Romania Libera* told Gross that "the communist elites, now the non-communist elites, are more skillful at manipulation," so they won the 1990 and 1992 elections.[10]

In Russia the press was considered by many to be the most democratic institution, and yet the government continued to use and abuse the broadcast media. National television was treated as the president's own house organ, but even private television was not immune. In 1995, the government threatened to take away the license of NTV, the nation's largest financially and editorially independent TV network, because of its factual reporting of the conflict in Chechnya.

The newly independent nations that had previously been an integral part of the Soviet Union—for example, the Baltics, Belarus, and Ukraine—had double difficulties. First they had to establish their own independence from Moscow, and then they had to free themselves from the old Communists and a totalitarian mindset at home. Sometimes this was so difficult that people returned the Communists to power and sought to reestablish their affiliation with "mother" Russia.

Belarus was an interesting case in point, and its media wars had a slightly different tone. Private media, especially print, had come into existence, but even at the end of the transition period, most of the state ministries were still controlled by former Communist functionaries. The speaker of Parliament was a former police general. In a 1994 article in *The People's Paper*, two police officials advocated strong presidential powers over the media. Belarus's economic problems were perhaps the most crucial factor in its struggle for democracy, and government officials used the weak economy as an excuse for their demand that the press should serve the party and the government. The prime minister publicly stated that he would only support that part of the press which supported the government. In early 1994 he issued orders telling journalists what to do as if he were giving a military order.[11]

The ruling government grew to believe that reunion with Russia would solve many of its economic problems, and when the media criticized that position, the prime minister lashed out against them. Even Moscow media criticized the Belarus position, saying Russia did not want Belarus with its economic problems. So the prime minister's press secretary went on television in Russia and told Belarus citizens that the two Russian TV channels received in Belarus were not presenting a true picture of Belarus. He said that certain external forces did not want a reunion so they distorted information. Throughout his speech he stressed the brotherhood of Russia and Belarus.

Newspapers in Belarus sometimes appeared with blank spaces where government censors had deleted stories. Several independent newspapers were refused the right to be printed at state-run printing plants. And when these papers were printed in neighboring Lithuania, the postal service was ordered to stop their delivery, supposedly because they were "foreign newspapers."

The Baltics also had to struggle against Russia as well as their own communism through the transition period, but they came through the transition better than most of the newly independent states.

In Latvia in January 1991, following the growing controversy between the Latvian government and the Communist Party, Soviet soldiers occupied and damaged the Press House in Riga, Latvia's best printing plant and editorial offices, temporarily disrupting the publication of many Latvian newspapers. At the same time, the Communist Party organized its own radio station in one of the Soviet army units in Riga. By May newspaper publishing had returned to normal. But in August 1991, the defeat of the attempted hardline coup in Moscow emboldened the Latvian government to clean hardliners out of its own house, not only old Communists but also any journalists who were critical of the government. Latvian soldiers (rather than Russian) occupied Latvian television, closed down the communist radio station, and the Republic of Latvia was officially declared independent on August 21, 1991.

"The illusion that independence would solve all problems soon began to fade," says Inta Brikse, head of Latvia's journalism school. In its place came the war between press and government. "The government accused the press of failure to understand political processes; the press in turn accused the government of dictatorship." For a time the government even reinstituted censorship.[12]

Both the press and the Popular Front government lost ground in the following months and years. The Popular Front, which had 70% of the vote in 1990, fragmented into many smaller parties, ending in defeat in 1993 with only 3% of the vote. The successor government was right of center, but not extremist.

In the meantime, the state of the economy proved to be a severe blow to Latvian media, especially after Russia imposed economic sanctions in 1992. Latvian government subsidies were reduced and inflation soared, driving up the cost of newsprint and ink. Newspapers had to raise prices at a time when newspaper readership was already declining. But stability slowly came to Latvia and private media began to thrive.

Lithuania went through similar struggles. Many political parties were organized, newspapers were privatized, and commercial broadcasting started. By the end of 1992, general elections to parliament resulted in a landslide victory for the leftist Lithuanian Democratic Labour Party, and in early 1993 Algirdas Brazauskas became the first freely elected president. Although the government was composed mostly of former Communists, it could not stop the advances of a free press.

The Lithuanian government did create a new organization of "Press Control," which did not censor or interfere with the press but simply registered publications. Censorship was not permitted, but a law protected state secrets. However, this law was changed so the burden of responsibility for protecting secrets rested with the government, not the journalist.

Of all the Baltic nations, Estonia's transition from Soviet communism was the most peaceful and stable. Its market economy developed more rapidly than Latvia's or Lithuania's. The mass media had played an important role in Estonia's move toward independence, and by the end of the transitional period, the media themselves had become more independent than they were in many of the other former Soviet states.

Considerable controversy over privatization of newspapers continued in Estonia into 1994, causing some of the same problems that characterized the Soviet period, according to Lisa Trei, a U.S. journalist in Tallinn who wrote for the European *Wall Street Journal* and taught journalism part time at Tartu University.[13] Even in Estonia, as in perhaps every country of the world, the government continued to seek control of media in general, but television in particular.

In Ukraine, even as late in the transition as Fall 1996, the government still owned 80% of all print distribution facilities, and most publications remained dependent on government subsidies. Local authorities in 1996 were able to shut down newspapers that were too critical, including *Nova hazeta* in Kiev, *Prykarpatska* in Lviv, *Vechirny Sevastopol* in Crimea, and *Gorod* in Donsetsk.

Of all the countries dealt with in this chapter, Albania remained the most repressive, the place where government most easily won its wars over the media. The ruling party continued to have complete control over all radio and television. Although private newspapers were allowed to publish, they were taxed heavily and had to limit their distribution to less than two dozen state-owned stores. In 1996, the government was still putting journalists in jail. The editor of one newspaper was convicted of slander for an article in which he accused a government official of corruption. Even the son of the former dictator, Enver Hoxha, was sentenced to a year in prison for giving an interview to a small newspaper, *Modeste,* in which he called the current Albanian government a "pack of vandals."[14]

NEW MEDIA LAWS

Since 1989, when Communist governments began to collapse, and throughout this transitional period, almost all countries of East/Central Europe struggled with laws defining legal rights, responsibilities, and limitations of mass media. Belarus, Russia, and Moldova passed new press or general media laws. Many countries continued with old press laws but passed legislation that would permit private broadcasting to exist along with government or public broadcasting. Among these countries were Bulgaria, the Czech Republic, Estonia, Hungary, Latvia, Poland, Romania, and Slovakia. Ukraine and Slovenia passed both types of laws.

As far as broadcast laws are concerned, East/Central Europeans looked to Western Europe for models. As Karol Jakubowicz points out, they tended to reject the German model as far too complex (with more than 30 different local broadcast laws, half a dozen treaties between the states, and the Constitutional Court also having a role to play). They rejected the British model, which required a complex legal structure and tradition. "Most countries," wrote Jakubowicz, "ultimately adopted the French legislative model, in which the Supreme Audiovisual Council is the main broadcast authority. . . . It thus offered them a 'respectable' solution that still allowed them to retain control over broadcasting."[15]

Often, journalists and media themselves in East/Central Europe have sought laws that would delineate their rights and provide some protections, usually through a revision (not elimination) of the existing Communist-era press laws. Journalists throughout East/Central Europe pushed for the public right to gather and publish certain information and participate in certain public proceedings during the transition period.

By the end of the period, in only a few cases in East/Central Europe (such as Belarus) was there any real censorship of newspapers or print media. There were ways in which pressures could be brought to bear on newspapers and magazines, especially in those countries where printing presses and distribution services remained public, or state-owned, rather than private. But, in fact, it seemed most governments were no longer really worried about most things newspapers or magazines might print. Reading was down, paper and printing prices were up, and, most important, everyone was watching more television. For these reasons laws about radio and television became the real battleground for media freedom.

The old Soviet Union was one of the first to enact new legislation; actually, the "Law on the Press and the Other Mass Media" was adopted in June 1990 when the Soviet Union still existed. According to Elena Androunas, the 1990 law was "the first legal document regulating the media in the history of the Soviet Union." The history of that law was long and complicated. Among its main provisions were the abolishment of censorship and affirmation of the right of anyone to establish a new medium, but it also required the registration of a new medium. The law also stated that "monopolization of any mass medium (press, radio, television and others) is not allowed." When the Union was dissolved, the new Russian parliament designed a new media law that Yeltsin signed in December 1991.[16]

Most of the reformers had themselves been communists, foremost among them Yeltsin himself. So, although they paid lip service to the idea of free media, in practice they tended to act like the party bosses they had been. They were, like many reform politicians in the rest of the former communist world, ready to strike back at critical journalists. As Mills notes in another chapter, true advances toward journalistic freedom were taken, not given, by the government. Freedom came first to print publications, only slowly to broadcasting, which initially was controlled by the new government.

The simple key to editorial freedom was usually economic independence. Newspapers and magazines, supported (although often inadequately) by readers, advertisers, or political parties (or some combination) were the first to break free. Television journalism had to await the introduction of NTV, the first private TV service in Russia.[17]

Development of press and media laws in Poland were fairly typical of the region. Its first press law had been adopted in 1938, but that law was invalidated by the Communists in their takeover after World War II. During the Communist era, according to Dr. Izabela Dobosz, an academic at Krakow's Jagiellonian University, the press was tightly controlled, by the police and by the Communist Party, even without a law.[18]

A new law passed in 1984 guaranteed certain media freedoms, and, says Dr. Dobosz, that law actually helped the process of breaking the Communist Party's monopoly because it gave more freedom to radio, television, and the distribution of print. A permanent commission was created in 1984 and that group continued to function, even after the Communist government fell. Censorship was abolished in 1990.

After 1989 legal questions of all sorts, including media, were the subject of continuing debate throughout East/Central Europe. Various agencies—journalists and their organizations, politicians, government experts, and academicians—worked on revising the press and media laws. Some of the questions being debated were: Should freedom of speech and press be limited? If so, in what direction? Where should press laws be located? Should press laws be linked with other laws?

The Poles and other Eastern Europeans often looked to Western Europe for models. Dobosz points out that not all countries of Europe had formal press laws—for example, Holland, Norway, and Sweden. But Germany, Austria, and Italy had such laws. Italian and German constitutions were quite clear about the direction of press control, she says. The Italian constitution allowed confiscation of media, required financial reports, and prohibited sensationalism. The German constitution allowed government to defend women and children from the press. In Germany each Land (or state) had a press law.

Common points characterized these press laws: They all required certain basic data in each issue, such as the printing of corrections, editorial responsibilities, certain fines and penalties, sending copies to certain libraries, and the printing of government decrees and laws. But there were also some essential differences; for example, in Italy, all publications had to be registered, whereas in Germany no registration was required.

One subject of media law debate concerned the profession of journalism itself and access to the profession. One faction held that journalism was not a profession to be licensed but rather an activity that should be freely open to everyone, Another faction argued that to be a professional journalist required higher education, an internship period, and licensing by a press council, made up of members chosen by the journalism profession. If the journalist was irresponsible, or unprofessional, this council could conceivably take away such a license.

Those in favor of licensing journalists sometimes used Italy as an example. In that Western European democracy, an 18-month internship and an examination were required before a person could be called a journalist; editors must have had 10 years of experience, and their editorships were for a limited term. The Italian law made a distinction between regular and specialized press.

Often East/Central European journalism organizations objected to rules about who could be a journalist. For one thing, said Jan Pieklo, president of the Krakow branch of the Union of Polish Journalists, "no one has 10 years of practice in Poland now. It is difficult to prove your experience in underground journalism."[19]

Some proposals for new media laws also required foreign correspondents to be accredited. Some proposals limited foreign media ownership, usually prohibiting foreigners from having a majority interest.

Many Europeans, having witnessed the horrors of fascism and the Holocaust, believed that the instigation of war and racism was justification for press limits.

Some journalists and journalism organizations pressed for the adoption of self-administered ethical codes rather than government regulations. In 1991, the Polish Journalists Association adopted such a new code, a "media charter." It differed from the Communist charter in Poland, which had several dozen articles; the new one had only 15. The previous charter was similar to the civil code, with specific penalties. The new charter had several general principles, and the last article said only that general punishment might be meted out.

Similar legal arguments and restrictions existed throughout East/Central Europe. In both the Czech and Slovak Republics, experts in 1991 began to draft a comprehensive new media law covering such topics as privacy, new technology, foreign investment, libel, right of privacy, monopolies, and source protection. In March 1991, the two Republics enacted new laws that ended state monopoly on land-based broadcasting, although the government preserved the right to license private broadcasters. But other aspects of press and media laws continued to be debated for several years without definitive action.[20]

In October 1995, the Czech cabinet passed a new press bill intended to update press regulations, but it did not assure media access to government nor the confidentiality of sources. When Czech journalists reacted negatively, Prime Minister Vaclav Klaus announced that the government would open information offices to facilitate the distribution of government information. The new law also did not change the defamation law, which allows journalists to be prosecuted for defamation of the president and other Czech officials.

In Romania a new constitution was adopted in November 1991 that guaranteed "freedom to express thoughts, opinions or beliefs" and forbade "censorship of any kind." However, the constitution also placed limits on public expression, making it unlawful to "defame the country and the nation, to incite war, national, racial, class or religious hatred, to incite discrimination, territorial separatism or public violence, as well as obscene acts contrary to good morals." The constitution also mandated that "the right to information must not jeopardize measures to protect the young or national security," and it obligated public and private means of mass communication "to ensure that public opinion is accurately informed."[21]

Romania also passed an "audio-visual law" in 1992 and a radio-TV law in 1994 that provided the legal structure for the broadcast media (see later discussion). When the National Salvation Front interim government took power in December 1989, it said it would abrogate the body of Communist laws. But one that remained in effect was the defamation portion of the penal code which had made libel and slander crimes for which one could be sentenced to prison. From 1990 to 1994, several versions of a new press law were unsuccessfully proposed, which most observers felt would be restrictive of the press. Most journalists were vehemently opposed to a press law, even though one part of it might guarantee journalists' access to government information.[22]

Romania's penal code also makes a crime of anything that could be characterized as an "offense against authorities." In 1995, two journalists were charged under this law because of articles they wrote in the newspaper *Ziua*, which alleged that President Ion Illiescu had been recruited by the KGB when he was a student in Moscow in the 1950s.

In Hungary's first five years of post-Communism, new laws to govern, regulate, protect, or affect the mass media were constantly and heatedly debated, yet much was left undone. The process actually started in 1989 under the Communist government but was not completed under the first post-Communist government's rule from 1990 to 1994. Even after the former communists came back to power in 1994, they too delayed and procrastinated in passing a "media law." Much of the debate was simply politics at work, the argument of liberals who wanted little restriction on media and conservatives who wanted a lot. Finally, at the end of 1995, the socialist government managed a coalition of interests to enact a media law that established a new framework for broadcasting, allowing private radio and television to be developed for the first time in Hungary. But a press law to regulate print media and journalists was never passed, and at the end of the transition period as this is being written it was no longer an issue.

In the Ukraine, a new "Law on Information" and a "Law on the Printed Mass Media" were passed in late 1993. These laws basically conformed to other international laws, forbidding censorship and guaranteeing the right to receive information. But by the time these laws were passed, according to the International Press Institute, economic controls had already assumed far more significance for Ukraine's media than government regulation.[23]

Lithuania passed the first new press law in Eastern Europe in February 1990. The other Baltic countries, Estonia and Latvia, followed suit quickly thereafter. Basically these laws stated that the government could not censor or interfere with the press but could register publications and protect state secrets. In the Baltics, as in many Central and Eastern European countries, the laws of libel shifted from government to individuals, resulting in the growth of libel charges as civil suits rather than criminal cases. For example, in Estonia the former head of the Communist Party was falsely arrested in Minsk; the arrest was reported but not the finding that the charges had been false. He sued and won.

In Belarus the passage of press and media laws was a source of continued political friction. Many drafts were prepared by Parliament and subjected to the argument and debate of various factions. The Soros Foundation funded a number of efforts to resolve the issues with conferences of foreign experts meeting with Belarus journalists and officials. The Belarus minister of information regarded the support of the Soros organization as an intrusion in his nation's affairs. "In the Soros report," he said, "they made it seem as if all we wanted to do was hide or censor everything. There is no censorship here, but a government still needs to protect some secrets."[24]

Serge Navoumchik, an anti-Communist and deputy member of Belarus Parliament's committee on mass media and human rights, in an interview in 1994, said his group had been able to write only one statement concerning the illegality of monopolization of the mass media in Belarus. Four times that statement had been put up for a vote, and each time it failed to get enough votes to pass. The chair of that committee in 1994 was an old Communist Party apparatchik. Parliament was under the control of the Council of Ministers in 1994, originally founded by the Communist Party, which hoped to pass a media law that would clearly enable government to control the mass media. The Presidium, the small upper house of Parliament, in February 1994 tried to name a former Communist police colonel as chair of the committee that dealt with the press. The Ministry of Information would report to this committee, insuring that government's control of information would be secure.[25]

The Belarus mass media law that was passed ultimately "affords the government broad, discretionary powers to engage in *a priori* control of the content" of the media, says legal critic Jakubowicz. It allows the government to "stop the activity of a mass medium" for "multiple breaches" of an article forbidding media from "calling for the usurpation of power; change by force of the constitutional order; breach of territorial integrity of the republic; kindling of national, social, racial, or religious dissension; propagation of war and aggression; [or the] encroachment on [the] morality, honor, and dignity of citizens."[26] Obviously, any critical article in the media could be accused of any of these "transgressions."

In Ukraine, the broadcast law states that "tele-radio organizations do not have the right in their programs to divulge information constituting state secrets or other secrets protected by legislation, to call for forcible change or overthrow of the existing state or public order, or [to call] for violation of the territorial integrity of Ukraine." It defines the duties of program makers to act as censors by not permitting the dissemination of such information.[27]

NEW PRINT MEDIA

Throughout East/Central Europe, the collapse of Communism ignited a veritable explosion of new publications. Some succeeded and survived the first six years of transition. Only a small handful became dominant in their markets or regions. Some grew fast and then slowly began a long fade. Others bloomed and died overnight. Some made enough profit to become truly independent of government and political parties or other interest groups. Many had to depend on government support. Many were constrained by government printing presses and distribution systems. Print media were quicker to privatize than radio and especially television. Broadcast frequencies were easier for governments to control, and most of the new governments refused to let go of television because they saw its control as essential to maintaining their new power.

As media privatized, of course, they became targets for foreign investors, and these investments were one of the reasons for proliferation. But daily newspaper circulation in general declined steadily throughout the period. The move toward advertising support also brought competition for the few advertising dollars. The development of private printing presses and distribution systems was also accompanied by the rising cost of newsprint, raising the price of publications to subscribers. At the same time, new and more attractive Western shows on television stole readers away from high-priced newspapers. Readership declined across the spectrum, and many publications, new and old, struggled desperately to survive.

Even before the new press law was passed in 1990 in the Soviet Union, new publications started appearing in Russia as a result of *perestroika*. By March 1991, Mills writes, 1,773 "All-Union" publications had registered under the new law, and half of them were new. Establishing ownership was impossible, however, because the new law required only that the "founder" be identified, not the "owner." So the statistics showed that 803 had been "founded" by state institutions, 233 by editorial collectives and publishing houses, 291 by public associations, 27 by political parties, 19 by religious organizations, "some" by cooperatives and businesses, and 241 by private persons.[28]

Androunas says that the most successful and the largest of the new independent newspapers at that time was *Nezavisimaya gazeta*, founded by the Moscow City Council and edited by Vitaly Tretyakov, a former journalist with the *Moscow News*.[29] The paper later fell on hard times and for a time suspended publication, losing out to more aggressive and market-oriented newspapers.

By the fall of 1996, Russian newspapers, like those in most other countries of the region, had sorted themselves out with their readers and their political patrons into a new order. The most widely read publication in Russia was no longer *Pravda* or *Izvestia*, each of which at one time had circulations in the tens of millions. Now it was the weekly paper *Argumenty i fakty*, with a circulation of 3.6 million.

In Poland, about 2,500 new publications were started after the fall of Communism, but fewer than half survived. Privatization of old media was a slow process. Poland established a commission to dismantle the old state press system, affecting 2,200 approved publications. By mid-1995, only 106 of Poland's dailies and weeklies had been offered to private buyers; only 69 had been sold.

Of the new media to become dominant in their region, the outstanding example was Poland's *Gazeta Wyborcza*; it had been started in 1989 to provide fair coverage for the first parliamentary elections, and it became the largest newspaper in Poland, with a circulation of about 700,000. But it also had a decidedly leftist bias.

A new Polish weekly, *Nie*, prospered with a circulation of about 600,000, largely as a result of its pornography, sensationalism, and heavy anti-Catholicism. Another weekly, *The Warsaw Voice*, became influential, although it was published only in English for a relatively small audience.

In the Czech Republic, two new publications achieved significance but by no means the largest circulations. They were *Lidove Noviny*, a daily with a circulation of about 125,000, and *Respekt*, a weekly reaching about 60,000. Like many new newspapers in the region, political partisanship was a common characteristic. *Lidove Noviny* started as a dissident monthly before the fall of Communism and then became a daily newspaper with the ambition to become "a newspaper of record and information as well as a journal of thought and opinion."[30] Increasingly, however, it was viewed as the voice of the Vaclav Havel government (some called it the "castle news") and circulation steadily declined.

Another new Czech newspaper, *Telegraf*, was started in June 1991 as *Sobotni telegraf*, closely affiliated with the Civic Democratic Party. Modeled on the British *Daily Telegraph* and expressing similar political views, it became a daily in January 1992.

Three new Slovak newspapers were politically aligned or dependent on government support. *Narodna obroda* was supported by the Slovak government, *Slovensky dennik* was the paper of the Christian Democratic Party, and *Verejnost* was founded by the Public Against Forum. Johnson writes that it was "plagued by amateurish journalism and its opposition to Slovak nationalism, rapidly losing readership as a consequence."[31]

The growth of new media in Romania since December 1989, writes Gross, was "nothing short of spectacular." By 1994, the Romanian press had nearly quadrupled, from 495 publications prior to December 1989 to about 1,800 in 1994. In the meantime the party press had declined from about 100 publications to about 10 in 1994.[32]

The first newspaper that truly freed itself from Communist control was *Romania Libera*, published by the first company to be recognized as a private business in Romania. It received a grant from the International Media Fund, which provided printing equipment to help it become a real independent newspaper. Another daily, *Adevarul*, was a new incarnation for the former Communist Party newspaper *Scinteia*. A sensationalistic tabloid, *Evenimentul zilei*, was started in 1992. These were among the most prominent dailies in the new era. Gross writes that the circulation of these and other new publications "skyrocketed" after the December 22, 1989 coup. By January 1990, *Adevarul* was producing 2 million copies per day, *Romania Libera* 1.2 million, and, within two months after it became established in 1992, *Evenimentul zilei* was printing 750,000 copies daily.[33]

However, in the next few years, after 1992, all print media in Romania were afflicted with the same economic problems that troubled the entire region: rising costs of newsprint, printing, distribution, taxes, and declining readership. By 1994, *Romania Libera's* circulation had dropped to 150,000, *Adevarul* to 90,000, and *Evenimental* to 180,000.[34]

In Hungary, the end of one-party socialism also brought a proliferation of media. That started in 1987, when 10 new publications appeared, picking up speed quickly. In 1988, there were 85 new publications, and in 1989 more than 250, called a "press bomb" by one Hungarian journalist.[35] By the middle of 1990, the Hungarian Post Office estimated it distributed 1,500 publications, whereas another 2,500 publications were sold on newsstands.[36] A more important indicator of publication growth is that in 1986, there were only four publishing houses; in 1990, there were 250.

Some of the new publications grew rapidly, although most fell quickly by the wayside. It is estimated only a third survived. One remarkable success was the new magazine *Reform*, a racy atypical weekly that reached a circulation of more than 300,000.

In Lithuania, soon after the fall of Communism, publications grew from about 190 to more than 1,500, with about 600 publishing houses where formerly there had been fewer than 10. *Respubliks* was a new independent newspaper started in 1990 and quickly reached the number two position with a circulation of about 85,000. This was a tabloid-type paper with sensational articles and investigative reporting. Its prestige and circulation grew after its deputy editor was murdered outside his home in a gangland-type assassination by a "Lithuanian Mafia" because "he knew too much." The newspaper was investigating organized crime.

Pozicija, a new weekly subtitled "Lithuanian People's Rights Defense Association Weekly," was an interesting example of Baltic journalism. It published long articles by prominent Lithuanian writers and poets and members of the Union of Writers, concerning family rights, social questions, demographic statistics, economics, and comparative market prices. One of its writers frequently interpreted new laws and was usually highly critical of them. One page was devoted to revelations from the KGB archives and to the memory of those who gave their lives during the Soviet occupation.

In Latvia, according to James Kenny, public affairs officer at USIS in Riga, half of all the papers published in 1991 were out of business by 1994.[37] One success was *Diena*, established by the Council of Ministers in 1990. It took the place of the former official party newspaper, *Latvias Republikas Laikraksts*, and became the largest circulation daily. Fifty-one percent was owned by a joint stock company and 49% by a Swedish newspaper. The Latvian edition had a circulation of 81,000 and the Russian edition 18,000 in late 1993.

In Estonia, in 1987, 217 periodicals were being published. From 1988 to 1993, nearly 500 new periodicals were started. Most were small local papers and newsletters, but 47 of them were national newspapers and 44 were magazines and journals. Many of them did not survive, and circulation of all newspapers and magazines dropped significantly after 1990.

Privatization was not as swift in some other countries as it was in the Baltics. By 1994, in Belarus, some 641 newspapers and magazines were being published, but only 123 were privately printed and only 71 published by private individuals; 471 were still being produced on state-owned printing presses. The nature of the publishers provided an interesting look at the lack of real free market journalism: 137 of the 641 were published by the council of people's deputies, 75 by "public" organizations, 51 by editorial boards, and 14 by religious organizations. In book publishing, 719 new books had been produced, but only 223 of these were privately printed.

One growing field, in Belarus and other countries in East/Central Europe, were publications that printed only advertising, usually small classified ads, as people were learning to buy and sell in a free market. Five such advertiser publications were being published in Minsk by 1994.

By mid-1994, there were more than 1,000 periodical publications in Bulgaria. Many large towns had 6 to 10 dailies or weeklies, and the national capital, Sofia, had at least 60.[38] Most of these publications were marginal at best. The leading new newspaper was *24 Chasa* , a nominally independent, sensational tabloid, mixing sex and in-depth political commentary. Together with its sister publication, a weekly *168 Chasa*, this enterprise, founded and managed by former Communists, became financially successful because advertisers wanted to get messages into their pages.

In Ukraine the economy was the main problem for all publications, new and old, throughout the transition. Newsprint was often in short supply, sometimes so critically that daily newspapers were not published every day. There was little promise that Kiev's eight dailies would survive the transition, but newer papers seemed to have a better chance than the older ones, and the most respected Ukrainian newspaper was not even in Kiev; it was *Postub*, in Lvov.

In spite of these problems, proliferation of print media continued in Ukraine. In 1996, the Minister of Information and Press reported that "about four or five new publications are registered each day." He did not say how many failed. As of June 1996, he said there were 5,325 registered periodicals, including 3,953 newspapers, 1,025 journals, and various other publications, but his report also indicated a drastic decline in household subscriptions from an average of five or six to less than one per day.[39]

RADIO AND TELEVISION

Unlike the print media, private broadcasting did not quite flourish in East/Central Europe in the first years of transition from Communism. Owen Johnson points out that "all of the post-communist rulers of Eastern Europe have tried fervently to hold on to state control of radio and television broadcasting."[40] In most countries, governments continued to control national radio and television, and private, independent broadcasting, if it got started at all, was limited to local or regional stations.

In Western Europe generally, radio and television have been viewed as public utilities, and it was easier for East/Central Europeans to follow that model than the more free enterprise U.S. version. Several factors encouraged the public utility model, including limited frequencies and expensive equipment. But perhaps most important, television (much more than radio) was seen as the most powerful and dominant medium and thus potentially the greatest threat to government, while at the same time the easiest to control.

Jakubowicz points out that except in Poland, "where a considerable effort to decentralize the system has been made, the old centralized, capital-centered broadcasting model has been continued or reinforced." He explains that "regulations giving public-service broadcasters lower advertising quotas than commercial broadcasters, enforced in the Czech Republic, Slovakia, Estonia, Hungary, Latvia, and Ukraine, demonstrate those broadcasters' dependence on other, usually inadequate, sources of revenue—often the state budget."[41]

The Czech Republic, Slovakia, Poland, and the Baltic countries were among the first to change their laws to allow private broadcasting. After the Czech and Slovakian governments passed new laws in 1991, dozens of private entities applied for new frequencies. The Czech Republic generally followed a free market model, whereas the Slovakian laws established radio and television as public rather than private institutions (similar to neighboring Austria).[42]

In Slovenia, television in 1996 was dominated by a public station, Televizija Slovenija, started in 1991 and by 1996 reaching 90% of the market, but still partially funded by the government and thus influenced by the state. Pop TV, a fully private company, was started in 1995, broadcasting mostly foreign programming, with a much smaller audience. In Croatia, the state-controlled media in 1996 were still treated like government services such as the army or police, and the government still had a monopoly on television channels.

In Romania the Communist Party had completely controlled all radio and television until the December 1989 coup. Romanian Radio (the national service) reopened some of the regional stations that the Communists had closed down and reformed itself as a "public broadcasting service" independent of party politics. In 1992, it was separated from Romanian Television, and in 1993 its status was redefined by Parliament to become "a partner to political forces."[43] By 1996, it was broadcasting five program channels—news and feature reports, cultural and artistic programs, youth and children's programs, local Bucharest news and features, and regional news and features. It also operated six regional stations around the country, broadcasting "minorities" programs in German and Hungarian, and transmitting internationally on medium and shortwave in 14 languages.[44]

Like Romanian Radio, Romanian Television broke with the Communist Party after the 1989 fall of Ceaucescu. It became Free Romanian Television, but that freedom lasted for less than two months. By February 1989, Gross writes, "Romanian Television was once again a valuable and manipulated asset" of the new government. By June 1990, according to the *Index on Censorship*, the government's role in the state-run television "reveal[ed] a persistent misuse of power."[45]

Romania passed a new Audio-Visual Law in May 1992 that demonopolized broadcasting, allowing private or independent agencies to apply for licenses from the Ministry of Communication, which established the frequencies. By the end of 1993 licenses had been given to 82 radio and 50 TV stations, and 196 private cable companies. But these licenses only went to local and regional broadcasters. National radio and television remained in the hands of the "public." A June 1994 law solidified this position by creating the Romanian Radio Society and the Romanian Television Society, two separate agencies operating as "autonomous public services of national interest," still technically under the control of the government.[46]

The first independent television station to broadcast in Romania was Free Timisoara Television in 1990, and by 1993, 16 local stations were on the air, transmitting what Gross called a "hodge-podge of programs ranging from local news and commentaries to foreign films and self-produced talk shows or interviews, from Worldnet to other U.S. produced programs."[47] Only one station became powerful enough to be a national force—Soti Television (Romanian Society for the Creation of an Independent National Television Company), established in September 1990. It was granted the right to broadcast programs on Romanian Television's Channel 2. It received a $400,000 turnkey production studio from the International Media Fund in 1991, as well as aid from the Soros Foundation. Soti-TV was the cause and center of a storm of political controversy, intrigue, and infighting. By the spring of 1994, it was permanently off the air, its permission to broadcast on RTV-2 revoked.

Romanian government's quasi-monopoly on television was seriously weakened in late 1995 when a private company, PRO-TV, reorganized itself to become a successful business and quickly became the most popular station in Bucharest and the surrounding region.

In Poland after the fall of the Communist government, pirate stations began to go on the air even before the government passed laws legalizing private broadcasting. Three privately owned commercial radio stations began operating in 1990 in Krakow and Warsaw, and attempts were made to start private television stations in Warsaw and Gdansk. Gradually between 1990 and 1993, more pirate radio and TV stations appeared, including a private station, TV Echo, in Wroclaw started in 1990, and plans were made for a religious TV station in Krakow. But Poland's national television continued to be dominated by two state-run channels, TVP-1 and TVP-2.

After much haggling by all parties involved, the Polish Parliament in 1993 finally approved a law that ended the state monopoly on radio and TV. By that time as many as 70 pirate radio and about 20 pirate TV stations were broadcasting. The first private TV network, Polonia I, began telecasting in March 1993. It was owned by Italian publisher/broadcaster Nicola Grauso, despite the fact that the new Polish law prohibited more than one third foreign ownership in broadcast stations.

The most controversial aspect of the new Polish broadcast law was the provision that required radio and television to adhere to a "Christian value system" and prohibited the promotion of "activities that violate the law or the interests of the state or opinions that conflict with morality and the public good."[48]

Poland's new laws, however, did not immediately bring big changes to secular broadcasting. Bernard J. Margueritte, a Franco-Polish journalist, in a paper presented at Harvard University, points out that old leftist-liberals of an earlier era continued to play large roles in national broadcasting in Poland. He quotes Jan Maria Jackowski, one of the country's bright young journalists: In spite of the legal restrictions in broadcasting on respecting Christian values, "It is more difficult for me to present on television not only Catholic programs, but programs about, for example, family values, than it was under communism!"[49]

However, much of Poland's independent broadcasting had a definite religious cast because many stations were operated by the Catholic Church. In fact, in a 1991 agreement the government gave every diocese in Poland a local share of radio frequencies. By 1994, the Church was operating 46 radio stations on 56 frequencies and had applied for a local TV station near Warsaw. The largest Catholic radio station in Poland, Radio Maryja, was given 60 frequencies and requested 50 more.[50]

Privatization of broadcasting developed fairly quickly in the Baltics. By early 1994, Lithuania had 30 television stations, of which 29 were private, the latter being mostly regional stations with limited power and reach. The one state-owned station still dominated national television, and although an initial effort in 1989 tried to make it into a "public" facility similar to Western European models, the new government tried to keep tight control over its programming.

Lithuanian Radio, the state system, was able to achieve more independence than television, partly because politicians did not regard it as important and partly because of competition from new private radio stations, three of which were broadcasting nationwide by 1994. The leading commercial station attracted about 75% of the audience, according to surveys.

In Latvia radio and television were still undergoing significant reorganization by 1994. There were two state radio stations and five or six private FM stations, mostly broadcasting popular music, "top 40" records, and the VOA (which USIA research said was the most popular Western radio program in Latvia). National TV was still state owned, but regional television was strong, fully private, and supported completely by commercial backers and advertising.

Radio was a bright part of Estonian media, according to Lisa Trei of the European *Wall Street Journal*. KUKU was the best of 16 local radio stations in Estonia, eight of which were privately owned by 1994. Television was weaker than radio, according to Trei, even though there were eight channels in Estonia, four of which were private. One of these, EVTV, came on the air in 1993 and had a good news program, the first of its kind in Estonia. News on the other stations made some improvement as a result of competition, but, said Trei, television still had lots of infomercials presented as news, and reporters were often paid by companies to write stories about them. Journalists wouldn't admit this but it happens, said Trei.[51]

Other governments of East/Central Europe were direct in their intent to control broadcasting. In Hungary, the government did not give up its monopoly on radio and television until 1996, late in the transitional period. And through the first six years of post-Communism, government constantly pressed its own officials of Magyar Radio and Magyar Television to follow a stricter government line. The first new post-Communist presidents of radio and television, Csaba Gombar and Elemer Hankiss, respectively, had been brought in during the era of liberalizing in 1990, but within a year or so of their administrations, the conservative government came to regard them as too liberal. The excuse given was that they were bad administrators, perhaps even corrupt. Gombar and Hankiss held their ground for more than a year but finally quit in early 1993 under the most extreme pressure. Immediate changes were made that brought radio and television more under direct government control.

Even when the Socialist Party returned to power in Hungary in 1994, the government retained control over broadcasting. When the new media law was finally passed at the end of 1995, it established a National Communication and Information Council for awarding radio and television frequencies to private operators, and it set up "foundations" to oversee Magyar Radio and Magyar Television as "public" broadcasting systems to be beyond the reach of political interference. Yet the government delayed in privatizing as long as possible and set up as many barriers as it could within the boundaries of the new law. By the end of 1996, about two dozen private TV and 30 private radio stations were in operation, but no private national television operation had yet been approved.

In Bulgaria national television remained nationalized and its two channels broadcast news that had little credibility, according to Byron Scott. The government agreed to license a few low-power TV stations, but those that had come on the air were not regarded as important media by most Bulgarians. The Bulgarian people, like most Central and Eastern Europeans, had access to other TV programs through satellite dishes. Two government radio networks distributed programming to local broadcast centers nationwide. Eight or nine independent radio stations had come on the air by 1994. The program formula for most radio was U.S. rock and roll music, and, like their U.S. counterparts, radio stations did little independent news reporting.[52]

In Ukraine, television remained the most controlled of the media. Two national channels, UT-1 and UT-2, as well as local channels in 20 regions, continued through the transition period as government dominated stations, producing 22 hours of television per day. A third channel, UT-3, was small and experimental but also still state controlled, and a few small independent stations existed that did not pose any threat to the establishment. Ironically, Ukrainians found Ukrainian television old style and boring, whereas Russian television, more technologically innovative and up to date, was far more popular with Ukrainian audiences.

The average Ukrainian viewer could get seven or eight over-the-air TV channels during prime time, including four or five independent stations. Satellite dishes and cable were also available to many viewers, and cable radio was accessible as well. Three national radio channels and local radio studios in 25 regions together produced more than 70 hours of programming in Ukraine per day. In addition, the government operated four short-wave radio transmitters for external broadcasting—in English, German, Romanian, and Ukrainian. By 1994, the government was trying to organize an external service TV station, using satellite, in a joint venture with Israel and the BBC.

In Belarus, the post-Communist government said it had licensed 226 radio and TV production units by 1994, of which 108 were non-state (public), 23 were private, and the remainder government. In fact, however, all broadcasting really belonged to the state, even though some were "independent" stations because even if a transmitter were purchased by a private party in Belarus, it had to be turned over to the Ministry of Communication, which operated it and charged rent from the user. After five years the state would buy the transmitter from the owner. Jakubowicz points out that "when private television stations in Belarus proved too critical of the government, the government would immediately close their transmitters 'for repairs.'"[53]

Use of a satellite dish, formerly prohibited, by 1994 was allowed, and about every fifth apartment had one. People complained, however, that having a satellite dish caused other problems because an expensive dish was a blatant signal to those who would rob apartments of the well-to-do.

In the USSR, national television, which was designated Presidential by its management (Gorbachev), would later in Russia be named in the same way, but referring to Yeltsin. "The Russian government," writes Mills, "directly prohibited privatization of TV, radio, and the communications infrastructure. The state kept exercising its ownership right to preserve its control of public opinion."[54] Yeltsin, for example, was able to issue decrees that narrowed the freedom of governmental television companies in commenting on national conflicts, such as the one in Chechnya.

As in the other countries of East/Central Europe, television in Russia was viewed as the most crucial political power. In a 1994 article, Y. N. Zassoursky, long-time dean of the Moscow State University School of Journalism, writes that television was the most decisive of the mass media in the dissolution process of the Soviet Union.[55] Gosteleradio, the central broadcast agency, had developed an extensive all-Soviet Union network, with more than 180 TV studios across the empire and an even vaster radio network. But by 1995, Gosteleradio had been dismantled to the point that it had just one national TV channel left. Competitors had developed and were growing stronger, including NTV, an independent national TV station that was so popular it drained advertising away from state broadcasting; RTR, the broadcast medium of the independent republics; and private enterprises to a lesser extent, according to Reino Paasilinna, a Finnish expert on Soviet television.

Paasilinna had found in 1995 that Russian television was still an important political factor, but more independent of the government. Although the freedom of television was frequently violated, he says, "now the violations get publicity." However, he concludes that "in Russia, there is such a heated struggle for power going on that one of its victims, in addition to the Chechen people, may also be the mass communications that were in the process of being liberated."[56] First among the media to lose would be television.

THE ROLE OF FOREIGN INVESTMENT

In 1991, Hungarian journalist Miklos Vamos wrote in *The Nation*, "All the socialist papers publicized for many years the famous Marxist slogan, 'Workers of the World, unite!' None of them adhere to this idea any longer. The new slogan should be: 'Capitalists of the World, invest!'"[57]

Throughout the transition, economic problems overwhelmed the media of East/Central Europe, in some countries obviously more than in others. Owen Johnson summarized the typical economic difficulties in the Czech Republic and Slovakia in 1991, early in the transition: The price of newsprint rose 377% between 1988 and 1991. Circulation declined by 34%. Cost of production increased 41%. Cost of distribution (in 1990 alone) rose 23%. Retail prices rose an average of 27%, or 65% for dailies.[58]

Indeed, in the first five years of post-Communism, those who were operating media in East/Central Europe eagerly sought an infusion of Western capital to keep their operations going. As the old system was collapsing, some apparatchiks made quick and secret deals, giving away or selling ownership or part ownership to Western investors. In this manner the German publisher Axel Springer acquired majority ownership of almost a dozen regional newspapers in Hungary, details of which are still not entirely public.

Margueritte wrote that "the press [in East/Central Europe] has routinely gone directly from the hands of the local communist elite to those of foreign media giants."[59] This is, however, a bit exaggerated.

Although the system was collapsing in Russia in the 1980s, the late Robert Maxwell established a joint publishing venture with the Soviet Academy of Sciences. Later Maxwell invested in the Hungarian newspaper *Magyar Hirlap* and established the first private printing plant in Hungary. Rupert Murdoch invested in a rival Hungarian newspaper, *Mai Nap*, and in private TV production facilities in Budapest. The German media conglomerate Bertelsmann acquired half ownership of the leading Hungarian daily, *Nepszabadsag*.

By mid-transition, writes Johnson, nearly 80% of Hungarian newspapers were owned by Western investors ("a development that happened so quickly in 1990 that neighboring countries moved to make sure it would not happen elsewhere."[60] Nevertheless, foreign investment spread throughout the region. In Poland, for example, by the end of 1996, the most popular weeklies were published by German companies, including Heinrich Bauer, Axel Springer, and Gruener & Jahr.

The Swiss company Ringier bought 17 Czech publications, including Euroskop magazines for women, the full-color magazine *Reflex*, and *Lidove Noviny*, the country's leading daily. The business manager of that newspaper, a year before its sale to Ringier, told Roger Cohen of *The New York Times* that "there's no choice but to sell this newspaper to foreigners and it had better happen as soon as possible." Its circulation had already fallen from 460,000 to 125,000.[61] In 1995, Ringier purchased *Expres*, a popular tabloid, and merged it with another Ringier tabloid, *Blesk*, to make it the third largest paper in the country.

Foreign investors would have put more money into East/Central European broadcasting if they had not been blocked by governments in many countries. Polish law prohibited more than 33% foreign investment in a broadcast station.[62] Silvio Berlusconi of Italy and Maxwell both sought national broadcasting channels in Poland but were turned down.

Margueritte points out that Berlusconi took charge of financial and advertising management, first for Soviet TV in 1989, then a year later for Polish TV. IP (a branch of Havas) acquired financial management contracts for Radio Danubius and TV-1 in Hungary, some regional TV stations in the Soviet Union, and two new public stations in Eastern Germany. Margueritte details how IP got control of advertising management of Estonian TV, two radio stations and one TV station in Latvia, Vilnius TV in Lithuania, Petersburg TV in Russia, Minsk TV in Belarus, Czech TV CTV, Slovak S-1, one radio and two TV programs in Ukraine, and Slovenia TV.[63]

Margueritte shows how the leading French media company, Hachette, started the first private radio station in 1990 in Czechoslovakia. It built Europa Plus Moscow, Europa Plus Petersburg, and Europa 2 in Prague. The French company L'Expansion invested in *Gazeta Bankowa* in Poland. Another French media company, Robert Hersant, acquired shares in eight major Polish newspapers, including *Rzeczpospolita*, the Warsaw government daily, and significant shares in Hungary's *Magyar Nemzet*, the Czech Republic's *Mlada Fronta Dnes*, and *Business in Russia*. The Luxumbourg satellite broadcaster Astra sold satellite receivers throughout Eastern Europe.[64]

In Russia, foreign investments might have been more difficult but not impossible. Greek millionaires Theodoros and Christos Giannikos acquired controlling shares of the former flagship of Soviet journalism, *Pravda*, in 1992. But they closed the paper in 1996.

U.S. companies also invested, but to a lesser extent than Western Europeans. HBO, a division of Time Warner, established "Global TV" in Warsaw, the first cable system in Eastern Europe. David Chase, a U.S. citizen and Polish Holocaust survivor, invested in cable TV systems in Warsaw, Gdansk, and elsewhere in Poland. Cosmetics magnate Ron Lauder purchased a major stake in the Czech TV Nova and increased his shares from 66% to 88% in 1996. The Stratton Group operated by American Michael Dingman purchased 15% of the Czech TV station Premiera in 1996. The Gannett Company formed a joint venture with the Swiss Ringier to publish *Blikk* (a sensationalistic tabloid) in Hungary. Cox Newspapers acquired a 10% interest in Poland's *Gazeta Wyborcza*. *Reader's Digest* and *Playboy* both started special editions in Hungarian, Polish, and Russian. (Within two years, the Hungarian *Reader's Digest* had become the largest circulation magazine in that country.)

Margueritte concludes that Western investors heavily penetrated the media markets in Poland, the Czech Republic, and especially in Hungary, where almost 90% of the national and 40% of the regional press were under western control by mid-1995.[65]

Unlike these three countries, however, not all others in the region attracted foreign money. Gross points out that the international media moguls did not see fit to pursue the purchase of newspapers in Romania or even to invest in them. Murdoch, Springer Verlag, Maxwell, and Berlusconi all stayed out of Romania, and only a small amount of outside money came into the Romanian mass media market from Romanian expatriates returning with foreign capital.[66]

Bulgaria was one of those slow to attract foreign money, but in late Summer 1996, a German press group, Westdeutsche Allgemeine Zeitung, purchased 70% of Bulgaria's largest press company, 168 Hours, publisher of 24 Chasa.

Print and broadcast media, however, were dealt with quite differently with respect to laws governing foreign investment. Most of the countries placed no restrictions on foreign investment in print media, newspapers, magazines, or books. (An exception is Moldova, which has a legal limit of 49% for foreign capital involvement in print.) Most countries, however, have limits on foreign investment in broadcasting, with the exception of the Czech Republic and Romania. Other typical limits are Estonia 49%, Poland and Slovenia 33%, Ukraine 30%, and Latvia 20%.[67]

OLD FORMS OF JOURNALISM

Many of the old Communist media survived and thrived in the transition period after the end of Communist governments East/Central Europe. Most of the old-line newspapers and other print media became privatized in most of the countries, although continued government subsidies, both overt and covert, were not uncommon. Almost all print media in all countries continued to be party-affiliated or partisan in their editorial leaning. There were some exceptions.

In some ways, Russia itself was the biggest exception. There, writes Dean Mills, a system of "establishment media" continued from the old regime through the transitional period, with the exception of very few newspapers (*Pravda, Sovetskaya Rossiya*, and *Rabochaya Tribuna*). The new government after the collapse of the old Soviet Union "inherited the loyalty of most of the [old] news media to the powers that be, regardless of their affiliation."[68]

In Russia, the twin pillars of Soviet journalism, *Pravda* and *Izvestia*, went in opposite directions. The result might serve as a metaphor for how much things have changed in Russian media. *Pravda*, the official Communist Party paper, once dominated the Soviet media landscape, both because it was the largest-circulation newspaper in the country and because other media always followed its ideological lead. In post-Communist Russia, absent the guaranteed subscriptions of millions of party members and other careerists, *Pravda's* circulation dwindled to virtually nothing. It published sporadically, then not at all, then was backed financially by Greek capitalists. In 1996, it apparently died its last death.

Izvestia, the former official government newspaper, underwent a complete ideological transformation under the leadership of Soviet-trained journalists with reformist sympathies. By 1996, it had become the most respected newspaper in Russia.

Another one-time organ, *Moskovskaya Komsomolets*, became the most popular newspaper in Russia under the leadership of a young editor, Boris Gusyev, who introduced a diet of crime stories, investigative reporting, and aggressive coverage of the Moscow area.[69]

For the print media, matters were not so bad in Hungary, but most of the dailies that existed under Communism were still in existence in 1996. *Nepszabadsag*, the former leading Communist party daily, stopped identifying itself as an official state paper in October 1989, but in fact continued to call itself a "socialist" newspaper on its flag until 1994. In 1996, it was still the most widely sold newspaper in Hungary, although its circulation had declined from the party figure of 900,000 in the 1980s to an audited circulation of about 340,000 in mid-1995.

However, among the old-guard national papers, *Nepszabadsag* made the quickest progress toward political independence and moved furthest toward objective news and separation of news and opinion. It continued to be most popular among all dailies because all readership declined during the period. Its chief foreign investor, the German Bertelsmann AG, gave the editorial staff a relatively free hand.

It is instructive to see how the other major newspapers of Hungary survived during the transition after 1989, because their development is not much different from some other East/Central European countries. *Népszava*, for many years second in national circulation, fell to third place briefly during this period and for awhile was not given much hope of surviving in a free market. It was the trade union newspaper, heavily subsidized in the past, with a large and loyal worker readership. As union subsidies dried up, the paper faltered, and it only became sustainable by getting foreign investments late in the period, enabling a strong comeback in 1994.

Esti Hírlap was an old and well-established newspaper that had been a serious contender early in the 1990–94 period. Robert Maxwell purchased 40% of its shares, but after his death it was speculated that government-owned industries and banks kept *Esti Hírlap* alive with contributions under the table so the paper would serve the interests of the MDF government. Within days after the MDF was defeated in the 1994 elections, the paper went out of existence.

Magyar Hírlap, which had been the government newspaper, also received a substantial Maxwell investment during the early part of this period. Maxwell installed a new printing plant in Budapest, and the new technology gave the newspaper a modern look, whereas the editorial staff gave it a Western-style content, aimed at a business/professional class. But its circulation dropped steadily, about 25% from 1992 to 1994.

In Poland *Trybuna Ludu* was the official newspaper of the Communist Party prior to 1989. As a concession to the political changes, it eliminated "the people" from its title, but as *Trybuna* it continued to have a large readership. In regional Polish cities, former Communist papers remained strong, including Krakow's *Gazeta Krakowska*, Poznan's *Glos Wielkopolski*, and Silesia's *Trybuna Robotnicza*. The Polish press had a socialist leaning throughout the transitional period, according to Magueritte, and this, he writes, was widening the rift between media and the church.[70]

In the Czech Republic, the former Communist youth paper, *Mlada Fronta Dnes*, became one of the most respected post-Communist newspapers, with a style comparable to *USA Today*. The former organ of the Communist Party Central Committee, *Rude Pravo*, transformed itself into an independent newspaper, but only after dismissing half its former staff. *Svobodne Slovo*, the Socialist Party's newspaper, continued its party affiliation and its readership declined.[71]

Slovakia's established newspapers of the old regime all continued relatively successfully into the transition period, including *Pravda*, the former Communist Party flagship; *Praca*, the trade union newspaper; and *Smena*, the party's youth paper. These three papers still had the highest readership in 1992.

In Lithuania all newspapers were privatized during the transitional period. *Tiesa* (the *Pravda* of Lithuania), former official newspaper of the Communist Party, continued under the editorship of Domas Skiakas, former head of the Union of Journalists and member of the ruling Socialist-Labor Party, formerly the Communist Party. The paper did change its political stance from far left to not-so-far left.

Not all the old papers toed old party lines. *Lietuvas*, with the largest circulation in Lithuania (about 118,000), was formerly the Communist youth party newspaper, "Truth of Komsomol," but during the transition its staff did not recognize its past, saying it had become a new newspaper with the end of the Soviet era. It expressed a variety of political opinions.

In Latvia *Neatkariga Cina* evolved from a former Communist Party newspaper, taken over by an agricultural firm and privately owned as a limited enterprise. However, like most newspapers in the entire region during the transition, its circulation dropped from 180,000 to 90,000 between 1992 and 1993. *SM-Segodnja*, the most popular and influential Russian-language newspaper, became privately published, gained much advertising, and was one of the first papers to focus on energy and economic issues, even though its circulation dropped from 170,000 in 1992 to 65,000 in 1993. *Rigas Balss* continued to be owned by the state in both a Latvian and a Russian edition. Its circulation dropped from 113,000 Latvian and 92,000 Russian in 1988 to 36,000 Latvian and 19,000 Russian in 1993.

In Estonia *Rahva Haal* [People's Voice], formerly the largest circulation newspaper (200,000 in 1990), fell to second place (64,000 in 1993). Until 1990 it was the official Communist Party newspaper; from 1990 to 1992, it was the official government newspaper. In January 1993, it was allowed to privatize. *Paevaleht*, formerly the organ of the Communist youth with a circulation of 186,000 in 1990, was still technically owned by the state in 1993, but operated independently from the government, and its circulation had dropped to 32,000.

The farther east one went, the more it seemed that the state continued to be involved in the control, or even in the actual publication and production, of print media as well as broadcasting. In Bulgaria during the transition period, two of the three largest dailies, *Duma* and *Demokratsia*, were published by the Bulgarian Socialist Party and the Union of Democratic Forces, respectively. Another newspaper, *Svoboden Narod*, was published by the Agrarian Union. These papers were seen as serving little more than the party faithful or union members, and their circulations had shrunk drastically to well under 100,000.[72] In Pleven, the principal weekly was published by the city and had its offices in city hall.[73]

In Belarus *Narodnaya Gazeta*, the largest newspaper with a circulation over 600,000, published five times a week in both Russian and Belarusian, belonged to the Supreme Soviet, or the Parliament, through the transition period. However, it was critical of and much disliked by the Council of Ministers. The editor, Joseph Seredich, was himself a member of Parliament, but he tried to be independent and printed controversial material. In 1994, for example, he printed a critical article about a political strike, telling how police arrested people who distributed leaflets on the streets even though this was not illegal. Parliament heatedly debated his dismissal.[74]

Sovetskaya Belorussia, a Russian-language paper whose title reflects its conservative content, was published five times a week by the

Council of Ministers and advocated rejoining Russia. Like all newspaper circulation in Belarus, its average print run declined in 1994, to 305,000 copies, down from its peak of 500,000.

NEW AND OLD JOURNALISTS

Most journalists in the transition period of East/Central Europe could probably be put into one of four categories: (a) old Communist journalists who had not changed (probably the largest group in 1990, though not by 1996); (b) old Communist journalists who had been converted into entrepreneurs and new journalists who were basically businessmen (probably the second largest group); (c) new journalists who were partisans and practiced advocacy journalism (third largest); and (d) old Communist journalists and new journalists who adopted a Western-style objective or adversarial journalism (probably the smallest group).

In general, it seems, prior to 1989, journalists in the region might have been upset about Communism's control of news, but they seemed much more upset and frustrated by Communism's restrictions on the expression of their opinions. Partly for that reason, the breakup of Communist power unleashed a torrent of pent-up political ideas. (And political parties proliferated; dozens of new parties were formed and put up candidates in the first multiparty elections throughout the region.) In East/Central Europe, as in most of Western and Northern Europe, journalism had been more often regarded as a political activity, rather than the packaging of information or the production of entertainment to sell as a product. In fact many figures in recent European political history were sometime journalist-politicians, or vice-versa (Winston Churchill, Karl Marx, and Adolph Hitler, to name a few).

The new journalism of East/Central Europe, like most Western and Northern European journalism, was not usually fact-based, nonpartisan, neutral, or objective. The usual article would be considered an essay, not a news report, and was usually literary or political. ("Articles of literary merit earn high acclaim," commented Jozsef Simanyi of the Hungarian Association of Journalists.)[75] Many of these journalists thought of themselves as writers rather than reporters, seeking to influence or develop a personal style rather than going out and getting the facts.

Janos Horvat, a Hungarian television journalist and astute observer of the media in transition, writes that a common concept in Europe was the journalist as active participant, "the journalist who sees himself as someone who wants to influence politics and audiences according to his own political beliefs." Horvat says this sense "is even stronger in Eastern Europe, where journalists are closer to artists and writers, and many poets and writers contribute regularly to daily publications." Horvat describes these kinds of journalists as people with a "messianic vocation: They want to become a mouthpiece for the people."[76]

Many of the old journalists continued to harbor deep suspicions of advertising or of a free-market economy. This, too, was somewhat typical of all Europeans. Of course, under Communism private advertising was discouraged, and advertising done by government was not very attractive. Many older East/Central European citizens continued to regard Western-style advertising as vulgar, intrusive, and exploitative. Throughout the transition period, the economy was in recession in most of these countries, and often there was not enough advertising business to support private free-market media.

Most older East/Central European citizens, journalists included, were not customer oriented, not interested in competition, wary of a free market, and worried about being exploited by Western capitalists. But not all. A new breed of post-Communist businessmen were entrepreneurs, some of whom more specifically should be called new "robber barons," and some of them saw huge potential profits in ventures of journalism and mass media.

Throughout the transition period in the region, journalists were not quite used to an adversarial role. One Bulgarian journalist explained to Byron Scott, "The assumption always was that anything not specifically permitted must be forbidden. In many ways we still behave as if that were true."[77]

If the government held a news conference, reporters showed up and dutifully took down everything but asked no hard questions, said Lisa Trei. There are, she said, very few attempts at news analysis and much one-source reporting, without getting the other side of the story. But in comparison to the Communist era, she regarded the press as very free.[78]

It should be said, however, that in some countries of East/Central Europe, the collapse of Communism did end the careers of many prominent journalists of the old regime. Johnson points out that "they were replaced by junior staff members and by a whole cohort of people who flooded into the profession, some with experience . . . and some with no experience whatsoever."[79] Some, of course, had experience only as dissident journalists working for *samizdat*, the underground press.

In some countries new journalists replaced the old more rapidly than in others. In Romania, for example, shortly after the fall of the Ceaucescu government, more than 90% of all working journalists were "leftovers from the communist era." However, writes Gross, by 1994, "a dramatic switch had taken place" and more than 90% of the journalists were now "new to the field and young, their median age in the mid- to late-20s."[80]

Journalism organizations in Central and Eastern Europe represented the dichotomy between the new and the old in the profession. In Hungary, for example, the Hungarian Association of Journalists (MUOSZ) was the oldest media organization in Hungary, with about 6,000 members. Prior to 1989 it was the Communist Party's journalism organization. It ran the only journalism training program in the country, and it was almost impossible to get into the profession without enrolling in the MUOSZ courses, most of which concerned political and economic indoctrination.

In 1990, the Association elected a new board and general secretary, Gabor Bencsik, a respected journalist who tried to steer the organization into a new non-Communist era. Nevertheless, the vast majority of its members had been journalists under Communist rule; they certainly were not the dissidents, and they did not get along well with the new conservative and nationalistic first post-Communist government. They were eager to express new opinions, but they regarded themselves as liberal and cosmopolitan rather than conservative and nationalistic. Although Bencsik did his best to keep the organization neutral, the government regarded the Association as a tool of the former communists and critical of the government's efforts at reform.

In 1992, a new organization was formed, the Alliance of Hungarian Journalists (MUK). It announced that it would be strongly pro-government and nationalistic to offset the "leftist" leaning of the old association. It proclaimed that the role of the journalist was to be patriotic, to support and promote the government. MUK gained about 500 members in its first two years and certainly had the encouragement and no doubt financial support of the government. After the socialists regained power in the 1994 election, MUK began to decline. Meanwhile, on election night in May 1994, when the socialist victory was assured, the journalist members of MUOSZ held a champagne party at the Association building to celebrate.

This dichotomy between new and old journalists was evident in separate journalism associations in other countries as well. In Lithuania two journalism societies existed. The Union of Journalists was the old-fashioned Soviet group, leftist, supporting the socialist government after it came back into power. The Association of Journalists, organized after independence, was rightist, and in opposition to the pro-socialist government.

In Slovakia the journalists' associations split into two factions quite similar to those of Hungary. The older Slovak Syndicate of Journalists, representing 2,700 members, came to regard itself as a professional, not political, organization concerned with freedom of the press. In November 1991, a new organization was formed, the Cooperative of Slovak Journalism; its few members felt that the journalist's duty was to help the Slovak nation successfully attain statehood.[81]

Romanian journalists had split into four different associations and unions, and during the transition, writes Gross, new journalism and media organizations sprang up every year. Gross says this proliferation was symptomatic of a lack of satisfaction with the leadership of the old organizations and a search for more proactive or professionally satisfying ones.[82]

In some countries new journalists hesitated to join the organizations of the old regime because of their negative reputations. Johnson says that was the case in the Czech Republic, where the old Union of Czechoslovak Journalists lost its credibility and many of its members.[83]

RISE OF ENTREPRENEURIAL JOURNALISM

Some of the new robber barons of post-Communist East/Central Europe were journalists interested in freedom of the press, but unlike those journalists who wrote political essays, the robber barons were interested in using media to make money. Many of them were former Communist Party officials who had learned how to manage and manipulate to their advantage. They turned to pornography, sensationalism, and niche media marketing to find their profits.

The rush to pornography was the first manifestation of this syndrome. Pornography had been officially forbidden under socialism, but by 1991, in Hungary for example, sexually oriented content constituted 25% to 30% of the newsstand market.[84] This figure was probably average for all the East/Central European countries in the early days of transition.

Playboy quickly got into the market with Russian-, Polish-, and Hungarian-language editions. The Hungarian edition of *Playboy* was one of the first new magazines to come onto the scene after the political change. The U.S. company soon sold to a Hungarian, who paid for the name and the right to continue the format. But within three years Hungarians had become bored with risque magazines, and the Hungarian *Playboy's* circulation dropped steadily from its initial surge. As the market outgrew this period quickly, many sex-only publications were short-lived.

In the daily newspaper field, pornography and sensationalism became a common format to attract customers and compete with television in a market where readership was declining sharply and the costs of publication were rising precipitously. Gross writes that economics led

"Romania's general circulation press to become more sensationalist in their approach to news coverage and more entertainment oriented." Porn publications sprouted quickly after the fall of Ceausescu, Gross writes, including *Bordel, Sexpress, Club Sex Caprice,* and *Pink House.* But as in other countries in the region, pornography declined before long, and by 1993, only *Pariunea* (formerly *Prostitutia*) was still on the newsstands.[85]

In Bulgaria, for example, in the first months of freedom, according to Bryon Scott, "many newspapers put nudes on their covers to attract attention." In time, the newspapers turned to less explicit but more sensationalistic techniques to gain customers. Scott called it the use of "outrageous headlines ungarnished by facts."[86] The largest circulation daily in Bulgaria, *24 Chasa,* was a tabloid that usually sold out within minutes of arriving at the kiosks. The reason for its success, most felt, was not that it had more accurate news, but that it had brighter graphics than any other Bulgarian daily. It was, wrote Scott, a "two-or-three color version of *USA Today,* and violently nonpartisan."[87]

A remarkable example of success in Ukraine was a new sensationalist Russian-language daily published in Kiev, the *Kievskie vedomosti.* Its "mixture of stories featuring scandals, sex and violence, as well as news and commentaries," sold a "staggering 500,000 copies a day." It was sponsored by a private company headed by a former communist counter-propaganda specialist.[88]

One of the most successful and controversial publications started in Poland, *Nie,* became popular because of its sensationalist negativism, fueled by a strong dose of pornography. It was highly critical of the church and the former president Lech Walesa, and there was considerable irony in the fact that its editor, Jerzy Urban, was the former spokesman for General Jaruzelski's martial law regime. In the Czech Republic, *Spigl,* a racy tabloid full of sex and sensational stories, rapidly gained popularity in the early years of the transition.[89]

Russia's entry into the free-market economy did not produce the journalistic cultural revolution that had been anticipated, according to an *IPI Report*; rather, it brought into being profit-oriented publications using sex and sensationalism to sell. But post-Communist Russia also created what IPI termed "the world's largest assortment of newspapers devoted to diverse purposes." Russia's freedom-of-the-press policies, coupled with the publishers' need to find new financing, led many new newspapers to seek niche markets. As a result, newspapers in Russia began to specialize in corruption, crime, and a full range of extremist political propaganda.[90]

Broadcasting also produced entrepreneurs, new business leaders who saw that the world of radio and television could be as lucrative in the new post-Communist world as it was in the United States. The main problem was that governments in East/Central Europe were not as quick to give up their hold on broadcasting, especially television.

CRIME, CORRUPTION, AND MEDIA ETHICS

When Communism failed, basically an economic system collapsed, but with it also came the end of a way in which human beings had socialized, related to each other, and coexisted in some agreed-on social harmony. Communism's failure left an enormous vacuum. Even in countries such as Hungary, where Communism's decline was more gradual, new systems of laws and standards and mores that harmonious societies require evolved slowly. As a result, crime, corruption, and, at a minimum, unethical behavior became the operating principle in the mass media as well as in other areas of life.

The economic collapse had the first and most profound effect on mass media. Whereas under Communism economic security was assured, after Communism there was no security. All media had subsisted on government money; now most of them were cut off from automatic support, especially print media. Not only did they lose direct government support, they lost much of their subscriber and reader base as well, while facing rising costs for paper, production, distribution, and personnel. And advertising was far from the economic mainstay of the media it had become in the United States.

In 1993, the Committee to Protect Journalists summarized the situation in Eastern Europe by saying: "Perhaps the most significant challenge to the press in these regions is the media's dependence on state support." In Russia, the report said, "very few print organizations and almost no broadcast media can survive without state subsidies. . . . This gives authorities free rein to use 'the power of the purse' and restrain publications which are in opposition."[91] Two years later, in 1995, the same group said: "Four years after the collapse of the Soviet Union, the Russian press, still the most democratic institution in Russian society, found itself threatened by violence, political intimidation, and financial pressure."[92]

The violence came from newly organized criminal activity, the so-called mafia of East/Central Europe, which was worst in Russia and in the countries of the former Soviet republics. David Satter wrote that in post-Communist Russia, "journalists are no longer threatened with long labor camp sentences for writing freely. But they risk their lives if they report on organized crime or corruption in the armed forces of if the financial interests of their media organization bring them into conflict with a corrupt group."[93] Satter estimated that there were 5,000 criminal gangs, 300 mob bosses, and 150 illegal organizations with international ties in Russia alone.

Ironically, the best investigative journalism was sometimes done by business media, often reporting on corruption in business and on mafia activities. As corruption grew throughout the period, journalists demonstrated extreme bravery to do some of their investigative work, even, according to Lisa Trei, in progressive countries such as Estonia. Throughout the region there were threats against journalists who were suspected of investigating corruption and a number of assassinations.

In October 1993, Vitas Lingis, 33-year-old founder and publisher of a popular Lithuanian daily, *Respublica*, was murdered outside his home. He had published a series of articles exposing organized crime in Lithuania. He was on his way to meet a government official, who was to give him crucial information about the criminal activity, when he was assassinated.

In Russia in 1994, journalist Dmitry Kholodov was killed by a briefcase bomb he had picked up from a source for a report he was writing on corruption in the Russian military. He was an investigative reporter for *Moskovski Komsomolets*, the most widely read newspaper in Moscow, and had already written extensively on the subject. The Committee to Protect Journalists called his assassination "especially chilling because it was so clearly linked to his activities as a reporter."[94]

Between 1993 and 1995, 19 journalists were murdered in Russia and one each in Belarus, Lithuania, and Ukraine; none of these were killed in battle but assassinated in civilian life. In 1995, four Russian journalists were also missing, as was one in Ukraine.

Not all journalists in East/Central Europe were brave enough to challenge either the authorities or the mafia. In fact, it seems, the majority were not. Survival, mostly economic, seems to have been the dominant motivation.

Both political and business forces grew increasingly effective at exercising threats to pressure journalists, and even young journalists not tainted with Communism fell victim to the pressures to survive. Examples in Ukraine are illustrative but not unique. In 1994, a private production company, Nova Mova TV, was awarded a contract to develop a Sunday evening prime-time news program called *Pisliamova*, managed and produced by a young journalist in his mid-20s, Oleksander Tkachenko. He had gained experience in Western TV news styles as a stringer for Reuters and created a slick, fast-paced analysis of the week's news.

Pisliamova scored many scoops, probably because its reporters had unusual access to Ukraine president Leonid Kuchma. It took on an increasingly pro-Kuchma slant, and people connected with the program attributed this to its economic, as well as political, self-interest. However, *Pisliamova* deviated once from its pro-Kuchma line, making a brief reference on December 24, 1995 to a controversial event in the administration that week. Nova Mova's contract was due to expire on December 31. It was never renewed, according to Chrystyna Lapychak in *Transition*.[95]

Lapychak states that during a 1996 briefing at the Ukrainian Media Club, "President Kuchma said he believes there are no independent media in Ukraine—that all publications and programs serve special interests—chiefly because there is no stable middle class to provide balance." Ironically, says Lapychak, "Kuchma's cynicism reflects the realities faced by the fourth estate all the more because of his own administration's increased bullying of journalists."[96]

Sometimes the bullying came from new media owners, often *nouveau riche* who bought media properties to exercise public influence. In the Czech Republic, for example, the owner of a huge steel company, Vladimir Stehlik, acquired ownership of *Prace*, a trade-union daily, and used the newspaper to attack the government and the national TV station Nova, both of which had been critical of his activities. Another businessman, Josef Kudlacek, took over what had been a widely respected newspaper, *Cesky denik*, and turned it into his mouthpiece, mainly for vitriolic attacks on the government.[97]

In all East/Central Europe countries, the dividing line between the business office and the editorial office frequently became blurred. At a journalism ethics seminar in Hungary in 1992 sponsored by the International Media Fund, Hungarian media representatives described the practice of reporters doubling as advertising salespeople when they went to business firms to write news stories. When U.S. journalists present expressed dismay at the practice, the Hungarians said it was common throughout the region and necessary for economic survival.[98]

In Russia and in all the other countries of East/Central Europe it was common for both news reports and editorials to be used to publicize their corporate or private investors and their advertisers. In many countries, business interests could buy advertising in the form of news reports. In many countries, reporters were used to sell advertising, and the implicit understanding was that the advertiser would receive a good news story in addition to the advertisement.

In 1996, the English-language weekly *Budapest Business Journal* broke a story that caused little sensation in Hungary. It reported that six out of the seven daily newspapers in Hungary (*Nepszabadsag, Nepszava, Magyar Nemzet, Uj Magyarorszag, Napi Gazdasag,* and *Vilaggazdasag*) regularly accepted money for publishing promotional articles without identifying the articles as advertising or promotion. Among Hungary's leading dailies, only *Magyar Hirlap* was not accused of the practice. In return for payments of about $500 to $2,000, the papers cited allegedly published favorable articles. Only one newspaper, *Nepszabadsag*, denied the accusation. According to the *Journal*, some Hungarian companies get five or six threats a year from newspapers that indicate they are writing reports about them.[99]

Zsofia Szilagyi, writing in *Transition*, reported that media experts in Hungary estimated such "camouflaged advertising" could represent as much as 10% of a newspaper's total income. "Public relations specialists calls the publication of paid-for stories 'an everyday practice,'" she wrote. Without it, she said, Hungary could not sustain seven national dailies.[100]

Such bribery went both ways in East/Central Europe. In the 1996 presidential election in Russia, although most pro-Yeltsin coverage was voluntary, according to *The Washington Post*, "evidence suggests that where volunteers were not be be found, the Yeltsin campaign spent hundreds of thousands of dollars" bribing journalists for favorable coverage.[101] Laura Belin, writing in *Transition*, points out that "most newspapers rely upon subsidies from the government or from business interests close to the Yeltsin camp, who also feared the consequences of a communist revanche." In fact, only a few Russian newspapers—such as *Argumenty I fakty and Moskovski Kmsomolets*—sell enough copies and advertising to be financially independent.[102]

Gross concludes that the media atmosphere in the transition period in Romania (and this was probably true for all of East/Central Europe) supported those who would do anything to make a buck. "In Romania today," he writes, "press freedom is absolute, but it is the freedom of the wild. Journalists can write anything they want, whether true or false, defamatory or laudatory. They can rant and rave." What has not happened, Gross suggests, is "to transfer the profession's freedom from that of a dangerous jungle to the civilized, ordered freedom demanded by democracy."[103]

Szilagyi writes that according to a media ethics professor at Eotvos Lorand University in Budapest, "aspiring journalists seem to be comfortable with the current [lack of] standards; their explanation is that they cannot afford to be ethical." This situation seems to prevail throughout East/Central Europe. What sociologists say about Hungarians could be applied to all in the region, namely, that they do not believe in the existence of the common good and feel that the state can only exercise a negative role. According to Laszlo Zsolnai of the Budapest Ethics Center, Hungarians' motto is "serve yourself, take care of your own profit, and do not respect anything."[104]

CONCLUSION

Despite the many problems, much progress was achieved in the transitional period, from 1990 to 1996, when this was being written. In many areas, especially in the rise of free-market advertising and public rela-tions, the development of real journalism (rather than propaganda), the privatization and independence of many of the media, and the begin-nings of some sound education and new training programs, much has already been accomplished.

More important, as Owen Johnson points out, the mass media were no longer centrally managed as servants of the Communist Party and government. No longer did they constantly disparage a free-market system. In some parts of the region, governments still had to provide support for media to be viable, but in other parts little remained of gov-ernment subsidies for print media except for some scientific, cultural, and scholarly publications.[105] Advertising on television had become suc-cessful enough to be seen as an important source of revenue for some governments.

Anne Nivet, introducing a special "Media Update" issue of *Transition* in the fall of 1996, concludes that "the vertical propaganda imposed by the ultimate voice, the Communist Party, has vanished. Compared with those dark days," she writes, "dazzling progress has been made. Yet compared with international standards of press free-dom, the region's media situation remains rather bleak."[106]

The countries of the former Soviet empire emphasized in this chapter are among the leaders in building democracies, free market sys-tems, and free media. Others not dealt with at length in our analysis could be much more heavily criticized. Charles Gati, in his 1996 article "The Mirage of Democracy," divides the countries into three groups. The "leaders" in the move toward democracy he says are the Czech Republic, Poland, Hungary, Slovenia, Estonia, Latvia, and Lithuania. The "laggards," placed far behind the leaders, are Slovakia, the seven countries in the Balkans (Albania, Bulgaria, Romania, Croatia, Serbia, Bosnia-Herzegovina, and Macedonia), Russia, Ukraine, Moldova, and Belarus. The "losers" are the eight countries of Central Asia and the Transcaucausus, an area Gati terms "essentially unreformed and oppres-sive."[107] This analysis applies to press and media freedom and develop-ment as well.

At the end of this transitional period, much remained to be done, but at least in many countries there was reason for optimism.

NOTES & REFERENCES

1. Teresa Sasinska-Klas, "Transformation of the Polish Media System," Unpublished manuscript, 1996, p. 1.
2. Karol Jakubowicz, "Media Legislation as a Mirror of Democracy," *Transition*, Vol. 2, No. 21, 1996, pp. 17-21.

3. Jerome Aumente, "Notes on Eastern European Media," unpublished manuscript, 1994, p. 8.
4. Elena Androunas, "The Struggle for Control Over Soviet Television," in *Mass Culture and Perestroika in the Soviet Union*. New York: Oxford University Press, 1991, pp. 185-200.
5. Owen V. Johnson, "Media in Czechoslovakia," unpublished manuscript, 1992, p.19.
6. Sasinska-Klas, *op. cit.* p. 2.
7. Aumente, *op. cit.*, p. 8.
8. David Satter, "Overview of Central Europe and the Republics of the Former Soviet Union," *Attacks On the Press in 1995*. New York: Committee to Protect Journalists, 1995, p. 160.
9. Owen R. Johnson, "East Central and Southeastern Europe, Russia, and the Newly Independent States," in John Merrill, ed. *Global Journalism*. New York: Longman, 3rd ed., 1995, p. 161.
10. Peter Gross, *Mass Media in Revolution and National Development: The Romanian Laboratory*. Ames: Iowa State University Press, 1996, Chapter 5, pp. 1-22, 41.
11. From the author's interviews in Minsk with journalists and government officials in February 1994.
12. Interview, February 1994.
13. Interview, February 1994.
14. *Attacks on the Press in 1995*, op. cit., p.148.
15. Jakubowicz, *op. cit.*, p.19.
16. Androunas, *op. cit.*
17. *Ibid*, pp. 44-48.
18. Interview, June 1995.
19. Interview, June 1995.
20. Johnson, "Media in Czechoslovakia, *op. cit.*, pp. 3 and 14.
21. Gross, *op. cit.*, chapter 3, pp.41–42.
22. *Ibid.*, pp. 58-61.
23. *IPI Report*, December 1993, p. 65.
24. Interview with Information Minister Butevich, February 1994.
25. Interview, February 1994.
26. See Jakubowicz, *op. cit.*, p. 20.
27. *Ibid.*
28. Dean Mills, "Russia," unpublished manuscript, p. 43.
29. Androunas, *op. cit.*
30. Johnson, "Media in Czechoslovakia, *op. cit.*, p. 8.
31. *Ibid.*, p. 9.
32. Gross, *op. cit.*, chapter 3, pp. 1–2.
33. *Ibid.*, p. 4.
34. *Ibid.*
35. Johnston M. Mitchell, "The Evolution of a Free Press in Hungary: 1989-1990." In Al Hester and L. Earle Reybold, eds., *Revolutions for Freedom: The Mass Media in Eastern and Central Europe*, Athens: University of Georgia, 1991, p. 141.

36. *Ibid.*, p. 142.
37. Interview, February 1994.
38. Johnson, "East Central and Southeastern Europe, Russia, and the Newly Independent States," *op. cit.*, p. 165.
39. See *Transition*, Vol. 2, No. 21, 1996, p. 61.
40. Owen Johnson, *Whose Voice? Freedom of Speech and the Media in Central Europe, in Creating a Free Press in Eastern Europe.*" In Al Hester and Kristina White, eds., *Revolutions for Freedom: The Mass Media in Eastern and Central Europe.* Athens: University of Georgia, 1993, p. 3.
41. Jakubowicz, *op. cit.*, p.19.
42. *Ibid.*, p. 8.
43. Gross, *op. cit.*, p. 20.
44. *Ibid.*, pp. 19-20.
45. *Ibid.*, pp. 26-27.
46. *Ibid.*, pp. 4–51.
47. *Ibid.*, p. 35.
48. Johnson, "Whose Voice," *op. cit.*, p.16.
49. Bernard J. Margueritte, *"Post-Communist Eastern Europe: The Difficult Birth of a Free Press,"* Cambridge, MA: Harvard University: Joan Shorenstein Center, Discussion Paper D, August 1995, p.11.
50. Sasinska-Klas, *op. cit.*, p. 6.
51. Interviews, 1994-96.
52. Byron Scott, "Bulgaria's Media," unpublished manuscript, p. 12.
53. Jakubowicz, *op. cit.*, p.21.
54. Mills, *op. cit.*, p. 5, 20.
55. See Reino Paasilinna, *Glasnost and Soviet Television.* Helsinki: Audience Research YLE, 1995, p. 192.
56. *Ibid.*, pp. 19-97.
57. Miklos Vanous, *The Nation.* Sept 30, 1991.
58. Johnson, "Media in Czechoslovakia," *op. cit.*, p. 4.
59. Margueritte, *op. cit.* p.9.
60. Johnson, "East Central and Southeastern Europe, Russia, and the Newly Independent States," *op. cit.*, p. 162.
61. Roger Cohen, *The New York Times*, December 28, 1992.
62. Carveth *et al.*, "Economic and Cultural Factors Affecting US Television Exports in Poland", paper delivered at Association for Education in Journalism and Mass Communication, Atlanta, 1994.
63. Margueritte, *op. cit.*
64. *Ibid.*
65. *Ibid.*
66. Gross, *op. cit.*, p. 3.
67. See Jakubowicz, *op. cit.*, p. 19.
68. Mills, *op. cit.*, p. 5.
69. *Ibid.*, p. 20.
70. Margueritte, *op. cit.* pp. 7ff.
71. Johnson, 1992, *op. cit.*, p. 9.
72. Johnson 1994, *op. cit.*, p. 165.

73. Scott, *op. cit.*, p. 10.
74. Interview, February 1994.
75. Interview, June 1994.
76. Janos Horvat, "Hot Issues in Hungarian Media as of July 1991," unpublished manuscript, 1991.
77. Scott, *op. cit.*, p. 10.
78. Interviews, 1994–96.
79. Johnson, 1992, *op. cit.* p. 12.
80. Gross, *op. cit.*, chapter 4, pp. 4–5.
81. Johnson, 1994, *op. cit.*, p.28.
82. Gross, *op. cit.*, chapter 4, p. 4.
83. Johnson, *op. cit.*
84. Mitchell, *op. cit.*
85. Gross, *op. cit.*, pp.13-14.
86. Scott, *op. cit.* p. 10.
87. *Ibid*, p. 11.
88. *IPI Report*, December 1993, p. 65.
89. Johnson, 1992, *op. cit.*, p. 8.
90. *IPI Report*, April 1993, p. 16.
91. Leonid Zagalsky, "Overview of Eastern Europe", In *Attacks On the Press in 1993*. New York: Committee to Protect Journalists, 1994, p. 186.
92. *Attacks on the Press in 1995*. New York: Committee to Protect Journalists, 1996, p. 165.
93. *Ibid*, p. 167.
94. Zagalsky, *op. cit.*, p. 146.
95. "Playing the Patronage Game in Ukraine," *Transition*, Vol. 2, No. 21, 1996, p. 60.
96. *Ibid*, p. 61.
97. See Jiri Pehe, "Money Talks in the Czech Republic," *Transition*, Vol. 2, No. 21, 1996, pp. 49-50.
98. It is interesting to note that this seminar was held at a Lake Balaton resort hotel owned by the Hungarian Journalism Association. The hotel had been confiscated from private owners in the early years of communism and given to the journalism association, no doubt as a reward for good behavior. Clearly, bribery of and by journalists was nothing new.
99. *Budapest Business Journal*, July 18, 1996, p. 1.
100. Zsofia Szilagyi, "Shady Dealings and Slow Privatization Plague Hungarian Media," *Transition*, Vol. 2, No. 21, 1996, p.4445.
101. June 30, 1996, p. 1.
102. "Private Media Come Full Circle," *Transition*, Vol. 2, No. 21, 1996, pp. 62ff.
103. Gross, *op. cit.*, p. 64.
104. Szilagyi, *op cit.*
105. Owen V. Johnson, "East Central and Southeastern Europe, Russia, and the Newly Independent States," *op. cit.*, p. 153.
106. Anne Nivat, "Money, Power, and Media," *Transition*, Vol. 2, No. 21, 1996, p. S.
107. Charles Gati, "The Mirage of Democracy," *Transition*, Vol. 2, No. 6, 1996, pp. 6–12.

4

Post-1989 Journalism in the Absence of Democratic Traditions

Dean Mills

In not quite post-Communist Europe, economic, social, and political institutions lurch uncertainly toward democracy. Some totalitarian artifacts live on past usefulness and logic. Rusty factories still turn out unwanted goods. Surly employees still staff government shops with mostly empty shelves. Others have assumed capitalist camouflage—state industries and bureaucrats transformed almost overnight into privatized firms and international wheeler dealers.

Adding to this neither-here-nor-there atmosphere seven years after the fall of the Berlin Wall, Communist parties (sometimes renamed, sometimes not) have risen from disgrace to recapture a big part of the political turf.

At the same time, almost as if in a parallel universe, pieces of genuine capitalism pop out all over the once uniformly grey landscape. Vigorous new private enterprises range from pirate cabdrivers and stylish mom-and-pop boutiques to multimillion-dollar corporations and banks.

The media, which both act on and are acted on by these vacillating realities, show the same chaotic and unstable pattern. Indeed, between the time this chapter is written and the time it sees print, much doubtless will have changed. Reformist managers at a government-owned television or radio operation will have been replaced by pro-socialist ones, or vice versa. Or one faction of reformers will have replaced another. Some private media outlets will have gone out of business, others will have been launched. A new law governing the media will have been passed in one or more of the countries under discussion. Or laws will have been repealed. Or, perhaps more likely, new laws will have been enacted and ignored.

Even if the target were not a moving one, accurate description of journalism in these countries would not be a simple task. As we are frequently and justifiably reminded by journalists and scholars from the region, Hungary is not Poland, Lithuania is not Estonia. Indeed, Czechoslovakia is not even Czechoslovakia. It is now the Czech Republic and Slovakia. Different historical, cultural, and professional traditions mean that attempts to democratize the media, like attempts to pluralize politics and to privatize firms, play out differently in different countries.

In broadest strokes, the degree of change in the media in these countries corresponds to the degree of isolation before the collapse of Communism. The Western-most countries—Czechoslovakia, Poland, Hungary, the Baltic states of the former Soviet Union—have moved the furthest toward both democratic media and the kinds of economic and political institutions that support them. The most isolated nations, geographically or politically—Albania and Romania, the Central Asian former Soviet republics—have the furthest to go.

Yet, some meaningful generalizations can be made about the process of change in the media within all of the formerly Communist countries. Some general patterns have emerged, patterns that seem to apply most of the time to media operations in most of the countries. These commonalities can be explained in large part by the legacy of totalitarianism these countries share, a legacy that has made it difficult for democratic media to take root. The countries all still lack, to greater or lesser degree, the stable economic, political, and legal structures on which free-market media depend. And many citizens, many politicians, even many journalists, of all ideological stripes, cannot—or will not—abandon the partisan, polemical approach to the news that they inherited from the Communist era. The result is that democratic journalism has taken much longer to set root, even in the most Western-like countries, than partisans of democracy on both sides of the Berlin Wall had hoped.

This chapter first explores how the establishment of free and independent media has been hampered by both the economic and political environment and by journalists themselves. Three factors in the environment in which the post-Communist media find themselves help explain the difficulties of the transition to truly free media:

1. Volatile and often hostile political climates
2. Unstable and often inhospitable economic climates
3. Political or economic enemies of free media, who will use whatever it takes, including physical attacks, even murder, to silence journalists.

As if those problems did not constitute challenge enough, would-be democratic journalists also must fight habits of the mind about the media that were formed during the Communist era, and which stubbornly live on in the post-Communist one:

1. Distrustful and apathetic publics, who have turned away from serious attention to the media, just as they have from serious attention to politics
2. Politicians, both reformers and Communists, who believe in free media only until they, or ideas they hold sacred, are criticized by the media
3. Journalists themselves, many of whom find it difficult to exchange their old roles as self-important commentators for new ones as fact-centered reporters.

In many ways, the media landscape of Central and Eastern Europe today resembles 19th-century United States, with many media dominated or owned by political parties, others by bankers or other commercial interests, and others by individuals with personal ideological agendas. Still rare are the media that are truly economically—and ideologically—independent. By July, 1995, according to a report of the State Press Committee, more than 85% of Russian newspapers were not financially independent. The report also noted the precariously low circulations of most newspapers. Of 10,500 in the country, most had a print run of fewer than 10,000 copies.[1]

The dissolution of the Communist system in Eastern Europe came so suddenly it seemed like a miracle. Six years later, it sometimes seems more like a mirage. Entrenched economic and political systems and individual attitudes have proven much harder to dismantle than a wall.

In retrospect, we understand that expectations for rapid and dramatic change were inflated beyond any reasonable expectation of quick fulfillment. These too-high hopes were themselves fed by the media. A euphoric sense of change was fed by the television images, seen in both East and West, of the tyrant Ceausescus being executed, of Boris Yeltsin on a tank, of crowds of demonstrators storming fearlessly onto the streets in many countries.

Euphoria in turn fed the media. In the first, heady days of freedom, in country after country, hundreds of new publications were issued to publics hungry for uncensored information and debate. Private radio and television stations sprang up almost overnight, usually without official license or blessing, to offer rock music, MTV, soft porn, and Western-style news reports. Underscoring the sudden change, news often came directly from the Voice of America, the BBC, CNN, and other once contraband broadcast sources.

Within months the honeymoon began to sour as postrevolutionary realities asserted themselves. Although the systems' managers had been changed, the systems themselves could not be replaced overnight with new economic and political systems compatible with the new ideals of political pluralism and the free market. The disenchantment was to some extent self-reinforcing. As reformers, constrained by the problems of the old system, failed to deliver quickly on the promise of a better life, voters turned nostalgically back to those politicians who wanted to turn the clock back to the old ways.

Even today, many media in the region still operate technically under Communist laws. Post-Communist governments often have not been able to pass new media legislation because of the instability of governments, the shifting political alliances, and, frequently, politicians' hostility to journalists who insist on a role as objective reporter and critic, in place of the accustomed role of public relations apparatus for the government.

THE CONTINUING STRUGGLE FOR POLITICAL INDEPENDENCE

Almost without exception, Communist-era media were in effect the direct public relations arms of the party and the government. (The exceptions were the Catholic press in Poland, where 98% of the population was Catholic, and the underground publications that emerged in the Soviet Union, Poland, Hungary, and some other countries beginning in the late 1960s. Those exceptions arguably provide another reason some countries—Poland, the Czech Republic, even Russia itself—were more ready than others for democratic change after the Communist governments fell.) That decades-old tradition did not die with the old systems. Whoever was in power, reformers or ex-Communists, the legal structure as well as habit continued to tie the media to the government. Journalists who insisted on exercising their new independence risked jail sentences, beating, even assassination.

Strictly speaking, many of the democratic changes that have occurred have taken place outside the law because media legislation in most of the countries has been tied up in parliamentary wrangling. And much of the wrangling has centered not on how to guarantee press freedom, but on how to limit it because of its presumed threat to other values.

It took until 1993, for example, for the Polish parliament to pass legislation to replace the 1960 law on broadcast regulation. Several unlicensed television and radio stations were already in business when the law was passed. And the Polish law codified the widespread feeling, not limited to Poland, that the media should not be completely free—although with a typically Polish twist. The content of both public and private broadcasting must adhere to "a Christian value system," the law said. The law also provides that broadcast outlets "should not promote activities that violate the law or the interests of the state nor opinions that conflict with morality and the public good."[2]

The Moldovan experience reflects the twists and turns in media legislation common to many countries. In December 1995, the Parliament voted to modify sections of legislation that prohibited publication of materials that "contest and defame the state and the people." The revision provided that only false materials published out of "ill will" would be subject to the law. Then, in February 1996, the Parliament voted to rescind that and other liberalizing modifications, thus subjecting journalists to what amounted to Soviet-era punishment should they publish materials officials found offensive.

The pro-democracy Concordia Human Rights Association in Moldova denounced the latest parliamentary decision as an attempt to "reduce to zero freedom of opinion" and to turn the press "into a simple toy handled by politicians and public servants."[3]

A member of Parliament who argued in favor of rescinding the modifications could have been reading from a book from the Soviet era. The less restrictive legislation, he said, would encourage irresponsibility by journalists and said that publications that "dare to offend state officials" should be closed down.[4]

For a variety of reasons, newspapers and magazines have claimed, and continued to enjoy, a greater latitude of freedom than other media. For one thing, they were not as dependent structurally and financially on the central government as were the broadcast media and the wire services. It required very little capital to start up a new newspaper, or to convert an existing one to new purposes. In the more Western (and Westernized) of these countries—Poland, the Czech Republic, Hungary, Estonia, Latvia, and Lithuania—newspapers remain largely free of direct government censorship. In the others, the degree of freedom changes with the shifting political winds.

In many cases, the appearance of independent newspapers was as simple as an underground newspaper coming above ground. *Gazeta Wyborcza*, the illegal organ of the Solidarity movement, already had the editorial talent and even a rudimentary distribution system that allowed it to become a commercially successful legal publication in the post-Communist era. The transition was not without its pain. Lech Walesa, Solidarity leader turned president, could not abide a newly independent *Gazeta* that insisted on its right to criticize him as it had the Communists, and the movement and the newspaper had to agree to go their separate ways.

Another route to independence was the transformation of one-time Communist Party organs, almost overnight, into independent newspapers through bloodless coups in the newsrooms, when professional journalists who had worked, however uncomfortably, in the old systems seized the moment and overthrew their Communist bosses. *Nepszabadsag* in Hungary, *Adverul* in Romania, and *Izvestia* in Russia took such a route to independence. The ironic, and for Western observers confusing, result was that newspapers that had represented the worst in toadyism to Communist authorities became almost instantly some of the most respected and professional newspapers in their countries. In a variant on that theme, *Moskovskiy Komsomolets* was transformed from a staid mouthpiece of the Moscow Communist youth organization into a breezy and enormously popular newspaper concentrating on local news about Moscow and its environs.

In some countries, the road to freedom for newspapers has had bumps along the road. Reformist President Boris Yeltsin closed down some Russian newspapers and instituted censorship at others in the wake of the abortive 1993 putsch against his government. *Nezavisimaya Gazeta*, using a standard play from the book of anticensorship fighters, printed blank space to symbolize censored material. In this case, the net result was increased press freedom. Yeltsin backed off in the face of both internal and external ridicule for his actions.

The degree of freedom for broadcast journalism also differs from country to country. But, unlike with the print media, not a single country has moved quickly toward totally independent broadcast news. The degree of state control ranges from Croatia and Serbia, where the government continues to control all television broadcasting, to the much freer Czech Republic and Poland, where political influence remains a powerful, but no longer all-powerful, pressure.

In most of the countries, private television stations popped up as pirate operations even before privatization was officially approved by law. Increasingly, private operations are being licensed, and even government television operations are moving away from direct government control to public boards that are at least nominally independent.

Nevertheless, politics continues to play a central role in the day-to-day realities of broadcast journalists. In Poland, the top officials of Polish National Television changed several times as new political factions came into power. In Romania, a bloated bureaucracy, heavily influenced by politicians, runs a "don't-rock-the-boat" national television operation.

In Hungary, until it was ousted from power by the Communists, a right-wing government tried to fend off criticism from the media by using very Communist-like methods.

> In broadcasting, relations were so bad for a while that the term "media war" came to be used. The heads of Hungarian radio and television who promoted what they termed objectivity and fairness in the broadcast media were seen by the government as simply being critical. Finally, the heads resigned, but the president of Hungary refused to accept their resignations. Nonetheless, the prime minister appointed people to take their places, people who followed his will and turned state broadcasting into an institution promoting the government's interests. In March 1994, just two months before nationwide elections, the Hungarian radio head fired more than 100 journalists for not meeting standards. Tens of thousands of people poured into the streets to protest what they saw as a simple case of politics. Four months later, a new radio head promised to rehire the journalists.[5]

In Russia, both the reformist president and the anti-reformist majority in the parliament continue to fight for influence over, if not out-right control of, broadcast journalism. In February 1996, President Boris Yeltsin fired Oleg Poptsov, the head of the official Russian Television and Radio's second television channel.

The incident underscored the complexities of media–government relations in the post-Communist era. Poptsov's television channel had given Yeltsin support during the anti-Yeltsin putsch of October 1993, broadcasting news of the pro-Yeltsin forces' efforts to end the putsch. But Yeltsin, in an unwitting throw back to the good-news philosophy of Soviet television, complained that the channel was failing to report enough about the successes of Russian industry, a shortcoming that Poptsov's successor was instructed to correct. Yeltsin also smarted under the channel's reports on his administration's handling of the anti-Russian rebellion in Chechnya.

Although Yeltsin's move was a temporary setback for journalistic independence, the fallout illustrated that the post-Soviet media, very unlike their predecessors, can and will fight back. Channel Two's employees sent an open letter of protest denouncing Poptsov's firing. And Igor Malashenko, president of one of the independent channels, NTV, used the occasion to strike a rhetorical blow for free media.

"This was the first alternative television channel in Russia," Malashenko said. "I don't think the state authorities like alternatives and they have shown this in this decree. . . . Some people advised president Boris Yeltsin to take a no-nonsense approach on the eve of elections because they think that it is very risky just to interact with the mass media when the mass media can be simply controlled."

Malashenko predicted victory for free media—but only after a struggle. "I said months ago that pressure on the media was going to increase. It is increasing now and it is going to be worse. Will freedom of speech survive in Russia? I think yes, it will, but it is going to be a very difficult struggle."

True journalistic independence in television news will probably emerge first at private broadcast outlets. And, although private television services have emerged in impressive numbers in many countries, that alone is not enough to guarantee vigorous journalism. The Yeltsin government's up-and-down relations with NTV, the first independent television station in Russia, serves as a prominent and probably instructive example.

In 1995, NTV officials were fighting with the Yeltsin regime. Its journalists had been banned from covering the Kremlin because their broadcasts were considered too critical by the Yeltsin people. And both Russian and Western observers gave credit to NTV for robustly critical coverage of the Yeltsin regime's blunders in the war against Chechnya—including extensive and damaging coverage of the protests against the war within Russia.

According to at least one report, a member of Yeltsin's team bluntly warned NTV to lay off its tough coverage of Chechnya or face being shut down. The NTV response showed the dramatic effect privatization can have on TV journalism, even if the private stations can be threatened with the revocation of their licenses by an unhappy government. Andrew Higgins, a Moscow correspondent for *The Independent*, the British daily newspaper, summarized the outcome of the Yeltsin–NTV dust-up, an outcome unimaginable in which television is under total government control: Like U.S. television networks during the Vietnam War 30 years before, NTV continued to hammer away, bringing the blood of what the government had wanted to keep a distant conflict into every living room—or at least those of the 100 million people in European Russia who can receive NTV. Its ratings and reputation soared; Yeltsin's popularity plunged.[6]

Yet NTV jumped happily aboard the Yeltsin bandwagon in the presidential elections of 1996, when he faced a drubbing by a Communist opponent. NTV's president even became a member of Yeltsin's campaign committee. Like many other journalists, he argued that journalistic objectivity was not as important as ensuring a defeat of the Communists, whose return would threaten the destruction of all free journalism.

In September 1996, Yeltsin signed a decree that freed NTV from a rule that had limited it to eight broadcast hours a day, permitting it to offer around-the-clock programming. The previous June, Gazprom, a government-connected natural gas company, bought a 30% interest in NTV.

In several other former Soviet republics, officials were continuing to use a combination of raw government power and judicial processes in attempts to stymy independent broadcasters. In the Republic of Georgia, the first nongovernmental television news was offered by an independent station in June 1996. Two weeks later, the Georgian Ministry of Communications revoked the station's license because, in the theory of the private station's owners, the government feared the competition would reduce revenues for the state television operation. Predictably, a group of 12 other independent stations, none of whom themselves offered newscasts, joined in a protest against the government's action. Unpredictably, so did journalists at the state's own television station—showing just how fluid the attitudes toward media issues have now become.[7]

In Belarus, which remains one of the most repressive of the former Soviet republics, the regime has used various tactics to threaten or silence independent journalistic voices. Government-owned printing plants have arbitrarily cancelled printing contracts with independent newspapers. The government has cut off independent radio station access to government-owned transmitters. In 1996, the Minsk regional government used its taxing power to freeze the bank accounts of five independent Belarus weekly newspapers.[8]

In many of the former Yugoslav republics, pressure on the media varies from virtually total control by the government in Serbia to heavy government pressure to toe the line in the other republics. In the Southern republics of the former Soviet Union, freedom varies from country to country, but it is generally far less than in Russia. In some countries, the leeway allowed newspapers seems only a bit more than in the Soviet days. Lip service is paid to press freedom, but, in practice, governments use a variety of weapons to discourage vigorous journalism. The arsenal includes prosecutions or civil actions in the courts to punish critical journalists, various schemes to deny "registration" to disliked journalists or publications, and physical intimidation.

Kyrgystan's president is Askar Akaev, a former physicist who bragged about his country's move to democracy after it declared its independence in 1991. Like many would-be democrats, though, he has since had second thoughts. Two Kyrgyz journalists were sentenced to prison in 1995 for "libelous publications insulting the honor and dignity" of the president. They had reported that Akaev owned a villa in Switzerland.[9] A court closed down the Kyrgyz newspaper *Svobodny Gory* in 1994 on charges that an illustration poking fun at the president and members of his cabinet had violated a 1992 press law that prohibits material that would incite violence, insult religious feelings, or increase ethnic tensions.[10]

Irena Lasota, president of the Institute for Democracy in Eastern Europe, described a trial of two journalists in Azerbaijan in 1995 that sounded, as she noted, straight from the Soviet days:

> I attended half a day of the trial of the journalists accused of publishing the satirical journal Chesme. They were sentenced to between 2 and 5 years of prison. It was a "normal Soviet-style" trial with the accused brought in from jail where they were in isolation for over 6 months, the judge (a woman) who was more aggressive than the prosecutors and the most vague accusation (offending the president, but no examples of offense were given and the president did not testify). In the courtroom, all the time there were between 8 and 12 uniformed soldiers with machine guns, clubs and pistols.[11]

In Albania, journalists can be jailed for criticizing the president or the parliament or even representatives from foreign countries. Romanian law prohibits journalists from insulting government officials.

In addition to the courts, Azerbaijani authorities used another tactic to keep journalists off balance and to make them think twice before publishing materials unfriendly to the government. By 1994, they had required media to re-register with the Ministry of Press and Information three separate times to prevent from being banned. The rationale, according to official Azerbaijani Radio, was that "the various media and publishers are rampantly exploiting freedom of the press and information."[12] Similarly, in the Oyrol Region of Russia, the regional legislature warned it would refuse accreditation of journalists if the deputies determine the journalists cover the legislature "unobjectively."[13]

In one way, journalists in post-Communist Europe are markedly worse off than in the old days of Soviet power. In the latter days of

Communism, working journalists were rarely physically endangered because of their profession. True, some underground journalists were on occasion beaten up by policemen or thugs working for security services, and the ringleaders of the samizdat press were frequently jailed or sent into exile. But few were killed as a direct result of their journalism.

In the chaotic post-Communist period, beatings have become an almost routine reward for aggressive journalism, and the number of journalists killed for practicing their craft grows almost daily. At least 41 reporters were killed while covering the Chechnya war, many of them by Russian forces.

It is usually impossible to pin down the motives because the murderers are seldom caught—whether because of police incompetence, police indifference, or as is suspected in some cases, direct police involvement in the murders. In most cases, speculation focuses on either organized crime figures who fear a journalist is getting too close to exposing their operations—or their revenue streams—or officials whose anger over their coverage explodes into violent retribution.

The most physically hostile environments for journalists today seem to be the former Soviet republics, particularly Russia itself and the former Soviet Central Asian Republics.

In one famous Russian case, a 27-year-old investigative reporter for *Moskovsky Komsomolets*, Dmitry Kholodov, was killed by a briefcase bomb. He had told co-workers he was picking up a briefcase full of incriminating materials from an official of the Federal Counter-Intelligence Service. Kholod had published articles that suggested high army officials were providing weapons and training to organized Russian crime. The newspaper's editor, Pavel Gusev, suggested the man ultimately responsible for the murder was Pavel Grachev, the Russian Minister of Defense.[14]

Izvestia, in a front-page article on October 20, 1994, described the murders of 12 Russian journalists that year. "This is censorship with fists and clubs, knives and brass knuckles, Kalashnikov automatics and explosives," *Izvestia* said. According to one estimate, more than 30 journalists had been killed by 1995 in Tajikistan because of their attempts to expose political corruption.[15] By the middle of 1996, 14 journalists had already been killed in the former Soviet republics, according to the Glasnost Defense Foundation Monitoring Group. All told, 41 journalists had been killed covering the Chechnya conflict, many of them presumably by Russian soldiers or authorities.[16]

THE STRUGGLE FOR ECONOMIC SURVIVAL

In a free-market society, lack of political interference is only one precondition to a free press. To survive, let alone thrive, the managers of media must also find ways to be economically self-sufficient. For most of the thousands of media that sprang up after the fall of Communism, economic independence remains a distant dream. In the meantime, most journalists find themselves in a continuing economic tug-of-war. Truly independent publications and broadcast outlets find themselves constrained by economic structures, practices, and often personnel inherited from the Communist past. Rare is the newspaper or broadcast outlet that can make it on its own financially. Most have to rely on government subsidies, overt or covert support from political parties, or shared ownership with Western media organizations.

The media's most pressing economic problem is the failure of most of the formerly Communist countries to find anything approaching a sound financial footing. Poland, the Czech Republic, Hungary, and Estonia have shown the most success at making the transition from command economy structures and practices toward a free market. Media in those countries, particularly the print media, have shown a corresponding growth in self-sufficiency—often with the help of major infusions of capital from Western media companies.

However, the economies in the other countries of the region have failed to take off. They are troubled by extortion by organized (and not so organized) crime, continued fights over privatization, meddling by political officials, raging inflation, and, perhaps most dangerous, hostility on the part of ordinary citizens who see, instead of the dreamt of Western luxuries, lost jobs, worthless pension funds, and little hope for more comfortable lives.

Media suffer doubly in such an environment. Falling economies deprive them of the independent financial support they need as readers opt for a loaf of bread over a newspaper. And advertisers are scarce in an unstable economy. What is more, government-controlled enterprises continue to control the supply of precious newsprint and the systems that distribute publications, and government ministries control or heavily influence which broadcasters are allotted air time.

Ivan Asyov, president of the CLK private radio-television center in Velingrad, in the Rhodopi Mountains of Bulgaria, knows firsthand the frustrations of trying to run a capitalist enterprise in the midst of the economic never-never land of a post-Communist country:

> Even if we knew how to attract advertisers, how can we even speak about advertisers here? Take a plant, for example. It is working

today but nobody knows whether it will be working tomorrow and whether there will be any products to advertise. Our economy is completely destroyed. How can you talk about marketing? Yes, we do work with a long-term budget but it doesn't make sense now, when things in the economy are changing catastrophically.[17]

Media also suffer, like all business enterprises, because even as they try to help invent new political and economic systems, they must deal with the almost crippling constraints of old ones. Olga Aksakova could be a role model for the modern media entrepreneur. Along with her husband, she founded *Tikhookeanskaya Curyor* [Pacific Courier], a business weekly in the Russian port city of Vladivostok. But in 1994, she was struggling to keep the newspaper in business in the face of confiscatory taxes, bankers who preferred to do business with the same old boys' network they had dealt with under the Communist system, and local politicians who, Aksanova said, threw roadblocks in the way of independent journalism:

We're the only truly independent newspaper in Vladivostok. The others are subsidized by the government or by a political party. But a free market needs reliable and neutral economic information. And a democracy needs objective news. Our politicians and our bureaucrats waste time fighting with each other while our economy and our businesses go to hell.[18]

In most of these countries, the economic straits of newspapers lead to continuing government subsidies. A typical pattern, in fact, is that only one or two newspapers of national scope find the advertising and circulation bases necessary to be independent—and then usually with an infusion of capital from a Western media firm. Other newspapers, if they are to survive, have to rely on financial help from the government, from political parties, or from private firms, often banks, that may have their own editorial axes to grind.

Dumitru Tinu, the editorial director of *Adevarul*, probably the most respected and most independent newspaper in Romania (although it is a direct descendent of *Scientea*, the Communist Party mouthpiece) explained the difficulties of economic survival under post-Communist conditions. The newspaper derives 23% of its revenue from advertising, a small proportion by Western standards—but many conservative readers resent even that much advertising as somehow cheating them of space that should be devoted to news and commentary. Unlike many newspapers in Romania and the rest of Eastern Europe, *Adevarul* is financially independent. "It would be very easy, financially and politically, if we supported the authorities," Mr. Tinu said. "If we supported power we would have no problem with power. If we supported the opposition we would get support from the outside. But we choose to go it alone."[19]

The Russian government continued to provide substantial subsidies to key print media. Drastic increases in paper prices, the high expense of delivery, and runaway inflation decimated Ukraine's newspapers and magazines, with the number of subscriptions dropping 75% from 1992 to 1993. More than half of the financial support for Ukrainian print media in the 1994 came from the Communist Party, the state, and industrialists.[20]

In some cases, political fighting between different organs of government has led to increased competition, but of a strange sort by Western standards. The Yeltsin regime took over control of the parliamentary mouthpiece, *Rossiiskaya Gazeta*, in the wake of the failed coup against Yeltsin. In October 1995, the State Duma founded its own 50,000-circulation weekly, *Narodnaya Duma*. The reason, according to a parliament spokesperson, was to increase public exposure to Duma legislation and "broaden the social base of legislation."[21]

Albania is the extreme example of the difficulties of independent media in a stagnant economy. Although 250 newspapers were officially registered in 1994, only about 60 were actually being published, and only one, the organ of the opposition former Communists, was published daily. All but two of Albania's newspapers depended on political parties for at least some of their support.[22]

Even in Hungary and Poland, which have arguably made the most progress of any formerly Communist country toward democratic media, unpredictable political and economic tides threaten media entrepreneurs. As in the rest of post-Communist Europe, the print media have moved the furthest toward economic independence. But even here the remnants of the old system block the path to the new. As Aumente notes, political parties and splinter groups in Poland fought for editorial control of former Communist papers even as they were being "privatized." And in Hungary, where the print media privatized rapidly, the reformed, nominally democratic government chafed so at aggressive coverage by an independent press that it started its own newspaper and magazine and secretly supported publications that supported the government.

Despite the economic and political obstacles, independent broadcast operations continue to start up in most of the formerly Communist countries. Some of them, such as NTV in Russia, provide news that is stubbornly resistant to economic, political, and physical intimidation. NTV's reporting of the Chechnya crisis, for example, often exposed the incompetence of the Russian military in Chechnya. And NTV reported the consequent anti-war demonstrations in Russia as well.

Hundreds of smaller broadcast operations are finding ways to survive, if not thrive, and still remain independent of political control. A Moscow-based Western media specialist reported in December 1995 that he had found independent commercial stations in six smaller cities in Kazakstan—hardly the most hospitable climate, either politically or economically, for independent broadcasting:

> In most of these small cities the commercial TV station is independent in the sense that it operates on its own revenue which it earns from (mostly classified) ads and owns its own transmitter, but since they're shoestring operations and production takes equipment which takes money, they produce very little (at best, news a couple times a week). Each of them was very pessimistic about our assertions that commercial TV *can* make it and can develop financially, but I think the examples we used to try to convince them their stations can be more than simply a movie theatre on the air had a little effect. At a minimum, e.g. the station in Dzehzkazgan called up the deputies running for parliament, discovered they did indeed want to buy advertising time, and sold some on the spot. Several of the station directors have already called or visited our office in Almaty to see what we "offer" so we're encouraged by their initiative.[23]

Government-supported wire agencies, although their monopolies have been broken by the widespread use of Western new services, remain in one form or another in most of Eastern Europe. The Czech Press Agency is still supported by subsidies from the state, even though it has been transformed into a public, nongovernmental corporation. On the Slovak side of the new border, the TASR Slovak wire service operates under government control.

One much-discussed threat posed by the economic instability of East European media—that Western media firms would soon dominate both the content and the ideology of media in the post-Communist era—seems for the most part not to have materialized.

True, the most popular television program in Poland, watched by 70% of the audience, is "Kolo Fortuny"—[Wheel of Fortune].[24] True, Russians have been entranced by recycled U.S. soap operas like "Santa Barbara" (even though it was first shown on Russian scenes out of sequence so that the story line did not make much sense) and "Dynasty." And true, in Hungary, nearly 80% of the newspapers and in Poland half of the major dailies are owned by Western firms.[25]

Yet few signs have emerged that many of the Western firms seek anything other than a return on investment. Indeed, those media most respected for their non-partisan approach to news often are those with substantial Western support—*Gazeta Wyborcza* in Poland, supported by the U.S. Cox newspaper group; the much respected English language *Moscow Times*, founded by Briton Dirk Sauer; and *Itogi*, a news weekly joint venture of *Newsweek* and NTV, Moscow's very successful television operation.

CHANGING ATTITUDES: THE MOST DIFFICULT TRANSITION OF ALL?

Media played a major role in the struggle for democracy in Eastern Europe, from the underground newspapers that, beginning in the 1960s, helped make alternatives to Communism thinkable, to the television broadcasts in 1989 that both documented and encouraged the mass demonstrations that ended Communist rule. Thousands of new publications then emerged to ride the crest of the postrevolution euphoria of freedom.

Seven years later, the euphoria has long since evaporated, replaced by the grimier vapors of post-Communist reality. Attempts to establish independent and free media have been hampered not just by the political and economic legacy of the Communist era, but by ways of thinking as well. The old ways of thinking about journalism—by ordinary citizens, by politicians and officials, and by journalists themselves—live on, slowing and sometimes thwarting the spread of democratic journalism.

One of the first casualties of the economic and political chaos that followed hard on the anti-Communist revolutions was the public's enthusiasm for the newly liberated media. Print media, easy to start on a shoe string, were the first to break out of the bonds of authoritarian control. Indeed, in many countries defiantly independent publications began emerging even before the overthrow of the old regimes was official. Citizens initially reacted enthusiastically to the novelty of uncensored publications. But the enthusiasm quickly waned as the novelty wore off, an accustomed cynicism returned, and ordinary citizens worried more about economic survival than the daily political bickering of the various political parties and factions.

Even in the Western-most countries, where economic, political, and media reforms took hold the most quickly, the public's honeymoon with the media was short. Johnson notes that the Czech public, trained through years of Communist polemics to be distrustful of the press, quickly turned distrustful of the post-Communist reform journalists, equally polemical in their own way. In any case, they were not much interested in public affairs. By 1992, ordinary Czechs and Slovaks were more interested in entertainment and information useful to improving their own economic and social conditions: "The most widely-sold newspapers in both the Czech and Slovak Republics were tabloids. With news much more readily available, readers and viewers no longer were [so] actively involved in finding out what was going on. The revolutionaries had won the right to say what they wanted, but the public was not so interested."[26]

Among public leaders, too, commitment to a free press could be less than whole-hearted. It is not surprising, of course, that Communist and ex-Communist politicians can quickly come up with rationales for fearing totally uncensored media. Perhaps only slightly more surprising, many politicians who grew up on the other side of the partisan fence can also find it difficult to accept media that are free to report on anything, to criticize anybody.

Gabor Demszky, a dissident publisher who became mayor of Budapest after the fall of Communism, notes that the end of Communist censorship has not meant the end of censors:

> New censors . . . appear day by day. They like to mask their activities as the defense of elevated values, the avoidance of unforeseen dangers and the ultimate protection of a brave new world. They refer to God, king or the homeland; always something sublime. They claim that it is for our common good that we not see, read and know everything we are interested in.[27]

Lech Walesa, anti-Communist revolutionary who became Poland's president, could never quite accept that his regime, and he personally could be subject to aggressive media examination and criticism. He eventually broke with *Gazeta Wyborcza*, the newspaper founded by his own Solidarity movement, over this issue. A 1993 law gave a national broadcasting council powers to regulate, and issue licenses and to govern the programming of Polish public broadcasting as a way of distancing the government from broadcasting. At one point, Walensa forced the head of the council to resign because he was unhappy with Polish broadcasting's failure to support his government sufficiently.

Johnson sums up the ambivalence with which a free press is regarded by many politicians of all stripes:

> Journalists and government leaders in these countries share a commitment to freedom of speech and press. But only for responsible people, especially themselves. Many government and political leaders do not think that a free and open press can be tolerated when the democracies and economies of their countries are still so fragile.[28]

In Hungary, the rightist government of 1990–94 chafed under the coverage it got from the public broadcast media. In March 1994, the head of Hungarian radio fired more than 100 journalists because of his unhappiness with what he viewed as unfair criticism of the government.

Journalists themselves are far from unambivalent about their proper role in post-Communist Europe and about the proper kind of journalism for post-Communist Europe. The lack of clarity stems in part from a blending of roles caused by many current-day journalists' individual backgrounds as partisan activists, and in part by a mindset that still views journalism as partisan by nature.

Adam Michnik, one of the founding leaders of Poland's anti-Communist Solidarity movement and now editor-in-chief of *Gazeta Wyborcza*, explained the difficulty of these transitions of attitude:

> It is difficult to change one's views; it is difficult for a dissident, a member of the underground to become the editor in chief of the most popular newspaper in a democratic state. The reality of democracy is so different from the world of dictatorship in which I lived from the day I was born. That world was inevitably a black and white one: Goodness struggled against evil, the truth struggled against lies, freedom staged the battle against enslavement.
>
> In the world of democracy, the prevailing color is gray. This world is ruled by arguments which are divided and not complete, by partial and contradictory interests.[29]

The more partisan journalists can take antifree expression views that are as extreme as those of any prereform Communist. The chairman of the Hungarian Journalists' Community, formed in 1992 to support a rightist government that thought it was being unfairly treated by the media, said bluntly: "We do not want free speech, because free speech is turning into spitefulness. . . . We want decency in the press" (Ray Hiebert, 1995, unpublished manuscript).

More typically, journalists today pay lip-service to the idea of a free press while indulging in practices and habits that undermine it. The bloated bureaucracies of most public broadcasting services, for example, continue to support, overtly or covertly, whatever regime is in power—even though various broadcasting boards or agencies have been devised in an ostensible attempt to free public broadcasters of direct government control.

Romanian National Television, for example, is seen by its critics as offering news and commentary that are almost as propagandistic as in the days of the Ceasescu dictatorship. The operation was described by Tia Serbanescu, a Romanian print journalist, as a "moral and professional misery."[30]

Western journalists and educators who have studied the practice of journalism in the area are struck by how stubbornly the Communist-era practices and habits stick among many journalists. Many journalists continue to take a very passive role by U.S. standards. News conferences are very tame and predictable affairs, with the reporters taking dutiful notes on long monologues from public officials, asking only very respectful questions.

U.S. journalists and educators who have worked with their colleagues in Poland are first bemused, then frustrated, by the continuing practice of having sources "authorize" stories written about them. That is, the reporters allow sources to vet stories before they are published.

For their part, the East European journalists are often mystified by the Western approaches urged on them by visiting colleagues. They defend the "authorization" technique as a way of ensuring accuracy, not caving in to politicians (or, as some Western critics argue, of being too lazy to report carefully and accurately in the first place). And Polish journalists, observes Jerome Aumente, the U.S. expert on Polish journalism, are appalled by what they regard as U.S. reporters' callous invasion into the lives of officials and their families.

Arnold Isaacs, a journalism instructor and former *Baltimore Sun* reporter who spent nine weeks working with journalists and journalism students in Poland, perceived a sharp divide between older and younger journalists in that country. The younger ones were eager to move toward a more straightforward, fact-based approach to news—although they could find few journalism educators or older journalists who would lead them in that direction. The older generation of journalists wanted to emphasize that lines still have to be drawn, that journalism cannot be totally free:

> older professionals [thought that] freedom of the press doesn't mean the press must now print "everything." The old timers are very uncomfortable with sensational reporting and graphic media images of sex and violence, or with reports focusing on the personal lives and peccadillos of public figures. And they are uneasy with the commercialization of journalism that has spurred that sort of popular, but not "serious" or "respectable" news.[31]

Another Communist-era tradition, that of mixing news with views, remains strong in newspapers and, to some extent, in broadcast news as well. In the view of many local as well as Western critics, it is the Communist-era mind-set that most gets in the way of providing citizens the unadorned news they need to understand the issues facing their countries.

Some of the more respected newspapers—*Gazeta Wyborcza* in Poland, *Nepszabadsag* in Hungary, *Izvestia* and *Moskovskiy Komsomolets* in Russia—are making efforts to separate commentary from the news columns at least part of the time. NTV, the Ted Turner-Russian joint venture in Moscow, introduced relatively neutral television news to Russia.

But for many journalists, the idea of entirely fact-based news remains an unwelcome U.S. import. Most newspapers exist financially only because of backing by political parties or corporations with ideological missions, so a partisan cast to the news is a given, and journalists working for government-controlled broadcast operations understandably believe their stories must toe the government line. In addition, many journalists argue, probably also with some justification, that their readers and viewers have come to expect a point of view along with their news—that they would find the news dull without it. Probably most important, many journalists consider fact-based journalism an uninteresting, even demeaning, pursuit. That is in keeping with a tradition in Western, as well as Eastern, Europe of journalism as a minor literary genre and the journalist as a minor philosopher.

A journalism professor at the University of Rostov in Russia defended this historic view of journalists after listening to a visiting U.S. professor's discussion of fact-based journalism. Such journalism, and the teaching of such journalism, would have no interest, he said in exasperation: "There is nothing to teach if you only want to teach them how to write facts."[32]

CONCLUSION

It has long been a cliche among Western defenders of democratic traditions, particularly the tradition of free expression, that democratic institutions are fragile and must be guarded carefully, lest they be taken away. The experiments with democracy in Eastern Europe and the former Soviet Union over the past seven years may suggest just the opposite—that given the tiniest toehold, democratic institutions can be stubbornly resistant to attack. The remarkable thing, perhaps, about democratic media and democratically minded journalists in these countries is that, despite the economic, political, and psychological obstacles in their way, they seem not only to be hanging on, but to be growing.

Although hundreds of newspapers and magazines have died in the face of rough times, some important ones survive. Some of them are beginning to thrive as they shake off the political and economic constraints of the old era. Although opposition journalists may face legal and even physical intimidation in some of the countries, they continue to practice. Virtually every country in the area has at least one serious newspaper not controlled by the government or a political party. Indeed, one sign that governmental monopoly of the news has been broken is that it is increasingly presidents or parliaments that complain they have to establish their own newspaper or television station because their views are not being heard. The idea of a government starting its own media may seem authoritarian to Western journalists, but for governments to feel so defensive that they want to start their own media represents a major change in attitude from the days when the government and the media were one.

Although governments, particularly Communist-dominated ones, try to retain control of broadcasting, journalists are finding ways to get out the news, either by fancy political footwork within the public broadcasting operations or by forming private operations. The very proliferation of new broadcast media seems to insure that diversity will win out over the stubborn attempts of governments to maintain control.

Finally, although ordinary citizens may be disappointed with the failure of the introduction of democracy to change their lives, particularly their economic lives, overnight, they show no signs that they would give up the new, wide spectrum of media that reforms have brought. Gabor Demszky writes:

> Under Communism most people thought of the freedom of the press as a kind of luxury—a pleasure to have, but something they could do without. Since then, however, citizens have learned by experience that the autonomy of the media and the right to speak freely are not perquisites but guarantees of freedom. They are the very token of liberty, a liberty won so late and at such a dear price in this part of Europe that people will never surrender it again. Freedom has become one of our most cherished values. I take this as the safest guarantee of the demise of censorship, which is destined to become a phenomenon so irrelevant that in the future it will arouse only the interest of media historians.[33]

The optimism may be justified. The Russian presidential elections of 1996 seemed to demonstrate that, despite the economic hardships caused by the collapse of the Soviet Union, the Russian people were not willing to consider a return to the totalitarian past. Even in the many countries where former Communists have returned to power, they have not shown an inclination to wipe out the gains in free expression. Perhaps even those politicians who have such an inclination know it is an impossible one to indulge in an age in which satellite and Internet technologies cannot be stopped by national borders.

Sometimes gradually, sometimes in sudden bursts, democratic journalism seems to be taking hold in the formerly Communist world. It is happening more quickly in the print media and in those countries that have had, or have, more contact with the West and Western traditions of democracy. In the more remote and economically less advanced areas of the formerly Communist world, governments continue to fight against independent journalism. But even there the journalists who are willing to fight for independence seem determined to hang on. In time, the idea of free media may indeed become, throughout the region, too common-place to have any but academic interest.

NOTES & REFERENCES

1. FSUMedia listserv, July 11, 1995, quoting Open Media Research Institute Daily Digest of July 11, 1995.
2. Owen V. Johnson, "Whose Voice? Freedom of Speech and the Media in central Europe," in Al Hester, and Kristina White, Eds., *Creating a Free Press in Eastern Europe*, Athens: University of Georgia, 1993, pp. 1-52.
3. FSUMedia, February 17, 1996, based on BASA Press account of February 16, 1996.
4. BASA-Press, February 6, 1996, transmitted by FSUMedia.
5. Johnson, p. 16.
6. "In Russian Media, Money Is the Key," *IPI Report*, September/October 1995, p. 21.
7. FSUMedia listserv, July 19 1996.
8. FSUMedia listserv, September 9, 1996.
9. Associated Press report, July 13, 1995.
10. The Knight International Press Fellowship Program Report, Center for Foreign Journalists, Reston, VA, 1994.
11. FSUMedia Listserv, October 24, 1995.
12. Open Media R I Daily Digest, January 15, 1996.
13. Express-Chronicle Human Rights News Agency Weekly Summary, September 7-13, as reported by FSUMedia Listserv, September 30, 1995.
14. Renfrey Clarke, "Censorship in the New Russian—with Bombs and Brass Knuckles," glas:austgreen in igc:reg.ussr, October 21, 1994.
15. Alvin Shuster, "They Shoot Journalists, Don't They," *IPI Report*, January/June 1995, p. 18.
16. FSUMedia listserv, July 14, 1996.
17. Ekaterina Ognianova, personal interview, June 7, 1994.
18. Dean Mills, personal interview, February, 1994.
19. Dean Mills, personal interview, May 18, 1995.
20. Owen Johnson, "East Central and Southeastern Europe, Russia, and the Newly Independent States," p. 181.
21. OMRI Daily Digest, October 5, 1996.

22. Owen Johnson, "East Central and Southeastern Europe and the Newly Independent States," p. 17.
23. Eric Johnson, "Letter from Kazakstan," FSUMedia listserv, December 10, 1995.
24. Johnson, *op. cit.*, p. 7.
25. Johnson, *op. cit.*, p. 12.
26. Owen V. Johnson (1995). "Dzechs and Balances: Mass Media and the Velvet Revolution" in Jeremy Popkin, ed., *Media and Revolution*, University of Kentucky, p. 18.
27. "Breaking Censorship—Making Peace," *Media Studies Journal,*Summer 1995, p. 79.
28. Johnson, "East Central," p. 10.
29. "Samizdat Goes Public," *Media Studies Journal*, Summer 1995, p. 74.
30. Peter Gross, "Romania," in Maurice Fliess, ed., *Looking to the Future: A Survey of Journalism Education in Central and Eastern Europe and the Former Soviet Union*, Arlington, VA: The Freedom Forum, pp. 56-59.
31. *Knight report*, p. 48.
32. Dean Mills (August 1994) "Russia," p. 61, in Maurice Fliess, ed., *Looking To the Future: A Survey of Journalism Education in Central and Eastern Europe and the Former Soviet Union*. Arlington, VA: The Freedom Forum, pp. 60-70.
33. Gabor Demszky, "Breaking Censorship—Making Peace," *Media Studies Journal*, Summer 1995, p. 85.

5

Before, During, and After: Journalism Education

Peter Gross

INTRODUCTION

Concomitant to the post-1989 mass media explosion in the former Soviet Union and East/Central Europe came a sudden mushrooming in journalism education programs. Both shared a range of problems, from the conceptual/ideational and facilities/technological, to staff and programmatic.

Previous chapters deal primarily with the mass media and their journalism in the many post-Communist[1] nations; their histories, role, and effects in the transition; and their evolution since 1989. They set the stage for the understanding of the evolution of journalism education in the regions under discussion.

This chapter deals with journalism education, the 96–110 journalism programs (university and vocational degree and certificate programs), 1,600–1,800 faculty, and 16,000–18,000 journalism students that by 1995 were part of the educational landscape of the new East/Central

Europe, the Baltics, Russia, and other former Soviet republics. As with so many other areas of development in the regions under consideration, journalism is still in a state of flux. Its evolutionary destination (the role it will play, its effects, ethics, and processes) is unclear. The transition from Communism is not proceeding according to a set scenario but is, instead, a trial-and-error process. Journalism education is no different. And, as is the case with journalism and the mass media, journalism education is affected by pre-Communist and Communist legacies, as much as by the transitionary period itself (i.e., the post-Communist authoritarian period, in those countries were it took hold, and the post-Communist pluralist period).

THE LEGACY

The Pre-Communist Era

The legacy of formal journalism education in East/Central Europe dates back to the post-World War I period. The earliest sign that formal journalism education was being contemplated as a prelude to media work is found in what is now the Czech Republic. There such education was proposed in 1910 and finally established in 1928 in the Free School of Political Science.[2] As it turned out in what was then Czechoslovakia, as well as in Poland and Romania, where some journalism education was reportedly carried out before World War II, it was conceptualized to provide a broad-based liberal arts and social science academic background. Skills training emphasizing reporting and journalistic writing, or professional ethics, and the philosophical underpinnings to news media's role in society was not included in the curricula.

In the Baltic countries, between 1890 and 1940, a number of professional organizations were formed and considered, among other issues, the establishment of professional standards and education[3] (see also Chapters 4, 5, and 6, this volume). However, no journalism training or educational programs were established.

Journalism everywhere in Europe, West and East, was practiced by intellectuals, academics, politicians, and those with varying degrees of talent for polemics, editorial writing, analysis, and some reporting. The latter served as a starting point for the former or as a followup to the specific editorial intent of an article. The Western and East/Central European tradition, as Horvat[4] explains, included, "the concept of the active or participant journalist, the journalist who sees himself as someone who wants to influence politics and audiences according to his own political beliefs."

In East/Central Europe, journalistic training was mostly offered by journalism associations that sprung up as part of a push to professionalize the news media in the 1920s. There were few such programs, all limited in scope. The majority of East/Central European journalists received their training on the job with a media whose journalism matched its cousin to the West: It was passionate, opinionated, polemical discussion of the days events from the point of view of the writer; a means for political, social, and cultural combat. It was to become even more so during Communist rule when, controlled by the indigenous ruling Communist parties, it became singularly purposeful, narrow, and one-sidedly ideological.

THE COMMUNIST ERA

In the aftermath of Communism's ascendancy in the late 1940s, journalism education was defined as political education and coupled with propagandistic techniques to be applied both in print and broadcast media. The earliest Communist journalism programs were launched in what is now Slovakia in 1948 and in Poland in 1950. Most East/Central European journalism programs under the Marxist-Leninist regimes were inaugurated in the 1950s.

Some, such as the Hungarian one that taught a literary type of journalism, were short-lived, shut down after the 1956 anti-Communist uprising. Hungary, concludes Hiebert,[5] "was one of the few communist-bloc countries that did not have university-level journalism education when the Iron Curtain crumbled." Instead, journalism training until 1991 was conducted by the Hungarian Association of Journalists, a government-subsidized organization that primarily indoctrinated journalists in Marxism-Leninism.[6] In Albania, a journalism program introduced at Tirana University in 1968 survived but six years. In Yugoslavia, formal journalism education was not introduced until the 1960s and 1970s (in Macedonia). And, in Romania, it was established as a political education tool in the 1970s and, appropriately, housed in the Stefan Gheorghiu Academy, a Romanian Communist Party "university."[7] In Poland, the Polish Journalists Association, among other professional associations, played a very active role in training and augmenting university-level programs of doubtful use and little standing.[8] The same was the case in Czechoslovakia and, as already mentioned, in Hungary.

The university-based journalism programs were either autonomous units as in most of the Soviet Union and Czechoslovakia, part of special party schools as in Romania, or placed in more traditional departments such as philology (e.g., Bulgaria, Latvia, Estonia), law and/or political science (e.g., Yugoslavia, Poland), international studies (e.g., East Germany). With very few exceptions these programs were theoretical, and Ognianova's[9] description of Bulgarian journalism education, its ideational source, and purpose perfectly describes each of the programs found in East/Central European Communist states and in the Soviet Union (inclusive of the Baltics countries). She notes, also flagging the pre-Communist tradition:

> The theoretical nature of journalism education was partly due to the East European journalism tradition in which general intellectual abilities and competence, as well as opinion and talent to present it have been valued more than the news itself. It was also due to the Bulgarian pre-communist tradition of a partisan press and newspaper's siding with a party's position since the last century. But, most of all, journalism education in communist Bulgaria was theoretical, since its purpose was to serve the ideological goals of the communist party. In this regard, journalism educators were seen by professional journalists as ideological gatekeepers and agents of the communist party and government.

The main impetus for definition and form of Communist journalism and journalism education, while holding on to some culture specific and historical characteristics, came to East/Central Europe, as to the Baltics, from the Soviet Union. There, as Mills[10] sums up the history of Soviet journalism education,

> Within a few years after the 1917 Bolshevik Revolution, workers were being trained by party schools in the Leninist methods of agitation, propaganda and organization. That tradition continued, in increasingly more formal training programs, until the collapse of the Soviet Union in 1991.

In the Ukraine, journalism programs were introduced at two universities, one in the 1930s and the other in 1954. In Belarus, the journalism program was started at the state university in Minsk in 1944. Other university and/or journalism union training programs were established in Moldova, Armenia, Azerbaijan, Georgia, Kazakhstan, Kyrgyztan, Tajikistan, Turkmenistan, and Uzbekistan. By the 1980s, the Soviet Union was reported to have 22 institutions of higher education that provided journalism training. Additionally, the Academy of Social Sciences and Moscow's Institute of International Relations also offered journalism education programs.[11]

In the Baltics, the Soviet occupation established a Stalinist media in the late 1940s, its staffs fed by a journalist program at the Latvian

State University started in 1947 (Faculty of Philology); at Lithuania's Vilnius University (Literature Department) in 1949; and at Estonia's University of Tartu (Department of Estonian Philology) in 1954.[12] According to Hiebert:[13]

> As the communists ended the thaw (in 1968) and became more repressive, they also came to perceive journalism education as subversive and began restricting some of the programs that had started in the late '40s and early '50s. In Riga and Vilnius, the journalism departments were discontinued for several years, and at Tartu the number of hours of journalism instruction was reduced. But journalism instruction slowly came back, although the curriculum was based on Marxist philosophy ("red subjects," the students called them).

In 1988, in a pioneering move in the world of Communist journalism education, the journalism department at Tartu University, Estonia, cut its Moscow-originated umbilical cord (see Chapter 2, this volume).

In most East/Central European nations, in the Baltics, as well as in the Soviet Union, the fusion of interests (party-state, media, journalism schools) was greater than anywhere else in the world.[14] It became, as Spielhagen[15] describes East German journalism, "pure politics."

Broadcast journalism/media were the most closely controlled and censored, with the least bit of latitude given to journalists in the nature and subjects of their reports. Exceptions existed. For instance, in Romania, radio journalism found itself somewhat neglected by the Ceausescu regime and had relatively more flexibility in practicing journalism. However, in print media the parameters of reporting afforded journalists varied from country to country, at various times by the 1970s and 1980s. It ranged from the absolutely restricted media atmosphere of Romania, Bulgaria, and Albania, to the relatively larger elbow-room atmosphere of Yugoslavia, Czechoslovakia, Hungary, Poland, and even the USSR in the post-Communist authoritarian period or glasnost.

THE SAMIZDAT–ALTERNATIVE JOURNALISM SCHOOL ?

Significantly, the official Communist media in some of the states east of the Elba were supplemented by an underground or alternative press, as described in Chapter 2 and in other works.[16] The strongest of these underground or alternative media were found in Poland, Czechoslovakia, Hungary, the USSR and Yugoslavia. In some cases, as for example in Czechoslovakia,[17] journalists worked for both the official and the underground or alternative media.

In the Soviet Union, the samizdat or underground press, which included books, magazines, and newspapers, was a considerable part of the media scene, particularly for urban, educated Soviet citizens.[18] In the Baltics, Hiebert[19] lists 30 regularly published underground newspapers between 1972 and 1988. In Romania, Bulgaria, and Albania they were nonexistent. These three societies and their mass media leaped from Stalinism directly to post-Communist pluralism in or after 1989.

This unofficial or illegal, predominantly print media also served as a quasi-training ground for some journalists. For whatever they were worth, they added an informal, unofficial "school of journalism" to the existing official journalism training/education programs. It is highly questionable whether they served as a vehicle for training journalists in concepts and techniques far removed from the Communist ones. The underground media were the antithesis of the Communist ones mainly in their opposition to the ideology militated for by the latter. The underground press did offer its readers information, but it was a combination informational and mobilization, opinion and recruiting messages on behalf of anti-Communism. It was mostly a "see, they are wrong again," or a "here's the real truth," approach to journalism. A journalism of information with a measure of objectivity and verifiability, a journalism of systematic inquiry and informed opinion was not to be found or only rarely found in any East/Central European or USSR media, official and legal or unofficial and illegal.

Still, as the Polish case illustrates,[20] the underground media was a recruiter and quasi-training ground for many new journalists who came from a variety of professions or educational paths.[21] For instance, during martial law from 1981 onward and in the years leading up to Solidarity, the underground press published hundreds of books and over 1,000 titles of short-lived or more permanent publications, employing hundreds of journalists and writers (see Chapter 2). In this environment, traditional journalism education at the universities seemed pale, further diminished by the perception that academics were too often in collusion with the established government order.

Czechoslovakia was yet another relative aberration in the communist world. In the aftermath of the failed Prague Spring in 1968, Johnson[22] found journalism education expanded, helping to create a sense of professionalism:

> Ironically, the influence of journalism education is perhaps the result of the regime's efforts to control the profession during the "normalization" after 1968 when hundreds of outspoken journalists lost their jobs. The number of young people admitted to the study of journalism to take their places increased and close ties developed between journalism faculties and political offices. Journalism education con-

sequently produced most of the journalists who joined the mass media. But in addition to professional skills, one of the most important lessons they learned in journalism education was to play it safe.

In the 1970s and 1980s, Czechoslovak journalists concentrated on "making their journalism more professional and less political,"[23] thus auto didacticism played a much greater role in journalism training than the existing journalism schools. By mid-1984, there were 129 oppositional periodicals published in Czechoslovakia, adding to this auto didactic school of journalism.[24]

In Hungary, the samizdat press, in existence since 1976, served as an outlet for noted writers and other intellectuals, many of whom became the leaders of the Free Democratic Party, the strongest opposition party in the 1990–94 period. Hiebert[25] indirectly makes the point that new standards were established by this underground press, standards that served as models of a sort for new journalists as they learned the craft. He explains,

> Gradually, however, the official media had to recognize the existence of the underground media and the government's inability to stop the samizdat. At first, the official media reported on the existence of the subversive media. Then, gradually, the lower ranks of the official media, such as small specialized journals, began increasingly to reflect the illegal media, even if in an informal manner. By the mid-1980s, the main official newspapers and periodicals often openly reflected upon and quoted the illegal publications. And, finally, by the end of the 80s, the illegal publications became legal.

Even in the Soviet Union, observes Mills,[26]

> Samizdat journalists were of far, far greater importance than their numbers would suggest in a Western context. They helped (along with Western radio services) to keep air in the system. Indeed, I think it could be argued that they constituted the first tiny core of the snowball that picked up heft and speed in the Gorbachev era.

Ultimately, there is no evidence the samizdat proved to be a significant training/educational institution for journalists and journalism, preparing both for a post-Communist pluralist society. Nevertheless, it was an alternative training/educational institution more significant for its counterbalancing role to the Communist media than for its professional uniqueness. It was a breeding ground for both political and media leaders of the post-1989 period, particularly in Poland, Hungary, and Czechoslovakia.

Finally, it is a well-established fact [27] that foreign media, particularly television and radio, have played a significant role in the informational and entertainment world of the Soviets and East/Central Europeans. How much these news programs, in particular, have influenced the journalism practiced in the post-Communist period (authoritarian and pluralist) is a question no one has pursued. Certainly, particular format changes a la the West are observable after 1989. But these may be more a function of the introduction of new technologies (e.g., the TelePrompTer, computers, etc.) than Western journalistic reporting and presentation techniques that are driven by the adoption and definition of a Western conception of the media and their journalism's roles in a democratic society. Individual journalists have attempted to adopt and adapt Western reporting and writing techniques, as well as an appreciation for professional standards and for journalism's responsibilities in an open society. They are still in a minority.

In short, journalists in East/Central European and the former Soviet Republics, as well as the existing institutions of journalism education, were ill prepared to step into a non-Communist world. Journalists were not accustomed to practicing their profession in a way consonant with the needs of societies in transition to democracy, that is, setting an example of democratic behavior, ethical standards; informing, educating, providing a vehicle for discourse, and emancipating the citizenry from the mentalities and behaviors instilled by Communism, as well as from the distant residues of the pre-Communist period. Journalism educators, with few, qualified exceptions, had no starting point or background for radically transforming professional education/training in their classrooms.

THE POST-1989 PERIOD

The Context of Journalism Education

In his perceptive, well-informed work, J.F. Brown[28] wrote, "In no country was there much to suggest the evolution of a constructive political culture. What was developing was combative, not competitive politics." The newly freed mass media and their journalism took their cues from, and themselves reinforced, this post-1989 development in East/Central Europe and the former Soviet Republics. Thus, the mass media remained agents of indoctrination and mobilization. Added to that was a measure of sensationalism for specific marketing purposes. Only minimally and selectively were/are the mass media purveyors of balanced, complete, verifiable information and nonpolitical analysis and fora for public debate and discussion.

The totalitarian mentality was simply atomized as Gross[29] describes the mentalities of Romanian journalists. In general, journalism was/is opinionated, polemical, partisan/subjective. Despite an oasis of good investigative reporting, journalism has retain the "oppositional," "advocate," and "attack dog" quality, rather than adopting the "informational" and "watch dog" one. The recurring theme of criticism all over East/Central Europe, Russia, the Baltics, and the other former Soviet republics is that (a) fact-based journalism is not the norm, and one needs to read several newspapers each day to gather enough information to know what is happening; and (b) television journalism is still strongly influenced if not outright controlled by the new governments.

The pressures the media and their journalists were faced with were immense,[30] and still remain so, making it very difficult if not impossible to reconceptualize journalism, its role in a post-Communist pluralist society, and its ethics, reporting, and writing. Jakubowicz notes, "journalists found it very difficult to adjust to the new situation, lacking the skills to do justice in their reporting to the immensely complex political and economic situation and to enable the audience to understand processes unfolding in public life."

Equally revealing, Robinson[31] describes the retooling problems of East German journalists, arguing that these journalists must develop a new role conception in which they change from passive conveyors of directives into active critics of the powers that be:

> Among these are the Eastern journalists' unwillingness to take personal responsibility for their reports, the ability to do independent research to establish the "facts" of a given situation, and fear of confrontation with authority. Together these result in an almost pathological indecision about how to "play" an issue. One Party reporting also taught journalists to be overreliant on press conference handouts and to practice an extreme division of labor in broadcast reporting that precludes understanding the whole picture.

Certainly, journalists in East/Central Europe and the former Soviet Republics, on the whole, are unwilling to take responsibility and severely lack reporting skills. Yet in East/Central Europe they generally have little fear of confrontation. In this regard, the case of the East German journalists may constitute a unique example in post-Communist journalism, but may be much more akin to the one found in many former Soviet republics such as Georgia.[32] Although old-guard journalists are still contributing to the mass media in East/Central Europe and in what used to be the Soviet Union, particularly in the television field, the explosion of print media and independent radio has relegated this group to minority status in most countries. For instance, in Romania, over 90% of journalists by 1995 had entered the profession after the overthrow of Ceausescu's Communist regime in December 1989.[33]

Far from fearing confrontation with authority or of being critics of the powers that be, journalists in most of the former Communist nations have been all to willing to confront and criticize those in power.[34] So much so, in fact, that even those new democratically inclined governments and enlightened leaders who made press freedom a central *cri de coeur* in pre-1989 days were inclined to argue for some degree of control over the press and continued government domination of national television. Sustaining this inclination all over the newly liberated countries was/is the growth of yellow journalism, "feeding on the wave of corruption, crime, and general crisis," as Jakubowicz[35] describes the situation in Poland: "After decades of sober and earnest journalism, dictated by a sense of decorum and straitlaced public morality typical of the communist era, some journalists are making up for lost time by pandering to low instincts and prurient tastes."

The inability or unwillingness of journalists all over the regions under considerations to establish, accept, and police professional standards have brought repeated calls for stringent press laws that spell out the dos and don'ts of journalism in a manner inhibiting to a responsible journalism in a democratic society. This can be avoided, as Kepplinger and Kocher[36] explain, by establishing standards that help "regulate the behavior of the professional group according to generally accepted principles." Equally as important, these standards "serve to protect the professional group from outside forces."

Yet, despite their inclinations to control the media, the new postrevolution governments were equally unprepared to outline media policy and define media roles and the rules governing them as were, and still are, the new media and their journalists. Brown[37] succinctly sums up the predicament East/Central European media find themselves in the post-1989 period, a predicament that directly impinges on the formulation of a democratic journalism serving a transition to democracy:

> Governmental attitudes toward the media were also a depressing reminder of how much still needed to be done. The media existed primarily to serve the government and report its views. Despite all of the protestations about press freedoms, this conviction was deeply held. Manipulation, therefore, was what governmental policy amounted to—skillfully applied in, say, the Czech Republic, fairly skillfully in Poland, crudely in Slovakia, hypocritically in Hungary,

blatantly in Croatia and Serbia. Television was mainly in state hands, anyway, and the governments were doing their best to keep it that way.

The social, political, cultural, and occupational nature and roles of journalists and journalism remain undefined and, therefore, not identifiable for purposes of internalization by them, by sociopolitical and other leaders, or by the audience. Also undefined and uninternalized is "the nature of democratic society, the function and structure of public dialogue, the needs of the public."[38]

It is in this atmosphere, compounded by the exigencies of media market requirements, the absence of developed civil society, nationalism, and economic hardships, that a new democratic journalism in the Western professional mode was supposed to be adopted and adapted. It is still missing from East/Central Europe, Russia, the Baltics, and other former Soviet republics. Also in this atmosphere, new journalism schools sprung up and old ones were reconfigured to meet the demands of a still growing mass media and interest in journalism on the part of many young people.

Journalism Education: What Is Available?

Journalism programs in East/Central Europe and the new nations carved out of the old Soviet Union have no problems attracting students.[39] Enrollments are up, and without controls on admissions found in most major university programs, they could well skyrocket in a number of countries.

There are four types of journalism training/educational facilities available to journalism students in the former communist nations. First, there is the old communist university programs now reconfigured away from serving as professional-ideological training grounds (this group also includes old Communist programs terminated for a period and resurrected after 1989). These programs are numerically dominating the journalism training/education field from Albania and Armenia to Ukraine and Uzbekistan. They are housed in state universities still laboring under varied degrees of central control. A recent Freedom Forum study[40] shows that 76 of the degree programs and those offering university-level courses are found at state universities in reconfigured or reestablished academic units (e.g., Albania, Hungary), independent or attached to another discipline. Of these 32 of them are in Russia.

Since 1989, many of these reestablished or reconfigured journalism programs are receiving some form of assistance (Fulbright professors, equipment, curricular help, etc.) from U.S. and Western European organizations.

Second, new university programs set up since 1989 are few in number and concentrated in only five countries: Belarus, Bulgaria, Hungary, Poland, and Romania:

- In Belarus, the European Humanitarian University launched a journalism program in 1992.
- In Bulgaria, a journalism program that graduated its first students in Summer 1995 was established in 1992 at the new American University in Blagoevgrad.
- In Hungary, two new programs were introduced after communism's demise in that country: one in 1990 at Attila Jozsef University in Szeged and another in 1992 at Eotvos Lorant University in Budapest.
- In Poland, a postgraduate School of Journalism was launched in 1993 at the Catholic University of Lublin; in 1995 the International School of Journalism was established at the Jagiellonian University in Crakow.
- In Romania, new journalism programs were set up at the universities of Timisoara (with help from California State University–Chico and the International Media Fund), Sibiu, and Cluj, with some courses also being offered at the University of Brasov and Iasi.

Third, journalism association and vocational schools offering vocational training programs have also been set up in a number of East/Central European countries and former Soviet republics. These journalism programs range from those attached to already existing journalism unions or theater and film academies (e.g., Hungary's Academy of Film and Theater, Romania's Academy of Theater and Film, Ukraina's Institute for Advanced Radio-TV Journalism Training) to those launched by new journalism unions (e.g., the Association of Romanian Journalists' Higher School of Journalism). These are certificate rather than degree programs.

Fourth, Western-sponsored journalism centers have been set up in nine countries: Belarus, the Czech Republic, Hungary, Moldova, Poland, Romania, Russia, Slovakia, and Ukraine. The center in Hungary closed in Spring 1995 with no indication if and when it might reopen. Three more were in the planning stages in early 1995 for Latvia, Lithuania, and Estonia. All of these new centers are sponsored mostly by U.S. organizations such as the Freedom Forum, the Soros Foundation, the International Media Fund, the German Marshall Fund, the Independent Journalism Foundation, the U.S.–Baltic Foundation, among other U.S. granting institutions and universities. They do not offer degree programs but an array of journalism courses for both journalism students and working journalists.

In addition to these journalism education/training facilities, some newspapers, radio, and TV stations in East/Central Europe and in the former Soviet Republics offer in-house training programs (e.g., Radio Romania, the State Hungarian Radio).

Technical, Material, Facilities Issues

Most of the reconfigured, reestablished, and newly established university journalism programs share some basic problems.[41] These problems are also common to the vast majority of journalism programs run by unions and by vocational schools: Some are ideational/conceptual, others are tied to facilities and faculty, all share a shortage of adequate financing. Outlined next are eight of the major, common problems.

First, there is a dearth of modern facilities ranging from buildings to computer labs, TV and radio studios, and journalism/mass communication libraries and the lack of financial resources to correct these deficits. Extensive Western aid since 1989, although significant, has not corrected the situation let alone met the ever-growing demand.

The poorest programs are practically homeless. The journalism program at Albania's Tirana University in 1994 was housed in an old, dilapidated building. It has at its disposal a couple of classrooms; their walls crooked, paint peeling, crowded with long tables, chairs, or benches, some crudely handmade and painted. It resembles a *fin de siècle* U.S. high school in a very poor rural district. An additional small room serves as a library/reading room. The (now-defunct) Washington, DC-based International Media Fund donated three computers, one scanner, and one printer. Even poorer, the journalism program at the Silesian University in Poland is housed in an old, cramped building and has no equipment whatsoever.

At the other end of the spectrum, the journalism department at Comenius University in Slovakia has 10 classrooms at its disposal, typewriters, radio and TV receivers, seven VCRs, three desktop computers, seven laptop computers, and two laser printers. At the Moscow State Institute of International Relations in Russia, the School of Mass Communication has large classrooms in a "fairly modern building that's well maintained," a TV studio, typewriters, and five computers.[42] The newly formed Postgraduate School of Journalism at the Catholic University of Lublin has completely refurbished classrooms, a radio station/laboratory, and a writing lab with 18 computers. In addition, at Bulgaria's Sofia University, the department of journalism and mass communication has a publishing center with five IBM computers, a computer writing lab, a language laboratory, two radio studios, a TV studio, a movie auditorium, and a library with 10,000 periodicals and books.[43]

The other programs in the regions under consideration range somewhere along the "very poor—relatively rich" continuum. The best equipped university programs are the ones funded by U.S. money. The American University in Bulgaria, for instance, according to Byron Scott and Ekaterina Ognianova[44] has

> a 14-station IBM classroom/lab with facilities for writing, editing and design, including digitized photo editing, a Freedom Forum Journalism Library. . . all facilities and faculty offices are networked on a UNIX backbone. . . a fully-computerized biweekly newspaper using mostly Macintosh hardware, and a 24-hour FM radio station that carries VOA-Europe and BBC news shows. A complete, two-station photo darkroom and satellite dish reception of international news (CNN-Europe, EuroChannel, etc.) . . . a six-unit videotaping and editing facility and multimedia production . . . a direct Internet connection via an agreement with IBM-Sofia.

The independent journalism centers set up by and with Western (predominantly U.S.) aid are also relatively well equipped. For instance, The Warsaw Journalism Center in Poland and the Center for Independent Journalism in Bratislava, Slovakia, have modern classrooms computer libraries, computers, copiers, fax machines, and U.S. radio and TV equipment. Best of all, they have Freedom Forum News Libraries, in which journalism students, faculty, and working journalists can access collections of scholarly books and textbooks on journalism and mass communication, U.S. daily and weekly newspapers and magazines on CD-ROM disks, and Internet connections.

Second, the salaries of full-time instructors and professors is so low as to force them to hold one or more other jobs to be able to survive financially. Therefore, their energies and talents are not focused exclusively on the demanding job of retooling, research, and teaching.

In Poland, as the director of the Journalism Institute at Warsaw University said,[45] "Professors' salaries are lower than that of a sergeant in the army." At Comenius University in Bratislava, Slovakia, Owen[46] dryly noted, "The financial situation of the faculty is challenging. The $300 monthly salaries offer no inspiration to improve teaching." Mills[47] described an equally depressing situation in Russia:

> Inflation has crippled the buying power of professors' salaries. Faculty members, who once led upper-middle-class lives by Soviet standards, now find themselves near poverty. "We intelligentsia were among the first to support the reforms," said one embittered senior faculty member at St. Petersburg University. "Now we're paid less than bus drivers. And our (paychecks) are often two or three months late."

Unless salaries are increased, it is unlikely that competent young people will be attracted to university teaching as a sole and permanent endeavor. With a majority of established faculty members busy with second and third jobs, and few PhD programs, the availability of top-notch research generated by journalism/mass communication faculty to be used in media policymaking or by the media themselves is also drastically affected.

Third, the size of journalism faculties varies from the behemoth-like one at Moscow State University with 219 full- and part-time professors and instructors, to the Catholic University in Lublin that only had one full-time journalism faculty in 1994, and the American University in Bulgaria that employed three full-timers that same year. In most all journalism programs full-time faculty is augmented by part-time faculty, many in both categories also wearing the hat of a working journalist.

The problem is not only finding people willing to teach but, more importantly, finding qualified people. At the Institute of Journalism at Taras Shevchenko State University in Kiev (Ukraine) there are no qualified teachers because, as Hiebert[48] quotes the deputy dean, "The best people tend to prefer the practice of journalism to teaching it. Journalists now get higher salaries than teachers."

The important question is how well prepared are these full- and part-time professors/instructors, from a professional and academic standpoint, to teach a new journalism capable of serving a transition to a pluralist, democratic society and to upholding that democracy? Many journalism professors, leftovers from the Communist period, are better prepared to teach propaganda techniques than modern democracy-oriented journalism; Communist mass media theories, rather than mass media theories for an open society; methods of Marxist-Leninist critique, rather than nonideological criticism and analysis; Communist ethics, rather than Western-type professional ethics. There is a real danger at some universities of reconfiguring programs into what may be a curricula of very creative anachronism. In Belarus a young journalist is quoted by Hiebert[49] as saying, "The old faculty at the university teach the same old thing; they just leave out the word communism" Adds Hiebert, "In the past, the priority was to promote communist ideology: Journalism was part of the party; journalists were party warriors. The faculty is still regarded as ideological, but now, members say, their priority is to promote Belarussian culture."

In Bulgaria, the Parliament's passage of the Panev Law that forbids former Communist functionaries from holding administrative positions in higher education until after 1999 hastened the departure of "longtime senior faculty and administrators."[50] However, in most of the old programs and in some of the new programs, the old guard that taught Communist journalism theory and practice are still teaching. Most are attempting to retool and are doing so with varying degrees of success and enthusiasm. Writes Mills[51] about Russian journalism faculty:

> The programs are still staffed largely by the same faculty who taught in the Soviet era. Some of them seem genuinely happy with the jettisoning of the polemical Marxist approach to education. . . . To many, the idea of objective journalism still seems foreign, both literally and figuratively.

The majority of journalism faculty in Russia and the former Soviet Republics, perhaps with the exception of the Baltics, and many still in East/ Central Europe are in a situation similar to their colleagues in Moldova. There, Dean Victor Moraru of the Faculty of Journalism at the State University of Moldova stated in 1994:[52]

> The future success of the university's School of Journalism depends now in large measure on its integration into the European process of instruction and professional education. . . . The overwhelming number of our faculty are isolated from the West European and North American process of preparing journalists.

It is not surprising that one of the needs and wishes generally expressed by journalism deans, chairs, coordinators, and faculty everywhere is for more faculty exchanges with Western universities and programs designed to "train the trainers."

There are some long-tenured faculty committed to retooling, rewriting curricula, reconsidering journalism pedagogy, and rededication to a new concept of journalism. They, along with new faculty members, are searching for direction, help, and a new standing within the academic community, in the mass media world, and in society at large.

New cadres of journalism/mass communication professors or instructors with appropriate academic and professional backgrounds have not yet been formed to supplant the old guard. In fact, there are very few PhD programs in mass communication/journalism (in Estonia, Russia, and Slovenia), and those that do exist are wrestling or should be with what the curricula should contain and what it takes to prepare future journalism/mass communication professors.

U.S. and Western European academics have since 1989 paid short- and long-term visits to journalism schools in Russia, the Ukraine, the Baltics, and the East/Central European countries, injecting a degree of new thinking into the programs and their faculties. Some programs such as the one at the University of Bucharest, Romania, and the

University of Ljubljana, Slovenia, have significantly internationalized their programs by the constant presence of foreign instructors. The same holds true for the independent journalism centers established and supported by U.S. and Western European groups.

Journalists, the other component of journalism faculties, are generally not practicing a journalism consonant to a democratic society (i.e., factual reporting is not standard, systematic inquiry, analysis, and informed opinion is replaced by polemics and off-the-cuff opinions). Therefore, they are hardly prepared to teach such a "new" journalism.

The problem of competent, adequately trained/educated faculty in both the academic and practical sense, is a long-term problem in the regions under discussion. It will remain so despite the already begun, yet limited, faculty exchanges with Western universities, until indigenous PhD programs are set up and the mass media themselves and their journalists make the leap from pre-professionalism to professionalism.

Fourth, an equally great problem to journalism training/education is the absence of indigenous textbooks and other pedagogical materials. The old textbooks used in the Communist institutions are simply useless. In Belarus, "Old texts are in Russian, many with a communist orientation, and most are 70 to 100 years old. Producing new ones is difficult, although the journalism faculty does print some student manuals."[53]

New ones have not yet been written and the money is not available to encourage indigenous publishing of textbooks or their purchase abroad, translation, and publication. When Johnson[54] writes, "There is still a lack of Czech language textbooks and other publications about journalism," he could just as well substitute "Czech language" with any of the other languages in the regions under discussion and be absolutely accurate. Besides, the orientation toward theory means few faculty members are interested or capable of preparing textbooks for practical journalism. Consequently, few journalism schools and faculty members have long-range plans (or express hopes) to publish new, original textbooks on news writing and reporting, interviewing, feature writing, and editorial/column writing. Only Peeter Vihalemm, professor of journalism and mass communication, and head of the Department of Journalism at the University of Tartu, Estonia, outlined such a plan, according to the 1994 Freedom Forum survey of journalism schools in East/Central Europe and the former Soviet Republics.

U.S. books, in particular, remain in high demand from Prague to Alma Ata. At Charles University in Prague, the Czech Republic, Otakar Soltys explains,[55] they "must overcome a shortage of suitable textbooks, especially those of our own creation. Today we use texts from other countries, mostly in translation."

Most of the books wholly or partially translated, mimeographed, or published in East/Central Europe and the former Soviet republics are U.S. ones. For instance, in Estonia a book translation project was initiated with Soros Foundation funds—"The department's most immediate project is to translate Denis McQuail's book on the theory of mass media."[56]

U.S. and Western European textbooks and other books on mass communication/media have flooded East/Central Europe and many of the former Soviet Republics via visiting U.S. scholars, and institutions that got involved in training journalists. The Freedom Forum News Libraries are additional, permanent, growing repositories of U.S. journalism and mass communication books. Freedom Forum News Libraries are located in Bucharest, Romania, at the Center for Independent Journalism; in St. Petersburg (Russia), at the Russian-American Press and Information Center; in Prague (Czech Republic), at the Center for Independent Journalism; in Lithuania, at the University of Vilnius; in Riga (Latvia), at the University of Latvia; and at the American University in Blagoevgrad (Bulgaria).

A handful of Western books specifically written for journalism education/training in East/Central European, Russian, Baltic states, and other Soviet Republics have been published in a number of languages. For instance,

- Malcolm F. Mallette. (Ed.). (1990). *Handbook for Journalists of Central and Eastern Europe*. Washington, DC: World Press Freedom Committee.

- Peter Gross. (1993). *News Reporting and Editing*. Timisoara, Romania: Editura de Vest.

- Sharon Yoder, Katie Milo, Peter Gross, and Stefan Niculescu-Maier. (1998). *Introduction to Public Relations*. Bucharest, Romania: NIM Press.

Still, the deficit of pedagogical materials, books in particular, will remain a troublesome feature of journalism education in East/Central Europe and all the former Soviet Republics for years to come.

Given the inclination toward theory, philosophy, and history, journalism/mass communication faculty members in East/Central Europe and the former Soviet republics have produced a number of scholarly works in mass communication since 1989. Some were published by them in the West,[57] some also in their respective countries.[58]

Fifth, the same lack of adequate financing that impedes journalism schools from purchasing Western journalism/mass communication books, translating and publishing them, or encouraging publication of indigenous books also has a profound effect on the availability of Western research journals, professional and general circulation magazines, and major newspapers. They are highly sought after by students and faculty alike and are included on any and all lists of "needs and desires."

In some cases, as at the Silesian University, journalism faculty desire access to foreign research and professional journals not only as a way of informing themselves in their research, but also in order to gauge outlets for their own work. The few research journals found in East/Central Europe and the former Soviet republics offer limited possibilities for researchers in the region to publish their work. Their status is mostly national or local. Consequently, another wish they have in common is the establishment of their own research/academic journals or to find funds to support the few existing ones.

For instance, at the University of Latvia, the Faculty of Communication was seeking funds in 1994 to publish a critical review of journalism as a scholarly quarterly. In Estonia, two annual journals, *Fact, Word, Picture* and *The History of Journalism,* have been suspended for lack of money, but faculty would like to again publish them.[59]

A few new journalism/mass communication research publications have sprung up since 1989. For example, in Slovenia the European Institute for Communication and Culture (Euricom) publishes *Javnost* [The Public]; in Romania the new *Global Network* is published as a regional/international publication of the newly formed East/Central European Network of Journalism Educators (see later discussion).

Sixth, many journalism programs produce their own newspapers for in-house or wider distribution, and some of the universities have universitywide publications, as do some of the journalism centers set up with U.S. help. Journalism program/department and university and journalism center publications range from laboratory newspapers (e.g., Center for Independent Journalism, Czech Republic) to bi-weeklies newspapers (e.g., the American University, Blagoevgrad, Bulgaria), monthly newspapers (e.g., Silesian University, Poland), quarterly newspapers (e.g., Moscow University, Russia), and monthly, quarterly, or semi-annual magazines (e.g., Charles University, Czech Republic; Catholic University, Poland; State University of Moldova). In the wake of changes brought about by the revolutions of 1989/90, the University of Bucharest journalism school publishes an English- and French-language version of its Romanian-language newspaper *Campus.* At the University of Timisoara, Romania, the journalism program's bi-monthly *In Other Words,* is a Romanian/English publication, reflecting the new program's marriage to the English department. In Poland, too, some of the university publications are in Polish and English.

Most student publication claim to be independent of their institutions' administrations. Some, like the ones published in Russia at Moscow University, St. Petersburg University, and Udmurt University are controlled by their respective administrations.

A significant number of student publications are online or are planned for with help from Western organizations. The European Journalism Network or the Soros Foundation are aiding publications at, among other venues, the University of Tirana (Albania), University of Minsk (Belarus), Tartu University (Estonia), University of Riga (Latvia), Charles University (Czech Republic), Vilnius University (Lithuania), University of Cyril and Metody (Macedonia), St. Petersburg University (Russia), Comenius University (Slovak Republic), and Kiev State University (Ukraine).

Only seven journalism programs/universities in East/Central Europe and the former Soviet Republics have student-run radio stations. The most interesting developments are to be found at Charles University in Prague (Czech Republic), where an e-mail weekly is produced both in English and Czech, and at Comenius University in Bratislava (Slovak Republic), where students (occasionally) put out an electronic newspaper. Western aid, particularly U.S. aid, has played a significant role in the creation of many student stations.

Seventh, student attendance and respect for the faculty and program are by no means uniform across East/Central Europe, Russia, or the other former Soviet Republics.

Albanian journalism students said in 1994 they attend classes but see little point in doing so given what is being offered by instructors who are mostly leftovers from the Communist regime.[60] They much preferred the U.S. instructors.

The situation is not much different in Bulgaria, where, according to Ognianova,[61]

> Journalism professors could not do much to change their teaching style because students did not go to school. Students preferred the practical experience of working in newspapers, magazines, radio and television stations. "They don't go to school because they don't believe any more that they will really learn something there. In the upper-level classes almost no students can be seen at school," Pogled, the weekly of the Union of Bulgarian Journalists, wrote.

In the great majority of programs theory is taught quite separate from praxis, partly because of tradition and partly because of the lack of facilities and staff (see later discussion). Consequently, students desiring to learn hands-on journalism do internships and/or hold part-time or even full-time jobs in media. Often this situation interferes with class attendance. In Russia, Mills [62] writes,

Journalism faculty complain that the students are so busy working at one or another of the new media enterprises, they don't devote enough attention to their school work. Or they drop out to become working journalists. More than half of Moscow's students have freelance or staff jobs in the media. Potential employers offering opinions about the value of journalism education would sound painfully familiar to faculty at U.S. journalism schools.

Additionally, the European tradition of simply showing up for end-of-semester exams creates a situation in which, at some universities more than at others, convincing students to regularly attend classroom lectures or labs is a difficult task. In Slovakia, according to Johnson,[63] students "often skeptical about the value of journalism education, skip classes and miss deadlines."

The formal relationship between students and faculty traditional to European universities, at least relative to the one found in U.S. universities, may also affect learning. After spending considerable time in Bulgaria, Scott[64] describes a situation that is quite apropos to most if not all university student–faculty relationships in East/Central Europe and the former Soviet Republics, to a lesser or greater extent:

> Students also were used to professors as distant gods and goddesses who gave lectures then disappeared. At first, when we invited them to our offices for conferences, they arrived dressed as if for a formal occasion. And when we sat down with them in the cafe to have beer and chat, they were aghast. Of course this was nothing compared to when the American faculty fielded a team in the intramural basketball league and began throwing hips and elbows in the traditional fashion.

Finally, contacts among journalism schools and faculty members in the regions under discussion are, generally, rare. Faculty members since 1989 are more apt to develop working relationships with their Western counterparts than with their colleagues in their own regions. Exceptions exist. For instance, journalism faculty members in the Baltic states have a working relationship with one another. Most faculty members in East/Central Europe, Russia, and other former Soviet Republics have a tendency toward self-isolation, some of it brought about by the lack of contacts and the severe shortage of funds.

In 1994, at the suggestion of a number of journalism program deans and directors gathered at a Freedom Forum conference in Arlington, VA, the East/Central European Network of Journalism Educators was organized. Its mission is to provide an East/Central European–former Soviet Republics counterpart to the American

Educators in Journalism and Mass Communication (AEJMC). Its initial membership was to include 40 journalism/mass communication schools and departments from 15 countries, nearly 400 faculty members.

Philosophical, Programmatic, and Status Issues

The demise of Communist rule did not herald the birth of democracy. The nations of East/Central Europe and the former Soviet Republics are in a transition phase, a kind of limbo in which the difficult process of overcoming the past, struggling with the present, and defining the future are tandem tasks. It is not at all clear if liberal democracy is, indeed, an option for all or even some of the nations newly liberated from Communism. Journalism's situation, its professionalization, parallels that of the nations in which it functions.

What to teach? The teaching of journalism has to be tied as much to a vision as to the operative reality of the profession in a particular society. A Western-type journalism, one of information (fact-based) and systematic inquiry (versus the shoot-from-the-hip, polemical, politicized, one-sided, advocacy commentary), is rarely practiced or encouraged. Can and should it be taught in journalism schools? If not a Western-type journalism, then what? The answer depends on:

- the degree of leadership and innovation journalism schools want and are able to assume vis-a-vis the media and society
- the nature of the journalism practiced by the media, their relationship with journalism schools, and their receptivity to graduates who are ready to practice the "new" theories and techniques
- the way the new political, intellectual, media, cultural, social, and economic leadership, as well as the various publics, choose to define and accept the role and nature of journalism.

Journalism, as it has already been suggested in this and in preceding chapters, is a helter-skelter craft in the regions under consideration, with no clear, uniform, and accepted definition of its form, role, practice, or ethics. It is in the main a mixture of Communist and pre-Communist-type journalism. Traces of Western-type journalism constitute aberrations in the panoply of the "new" journalism. In the post-1989 period, discussions of professional journalism and democracy are carried out on the same level: on the idealized, often misunderstood and misinterpreted, incongruent to local reality, academic level.

A sampling of opinions among journalism educators and journalists offers a glimpse of the problem in all the countries under discussion:[65]

- "Advocacy journalism existed before 1989 and it exists today. The old and new journalists approach the profession the same way"—Karol Jakubowicz, vice president of the Board of Directors of Polish Television, chief advisor to the National Broadcasting Council and a journalism instructor at Warsaw University.
- "The totalitarian approach (to journalism) still prevails"— Anatoli Mikhailov, rector of the new European Humanitarian University, Minsk, Belarus.
- "Journalism is an intellectual passion not a real profession in Albania"—Ylli Rakipi, head of the Union of Albanian Journalists.
- "[academic institutions such as journalism schools] are feared because they could bring a new philosophy and new practices that could endanger the existing media system"—Mihai Coman, dean of the School of Journalism and Communication Studies at the University of Bucharest, Romania.

In such a media world, it is very difficult if not impossible to define, as Owen[66] suggested for Czech journalism schools, "the purpose and goals of journalism education." A conclusion echoed by Gross and King[67] in their examination of Romanian journalism education in the post-1989 period.

Fact-based journalism is sparsely taught or ill taught even when its value is recognized, partly because journalism instructors themselves do not understand it, know enough about it, have not practiced it, or do not know how to teach it. For instance, in the Department of Journalism at the University of Tartu, Estonia, the head of the program admitted[68] that "fact-based journalism has been a weak point, and that education has been too technology-based." His students, he feels, need to spend more time learning how to gather and analyze facts and produce meaningful content.

The journalism program at Adam Mickiewics University in Poznan, Poland, said its faculty, "intends" to teach fact-based journalism.[69] The absence of fact-based journalism, or its minor status in curricula, is not only tied to a pre-Communist and Communist journalistic legacy but also to the literary tradition that was dominant in both eras. Therefore, writing classes were and still are emphasized over reporting classes. Stressing reporting and interviewing may constitute an important step in the process of changing journalism education.

The issue of "objectivity" is one that pervades debates over journalism in the regions. It goes beyond the philosophical conflict that separates European and U.S. journalism—whether journalists must or should provide interpretation, comment, and analysis within news reports. Quite the contrary, it centers on the general notion that journalism means that some news and facts (often inaccurate, unverifiable, incomplete, skewed) is included in interpretative, analytical, polemical reports.

Ultimately, however, teaching journalism, together with the learning of a set of professional ethics, is today only marginally relevant from a practical perspective because it is on only seldom allowed application. "Once some of these students get jobs, they're on staffs that don't uphold the values they've recently been taught," explained Josephine Schmidt, associate director of the Center for Independent Journalism in Prague,[70] buttressing Coman's previously mentioned views of media fearing new ideas.

The statement only partially holds true elsewhere in East and Central Europe and in the former Soviet Republics. In Croatia, Macedonia, Moldova, Slovenia, and the Ukraine, the relationship between media and journalism programs remain stronger. The reason rests in the similarities of what is taught and what is practiced. In these cases the media, systemically changed but professionally less so, set the norms, instead of the journalism programs pioneering a drastically different approach to the practice of journalism. In Slovenia, journalism is far more Western European and so is its teaching at the university in Ljubljana. In the other four nations it is not, remaining a mixture of Communist, pre-Communist, and post-Communist/transition journalism. In Russia, writes Mills,[71]

> University-media ties are strong, with journalism graduates in many of the key positions at Russian media outlets. Nearly 60 percent of the country's professional journalists were educated at journalism schools. To an extent unheard of in the rest of Europe, newspapers and broadcasters look to journalism programs to deliver the "cadres" of young talent, just as they did in the Soviet period.

Yet, aside from the presence or absence of media support for journalism schools and what is being taught by them, there is also the issue of the absence of media as progressive professional role models for journalism students. Unless the media themselves change how they practice journalism, what Gross and King[72] found in Romania, in part also paralleling Schmidt's earlier statement, will remain so in all the countries under discussion: "There will be no indigenous models for aspiring journalists to emulate, and little support for graduates of journalism schools in applying modern methods and processes of news gathering and dissemination capable of serving people in a democratic society."

Clearly, developing close ties with media, educating them to the benefits of journalism education and the role journalism programs can play in helping them is part of rebuilding or establishing a new journalism education program. In fact, it may be a central function for journalism schools if they are to secure a future for themselves.

There are journalism programs that resist outright the teaching of Western-style, fact-based journalism. At Rostov-on-Don University, Mills[73] found journalism faculty to reject the teaching of fact-based journalism. He explains, "Literary methodology has always played an important role in both the teaching and the practice of journalism, so that traditional faculty as well as traditional journalists tend to look down on fact-based reporting as mere stenography."

For some journalism programs and faculty, journalism is still defined according to a pre-Communist model: Its not a profession but an intellectual pasttime, a mode of expression on behalf of personal, party, politico-ideological interests. Bartlomiej Golka, director of the Journalism Institute at Warsaw University,[74] speaks for many journalism educators in the transitionary nations when he said he does not want his program to "become a vocational school."

The upshot of all of these legacies, problems, and journalistic and educational concepts (or lack of) is a shortage of professional skills classes, those available being tilted, as already mentioned, toward writing and the technical aspects of broadcast media and not sufficiently toward reporting and interviewing. In many cases even these skills classes are more theoretical than practical, and even these "theories" are often questionable. There is an emphasis on literature and other humanities and social science courses in most journalism curricula. Rare are curricula that include at least the theory of Western journalism and journalism ethics, such as is the case at Lithuania's Institute of Journalism, University of Vilnius.

Another key element of journalism education is, for all intents and purposes, lacking in the regions' programs: media management and marketing. Some Western instructors have and are offering some courses in these areas at the universities or at the independent journalism centers set up by predominantly U.S. groups.

Existing university and vocational school journalism curricula are constantly changing and will continue to do so in an attempt to find a purpose, a direction, and, ultimately, acceptance. There is no generalizable approach to teaching journalism at this point in the evolution of journalism education in East/Central European and in the former Soviet Republics. What binds these programs together are their pre-

Communist, and post-Communist legacies. There is much experimenta-
tion. The same is true of Western-sponsored journalism centers where
there are no set faculties. In some university programs the curricula has,
in fact, not yet been outlined for the duration of their 3- to 5-year B.A. programs (i.e., in Albania, the Czech Republic, Latvia, and at some Romanian
and Polish universities). Roughly 11 M.A. programs and a handful of
postgraduate certificate programs add one to two additional years to programs found in Bulgaria, Croatia, the Czech Republic, Estonia, Hungary,
Lithuania, Poland, Romania, Russia, Slovakia, and Slovenia.

   Theory vs. praxis. The traditional theoretical approach to the
teaching of journalism creates another serious vacuum in university
journalism education, as well being part of the failure in bridging the
gap between education and its application. Mills'[75] analysis of the
Russian system encapsulates the problem for all the countries under
considerations:

> The European bias for "real" academics—those with advanced
> degrees—seems to distance classroom education from the real-world
> reality, even in those classes that are devoted to the practice of jour-
> nalism. Add to this the formal, arms-length relationship that is tradi-
> tional in European lecture halls, and students get little help in bridg-
> ing an apparently first-rate humanities education to the professional
> world that they want to enter.

The majority of programs surveyed by the Freedom Forum in 1994 indicated their programs are a combination academic–professional. Most of
them put the emphasis on "academic," even if they claim to have a
50–50 division in their academic versus professional or practical versus
theoretical approach. As already mentioned, the general shortage of laboratory equipment and facilities is at least partially responsible for journalism education, such as it is, more or less tilting in favor of the acade-
mic/theoretical. The shortage of faculty able to successfully combine
theory and praxis is another reason for the imbalance.

   There are exceptions to the general rule—at least on paper. In
the Department of Journalism Studies, Zagreb University (Croatia), "of
the core courses, 80 percent are skills oriented, 20 percent research and
theory," reports Ricchardi,[76] without, however, spelling out the nature
of these skills classes. This may be the most unique journalism program
in East and Central Europe and in the former Soviet Republics.

   A small sampling of students and journalists opinions expresses
what may be the dominant opinion on the theory versus practice imbalance and the value of many programs from Albania to Uzbekistan:

- "Students here are not adequately prepared"—a Lithuanian journalist.[77]
- "I would never hire a Moscow State journalism graduate"—a Russian editor.[78]
- "The best journalists are not from the Department of Journalism"—a Slovak academic.[79]
- The journalism program "fundamentally does not differ from academic programs in the developed world. . . . However, in terms of possibilities for practical work for students, the differences are great"—a Slovenian academic.[80]
- Slovak students have complained "about the content of their studies—particularly the absence of practical experience" even before 1989.[81] "I think that the duty of the university is to prepare specialists for work . . . not to make them walking encyclopedias"—a Slovak student.

To reiterate, skills classes do not dominate most curricula and are themselves more theoretical than practical. The very theory being taught is questionable given its grounding in concepts that lack efficacy in, and may even be inimical to, liberal democratic societies. At those very few universities where student media exist, practical training starts with those publications or broadcast media. Generally, in line with tradition, much of the practical training occurs on a job, as part of formal or informal internship arrangements or in a part- or full-time job. For instance,

- In Albania, sophomore journalism students will spend every second week working at Albanian Television, Radio, or one of Tirana's newspapers.
- In Bulgaria, Sofia University journalism students will spend their third, fourth, and fifth years in practical training, working in media, sometimes full time.
- In Latvia, most journalism students work in the field while studying.
- In Moldova, journalism students complete four internships with various media during their five-year university program. In 1994, 62% of journalism students were employed by media in the capital city of Chisinau.[82]
- In Poland, mandatory internships during the academic year, in the summer, or during the last two years are built into university journalism programs.
- In Romania, although internships are not built into the curricula, many journalism students hold part- or even full-time jobs with newspapers or the growing number of radio and local television stations.

Hands-on journalism is more likely to be emphasized in nonuniversity programs, those vocational in nature, attached to film/theater institutes, and those established by Western institutions (the independent journalism centers that have sprung up in a host of East/Central European, Baltic, and other former Soviet Republics). There, too, however, the technical aspects of broadcasting and print and broadcast journalistic writing are emphasized over reporting. The quality of teaching, as well as the specific conception of journalism, is largely dependent on who is teaching, Western or indigenous instructors.

Status in the academic and professional world. The debate over the need for university-level journalism degrees began almost immediately after the various Communist regimes collapsed. It was fueled in some countries by journalism schools' negative reputation as indoctrination institutions during the Communist period. And, in others, by the return to a journalism that traditionalists viewed as requiring no university-level professional training. The debates, to some extent, parallel those in Western Europe and the United States.

In Romania, there are many in and outside the journalistic profession that will argue journalists are "born" and not "made."[83] Therefore, they argue, "there is no need for journalism schools per se. A degree in one of the traditional fields is sufficient (perhaps even better) grounding for a journalism career."[84] In a similar situation, in the Czech Republic:[85]

> Some critics question whether journalism education is necessary at all today. Others say there should be journalism education in the university, but that it should reflect its academic home and emphasize study in the humanities and social sciences.

Closer ties between journalism schools and mass media need to be developed in most East/Central European nations. The role of these schools as educators and producers of credible, useful research needs to be established and sold to the mass media. In a unique attempt to develop a relationship with the press, the journalism program at Sofia University (Bulgaria) has established a national journalism awards program. The media pays close attention to what this program does, as well as to its views on journalism standards. It is a program worth emulating by other East/Central European journalism schools.

The yet-to-be established credibility and value of journalism programs in the majority of the countries under discussion adds to the difficulty they have in achieving a degree of autonomy that, in turn, allows them to create curricula divorced from the political pressures of a mother department/school or governmental institution. With only a few exceptions, journalism programs in East/Central Europe are housed in or married to Faculties or Colleges and Departments that encompass other disciplines, for example, Political Science, Law, Social Policy, Philology, Letters, History, International Relations, and/or Social Sciences. Few are lucky enough to be constituted in separate departments, others in more or less independent institutes. Journalism is sometimes looked on as the poorer cousin to other disciplines and, in fact, is not always considered a distinct academic discipline. There are exceptions, most notably in the former Soviet Republics such as the Ukraine and Russia, where,[86]

> Journalism education also enjoys respect within the academy unmatched anywhere in the world, including the United States. . . . Even critics of journalism education concede that such universities provide the solid—and prestigious—broad liberal-arts education that are pre-requisites to successful professional careers. . . . What's more, journalism programs have been freed of centralized control and encouraged to experiment with ways of educating journalists for the market economy.

This centralized control remains a feature in a number of countries, where in greater or lesser measure the Ministry of Education, or Ministry of Education and Culture, still looks to be a gatekeeper to all university programs. In an exceptional situation, control of the journalism program in Belarus extends to more than one ministry: the Ministry of Education, the Ministry of Information (for ideological direction), and the Ministry of Communication.[87]

Thirteen of the university programs surveyed by the Freedom Forum[88] in 17 East/Central European and Baltic countries, plus Russia, Belarus, and Ukraine were accredited by ministries of education; most were not accredited. In Slovakia, the journalism program is approved as a major within the university, and in the Czech Republic the B.A. and M.A. programs at Charles University received approval from the university's Academic Senate.

Accrediting institutions in the regions under discussion have as difficult a time defining accreditation criteria as do the educational units in question and the journalism profession itself.

WESTERN AID

Western aid to journalism education and training, extended to educational facilities as well as to mass media and their journalists, has been extensive. It has consisted since 1989 in conferences and workshops, long-term and short courses and programs at universities and media organizations in the regions under discussions and in Western countries. Additionally, it has taken the form of new centers for journalism training and journalism libraries.

Among the European-based and international organizations that have aided the education and training of print and broadcast journalists, editors and publisher in all aspects of the media include:

European Union	Danish International Development
Friedrich Ebert Foundation	Agency
(Germany)	
BBC (England)	Council Of Europe
International Federation of	British Know-How Fund
Journalists	(England)
European Journalism Network	Swiss News Agency
United Nations/UNESCO	Reuters Foundation (England)
International Federation of	Radio Deutsche Welle (Germany)
Newspaper Publishers	Newspaper Society (England)

U.S. organizations, both private and governmental, have played a significant role in the development of media, journalists and journalism, and journalism education in East/Central Europe and the former Soviet Republics. So also have many U.S. universities by hosting groups of or individual journalists under sponsorship of one or another U.S. governmental or private funding agency. They have provided, or are providing, training in the regions under discussion, helped establish journalism programs and developed existing ones. Among U.S. universities that have and continue to play a significant role in the evolution of journalism education and training of journalists in the regions are the University of Maryland, University of Missouri, California State University–Chico, Rutgers University, University of South Carolina, and the University of Georgia.

Despite the limited opportunities to practice a Western-style journalism, young journalists have shown themselves particularly receptive to U.S. training. For instance, as Aumente notes[89] of Polish journalists, "They welcomed the brand of U.S. enterprise and investigative journalism we were bringing." The most successful American programs proved to be those that took into account the historical and cultural background of journalists from East/Central Europe and the former Soviet Republics and shied away from the "we know best" attitude and the "we have come to lecture you" approach. Most in demand were and still are courses, workshops, and lectures in investigative, public affairs, and environmental reporting, coverage of political elections, media management, marketing strategies, and advertising.

In spite of the obvious differences in the interpretation and practice of journalism, journalists from the regions under considerations have flocked to a variety of U.S. training programs, lectures, and media/journalism-related conferences since 1990. They continue to reinforce the feeling shared by foreign and indigenous journalism educators that training and continuing education programs for working journalists should be a priority for journalism education programs, a function now filled primarily by the independent media centers established with Western help.

The Voice of America International Training program alone has facilitated a variety of training programs in the United States and "in country" beginning in Summer 1990. These programs have exposed nearly 2,000 print and broadcast journalists, editors, and publishers/managers from East/Central European and the former Soviet republics to U.S. journalism education, practices, media management, and sales techniques.[90]

The U.S. Information Agency has also facilitated a wide range of aid programs to the countries under discussion, making possible the translation and publication of journalism texts and the establishment of new university programs and lectures by visiting U.S. scholars. U.S. journalism professors on Fulbright grants have played and continue to play an important role in journalism education in the new East/Central Europe and the former Soviet Republics, supplementing indigenous faculty.

In the summer of 1990, the International Media Fund was created by the President's Initiative on East/Central Europe. Its primary duty was aid to mass media organizations and journalism education/training institutions. It has carried out over 103 projects in 14 countries, providing media equipment and training and facilitating the establishment of educational facilities.[91]

The Freedom Forum (formerly the Gannett Foundation) also entered the journalism training world of East/Central Europe and former Soviet Republics in May 1992 when it opened its European office in Zurich, Switzerland. It established the valuable Freedom Forum News Libraries (See earlier discussion), facilitated the establishment of independent journalism centers, and sponsored lectures at universities. It is aiding university journalism programs in a number of ways, inclusive of its sponsorship of the new East/Central European Network of Journalism Educators. The Freedom Forum also instituted its International Professional and Student Journalism Program that allows journalists and journalism students from East/Central Europe and the former Soviet Union to spend up to a semester in a U.S. university journalism program.

Major players in the evolution of mass media and journalism education in the regions include the Soros Foundation for an Open Society, the German Marshall Fund, the World Press Freedom Committee, the Center for Foreign Journalists, and the John S. and James L. Knight Foundation. Other U.S. organizations that have sponsored or carried out a variety of journalism education programs include:

National Endowment for
  Democracy
International Republican Institute
Atlantic Council of the United
  States
National Forum Foundation
U.S.-Baltic Foundation
Institute for Democracy in Eastern
  Europe
U.S. Agency for International
  Development (USAID)

Foundation for American
  Communication
World Association for Public
  Opinion Research
National Democratic Institute
Environmental Health Center
Radio Free Europe/Radio Liberty
Internews
Thomson Foundation

U.S. university and private and governmental organizations should continue their aid. Having already invested enormous financial and personnel resources, they have a vested interest and obligation to complete the process of helping change mass media and journalism in these regions. All indications are that the major contributors will remain active: The Soros Foundations has permanent offices in the region; the Freedom Forum established a European office to oversee its programs in the regions; the Knight Foundation has established fellowships; U.S. AID and the U.S. Information Agency and the VOA International Training program continue to support a variety of programs for journalists. U.S. universities, too, will continue their cooperation and collaboration, having established solid formal and informal institution-to-institution as well as faculty-to-faculty relationships.

CONCLUSION

There is a sense that university and vocational journalism education will remain an integral part of the landscape of the new East/Central Europe and the new nations of the former Soviet Union. However, what these programs will teach, with what success, and what role they will play within academia, mass media, and society at large is an open question. It will depend in large measure on how successfully each society, its sociopolitical and cultural leadership, its mass media, and journalists will be in agreeing on a definition of journalism's meaning, practice, expected effects, and standards. They will also depend on the role assumed by existing journalism education institutions and their faculty and the forcefulness with which they will play it out.

Additionally, the future and nature of journalism education at the university will depend on the ability of East/Central European and former Soviet Republic institutions of higher learning to establish graduate degree programs in journalism/mass communication (inclusive of PhD level programs) that will feed the need for academically prepared faculty. In fact, one of the major assistance packages the West should focus on is the training of PhDs in Western universities who can then enhance and augment the corps of journalism/mass communication educators and establish and service their own graduate programs. The future and nature of journalism education will further depend on the relationship these institutions develop with a mass media that can serve as a model for and an additional bona fide training ground for journalism students, one that is on the level with that of the academic side of journalism education. As part of this process of developing a working relationship, they should establish continuing education programs for working journalists, programs that are in high demand.

Journalism education programs also needed to resolve their status in academia and gain a level of respect within it now enjoyed by the traditional disciplines. In that sense they need to move in the direction many Western European programs have inched toward since World War II.[91]

U.S. and other Western aid to journalism education and the education of journalists should continue. It should be an assistance program that seeks to enhance the relationship between the mass media and the journalism education institutions. It should be rooted in these institutions, and it should be a long-term commitment. As part of this relationship, growing collaboration in media/journalism research projects would also enhance the status of journalism/mass communication educators from East/Central European and the former Soviet Republics by producing work that has utility in media policy making and the practical, day-to-day operations of the news media. In this context, the West can and should aid research projects and the development of academic and professional journals and books serving the mass communication/journalism field.

Other areas in which the West can and should aid the evolution of journalism education and journalism is increasing student exchanges, continued technical assistance to universities, and help with establishing programs in high demand areas such as advertising and public relations.

Finally, the success or failure of journalism education programs in East/Central European and in the former Soviet Republics will also largely depend, perhaps more fundamentally, on economic and political developments in these nations. Lack of economic development will mean the continued absence of financial assistance to universities and other educational institutions, a fact that will drive faculty and prospective faculty to other professions and make it impossible for them to acquire modern equipment and facilities necessary for journalism training. The absence of some progress toward a liberal democracy could affect the role and nature of journalism and, in turn, the evolution of journalism education.

The development of journalism education programs and of journalism should be of high interest to Western European and U.S. journalism educators and journalists. They should because it can inform the continuing debates in the United States and in Western Europe about the role, nature, and effects of journalism and journalism education in these regions. They provide a lesson in transition, in mass media roles within this transition, and offer an opportunity for self-examination through the lens of struggling journalism education systems.

NOTES & REFERENCES

1. The term *post-Communist* encompasses the authoritarian (i.e. pre-1989) and the pluralist (i.e. post-1989) post-Communist periods, as Brzezinski (1989) defines the term. Zbigniew Brzezinski. *The Grand Failure. The Birth and Death of Communism in the Twentieth Century*. New York: Collier Books.
2. Owen V. Johnson, "Czech Republic," "Slovakia," in *Looking to the Future: A Survey of Journalism Education in Central and Eastern Europe and the Former Soviet Union*. Arlington, VA: The Freedom Forum, August 1994, pp. 22-26.
3. Svennik Hoyer, Epp Lauk, and Peeter Vihalemm, *Towards a Civic Society. The Baltic Media's Long Road to Freedom*. Tartu, Estonia: Nota Baltica Ltd., 1993.
4. Janos Horvat, "The East European Journalist," *Journal of International Affairs*, Vol. 45, 1991, pp. 191-200.
5. Ray Hiebert, "Hungary," in *Looking to the Future: A Survey of Journalism Education in Central and Eastern Europe and the Former Soviet Union*. Arlington, VA: The Freedom Forum, August 1994, pp. 32-37.
6. Ray Hiebert, "Belarus," "Estonia," "Hungary," "Latvia," "Lithuania," and "Ukraine," in *Looking to the Future: A Survey of Journalism Education in Central and Eastern Europe and the Former Soviet Union*. Arlington, VA: The Freedom Forum, August 1994, pp. 7-12, pp. 27-31, pp. 32-37, pp. 38-41, and pp. 42-45; see also Paul Lendvai, *The Bureaucracy of Truth. How Communist Governments Manage the News*. Boulder, CO: Westview Press, 1981.

7. Peter Gross and Stephen King, "Romania's New Journalism Programs Raise Old Questions for United States," *Journalism Educator,* Vol. 48, No. 3, 1993, pp. 24-31.
8. Jerome Aumente, Notes to the author. Mimeo, January 15, 1994.
9. Ekaterina Ognianova *"Journalism Education at Sofia University in Bulgaria."* Mimeo, 1994.
10. Dean Mills, "Russia," in *Looking to the Future: A Survey of Journalism Education in Central and Eastern Europe and the Former Soviet Union.* Arlington, VA: The Freedom Forum, August 1994, pp. 60-70.
11. John C. Merrill, *Global Journalism.* New York: Longman Publishers, 1983.
12. Hiebert, 1994, *op. cit.;* Hoyer, Lauk, Vihalemm, op. cit.
13. Hiebert, 1994, *op. cit.*
14, Lendvai, *op. cit.;* Tomasz Goban-Klas, *The Orchestration of the Media. The Politics of Mass Communications in Communist Poland and the Aftermath.* Boulder, CO: Westview Press, 1994; Peter Gross, "The Still Applicable Totalitarian Theory of the Press: The Case of Romania," in Slavko Splichal, et al., eds., *Democratization and the Media.* Ljubljana, Yugoslavia: TV Capodistria, 1990, pp. 94-106; Peter Gross, "Romania," in David Paletz, Karol Jakubowicz, and Pavao Novosel, eds., *Glasnost and After. Media and Change in Central and Eastern Europe.* Cresskill, NJ: Hampton Press, 1995, pp. 199-220; Peter Gross (1996) *Mass Media in Revolution and National Development: The Romanian Laboratory.* Ames, IA: Iowa State University Press, 1996.
15. Edith Spielhagen, "Mass Media and Politics in East Germany: Observations of a Revolution." Paper presented at the International Communication Association Annual Conference, Washington, DC Mimeo, May 27, 1993.
16. Dean Mills, "Mass Media as Vehicles of Education, Persuasion, and Opinion Making...in the Communist World," in L. John Martin and A.G. Chaudhary, eds., *Comparative Mass Media Systems.* New York: Longman, 1983, pp. 167-186; Oleg Manaev, "The U.S.S.R. (Republic of Belarus)," in David Paletz, Karol Jakubowicz, and Pavao Novosel, eds., *Glasnost and After. Media and Change in Central and Eastern Europe.* Cresskill, NJ: Hampton Press, 1995, pp. 65-96; H.G. Skilling, *Samizdat and an Independent Society in Central and Eastern Europe.* Columbus: Ohio State University Press, 1989.
17. Rudolf Prevratil, "Czechoslovakia," in David Paletz, Karol Jakubowicz and Pavao Novosel, eds., *Glasnost and After. Media and Change in Central and Eastern Europe.* Cresskill, NJ: Hampton Press, 1995, pp. 149-172.
18. Mills, August 1994, *op. cit.*
19. Hiebert, August 1994, *op. cit.*
20. Karol Jakubowicz, "Solidarity and media reform in Poland," *European Journal of Communication,* vol. 5, No. 2-4, 1990, pp. 333-354.
21. Jerome Aumente, Notes to the author. Mimeo, January 15, 1994.
22. Owen V. Johnson, "Media." Unpublished manuscript. Mimeo, 1992.

23. Owen V. Johnson, "Czechs and Balances: Mass Media and the Velvet Revolution," in Jeremy Popkin, ed., *Media and Revolution*. Lexington: University of Kentucky Press, 1995, pp. 220-232.

24. Prevratril, *op. cit.*

25. Hiebert, 1994, *op. cit.*

26. Dean Mills, Notes to the author. Mimeo, January 29, 1995.

27. Johanna Neuman, *The Media: Partners in the Revolution of 1989.* Washington, DC: The Atlantic Council of the United States, June 1991; see also Gross, 1995, op. cit.

28. J. F. Brown, *Hope and Shadows. Eastern Europe After Communism.* Durham, NC: Duke University Press, 1994, p. 34.

29. Gross, 1995, *op. cit.*

30. Karol Jakubowicz, "Media as Agents of Change," in David Paletz, Karol Jakubowicz, and Pavao Novosel, eds., *Glasnost and After. Media and Change in Central and Eastern Europe.* Cresskill, NJ: Hampton Press, 1995, pp. 19-48.

31. Gertrude J. Robinson, "East Germany," in David Paletz, Karol Jakubowicz, and Pavao Novosel, eds., *Glasnost and After. Media and Change in Central and Eastern Europe.* Cresskill, NJ: Hampton Press, 1995, pp. 173-198.

32. Mike Buffington, "A Needs Assessment: The Press of the Georgian Republic," in Al Hester, et al. eds., *The Post-Communist Press in Eastern and Central Europe: New Studies.* Athens, GA: The James M. Cox, Jr., Center for International mass Communication Training and Research, The University of Georgia, 1992, pp. 147-158.

33. Gross, 1995, *op. cit.*; Gross, 1996, *op. cit.*

34. Ibid; Goban-Klas, op. cit.; Ildiko Kovats and Gordon Whiting, "Hungary," in David Paletz, Karol Jakubowicz, and Pavao Novosel, eds., *Glasnost and After. Media and Change in Central and Eastern Europe.* Cresskill, NJ: Hampton Press, 1995, pp. 97-128.

35. Karol Jakubowicz, "From Party Propaganda to Corporate Speech? Polish Journalism in Search of a New Identity," *Journal of Communication,* Vol. 43, No. 3, 1992, pp. 64-74.

36. Hans Mathias Kepplinger and Renate Kocher, "Professionalism in the Media World?," *European Journal of Communication,* Vol. 5, No. 2-3, 1990, pp. 285-311.

37. Brown, *op. cit.*, p. 34.

38. Gross and King, *op. cit.*

39. The author has met with journalism educators at universities in Poland, Hungary, Romania, Albania, Bulgaria, Slovenia, and the Czech Republic.

40. Maurice Fliess, ed., *Looking to the Future: A Survey of Journalism Education in Central and Eastern Europe and the Former Soviet Union.* Arlington, VA: The Freedom Forum, 1994.

41. From discussions with journalism educators, students and administrators in Eastern European journalism schools in the last six years.

42. Mills, 1994, *op. cit.*

43. Ognianova, *op. cit.*

44. Byron T. Scott and Ekaterina Ognianova, "Bulgaria," in *Looking to the Future: A Survey of Journalism Education in Central and Eastern Europe and the Former Soviet Union*. Arlington, VA: The Freedom Forum, August 1994, pp. 13-17.

45. Peter Gross, "Albania," "Moldova," "Poland," "Romania," and "Slovenia," in *Looking to the Future: A Survey of Journalism Education in Central and Eastern Europe and the Former Soviet Union*. Arlington, VA: The Freedom Forum, August 1994, pp. 4-6, pp. 48-49, pp. 50-55, pp. 56-59, and pp. 77-78.

46. Johnson, 1994, *op. cit.*

47. Mills, 1994, *op. cit.*

48. Hiebert, 1994, *op. cit.*

49. *Ibid.*

50. Scott and Ognianova, *op. cit.*

51. Mills, 1994, *op. cit.*

52. Gross, 1994, *op. cit.*

53. Hiebert, 1994, *op. cit.*

54. Johnson, 1994, *op. cit.*

55. Fliess, Ed., *op. cit.*

56. Hiebert, 1994, *op. cit.*

57. Goban-Klass, *op. cit.*; Slavko Splichal, *Media Beyond Socialism*. Boulder, CO: Westview Press, 1994.

58. Hoyer, Lauk, Vihalemm, op. cit.; Slavko Splichal, John Hochheimer, and Karol Jakubowicz, eds., *Democratization and the Media. An East-West Dialogue*. Ljubljana, Yugoslavia: TV Capodistria, G. Szoboszlai, ed., 1990 *Democracy and Political Transformation: Theories and East-Central European Realities*. Budapest, Hungary: Hungarian Political Science Association, 1991.

59. Hiebert, 1994, *op. cit.*

60. Gross, 1994, *op. cit.*

61. Ognianova, *op. cit.*

62. Mills, 1994, *op. cit.*

63. Johnson, 1994, *op. cit.*

64. Byron T. Scott, *"Bringing American Journalism to the Balkans."* Paper presented at Meredith Corporation, Des Moines, IA. Mimeo, July 9, 1993.

65. Fliess, Ed., *op. cit.*

66. Johnson, 1994, *op. cit.*

67. Gross and King, *op. cit.*

68. Hiebert, *op. cit.*

69. Gross, 1994, *op. cit.*, interview with the dean of the journalism faculty.

70. Johnson, 1994, *op. cit.*

71. Mills, 1994, *op. cit.*

72. Gross and King, *op. cit.*

73. Mills, 1994, *op. cit.*

74. Gross, 1994, *op. cit.*, interview with the director of the Journalism Institute.

75. Mills, 1994, *op. cit.*

76. Sherry Ricchiardi, "Croatia," in *Looking to the Future: Survey of Journalism Education in Central and Eastern Europe and the Former Soviet Union.* Arlington, VA: The Freedom Forum, August 1994, pp. 19-21.

77. Hiebert, 1994, *op. cit.*

78. Mills, 1994, *op. cit.*

79. Johnson, 1994, *op. cit.*

80. *Ibid.*

81. "Slovakia," Looking to the Future. . . , *op. cit.*

82. Gross, 1996, *op. cit.*

83. Gross and King, *op. cit.*

84. Johnson, 1994, *op. cit.*

85. Mills, 1994, *op. cit.*

86. Hiebert, 1994, *op. cit.*

87. Fliess, Ed., *op. cit.*

88. Aumente, 1994, *op. cit.*

89. Bobbie Win, Notes to the author. Mimeo, March 28, 1995.

90. Aurelius Fernandez, Notes to the author. Mimeo, March 8, 1995.

91. Gunter Reus and Lee B. Becker, "The European Community and Professional Journalism Training," *Journalism Educator*, Vol. 47, No. 4, 1993, pp. 4-12.

6

Lessons Learned and Predictions for the Future

Our goal in this book has been to find common denominators characterizing the mass media evolution during the singularly important years of transition in East/Central Europe from Communism to democracy, from 1989 to 1997. In this last chapter we examine the broad outlines we have discovered, to see what principles will help explain mass media in transition in all societies, including a model of the process to help understand relationships between social movements and media developments.

First we present some broad generalizations about East/Central Europe. We have found that, despite obstacles of all sorts, on the whole the media have made significant strides toward freedom. At the end of 1996, there was still considerable financial instability; there were still attempts by governments at media control; there was still considerable hostility toward journalists who would expose unpopular truths, sometimes expressed in the murder of journalists by mafia gangs rather than exile to Siberia by Communist apparatchiks. However, one could say that financial instability, government manipulation, and public anger toward messengers who bring bad news are universal, characteristic of the United States media as well.

We have discovered many ways in which the post-Communist press of East/Central Europe resembles the 19th-century press in the United States. A partisan press still exists, as it did in the United States. Yet there is an apparent move away from dependence on political parties, as happened in the United States. There is also a growing commercialization of news, perhaps as a result of increased independence from political parties that was also characteristic of the United States.

In fact, commercial motives (exploiting the facts to make a profit) seem more apparent than either journalistic motives (telling the facts so readers will be informed enough to make up their own minds) or political motives (shaping the facts to influence the public). But this, too, is in a state of flux, as it was in the United States.

As we have said elsewhere in this book, one cannot make sweeping generalizations covering all countries of the region. Russia is obviously quite different from all the others, because of its size and its power. The Balkans in the south are very different from the Baltics in the north. The countries on the western side of the region are different from those on the eastern side.

In the case of Russia, it may be moving more easily toward a journalism of fact and investigation than most of the other countries because Russian journalists have had more real professional education and training. In fact, by the end of the transition period we are writing about here, there has been quite an outbreak of good investigative reporting in Russia.

Finally, we should point out that other scholars have also attempted to find generalities about media in transition in East/Central Europe, and our effort here is to present our typology and then provide a concluding analysis of the differences and similarities in ours and other models of the process.

We have designed a typology with six parts: media systems, media laws, media audiences, media content, media economics, and media personnel (see the accompanying chart for a brief summary).

MEDIA SYSTEMS

For the most part, the mass media of East/Central Europe had been originally formed within an authoritarian socio-political-economic structure. Before Communism, with few exceptions, the countries in this region of the world were monarchical, top-down societies, and the mass media that existed were either privately or publicly owned but in either case operated with the permission and largely for the benefit of the country's rulers. One exception to this was Czechoslovakia, which for a time early in the 20th century had a lively democracy with more press freedom than the region had ever experienced. In this authoritarian period for most of the region, a highly literate society supported a variety of newspapers, magazines, and books, and the enlightened monarchies permitted a variety of opinions to be expressed.

With the takeover of the Communist system, the media were removed from the hands of private owners and made completely subordinate to the party and state. Some media might have represented government, others the party, others trade unions, but no matter the external representation, ownership was "public" and control was completely under the authority of the party's leaders and apparatchiks. As radio and television emerged in this period, they developed completely within the totalitarian notion of "public" ownership and party domination.

With the end of Communism, during the years of transition, no single media system came to dominate. Rather, what typified the transition period was a situation that allowed a variety of media systems to operate more or less simultaneously. The only thing that vanished completely was the absolute totalitarian control by a single political party. However, political or partisan media flourished; even the old communist party continued to control some media, and with the fragmentation of politics into a multitude of parties, each political entity felt entitled to control its own media.

Print media, in particular, operated in a variety of systems. A partisan media system developed as political parties were often able to maintain some sort of print communication, either simple and limited-audience occasional magazines and books or full-blown daily newspapers, some with large circulations.

Print media also developed for purely commercial reasons in a classic free-market system. Newspapers, magazines, and books were published by entrepreneurs who had no interest other than making a profit. Gossip, sensation, and pornography were used to build an audience. Advertising was developed to sell goods and services. In some economies, some media were able to support themselves entirely with advertising, but these were exceptional situations, for economic reasons (as we discuss later in this chapter).

The transition to a private broadcasting system was the hardest to achieve. With no tradition of private broadcasting, it was easier for new governments to take radio and television away from the Communist party and turn them instead into instruments for the support and purposes of the new party in power. As time went on during the transition, public pressure for nongovernment broadcasting developed in many societies, aided and abetted by opposition political parties and groups seeking political influence, by commercial interests seeking a share of broadcasting's advertising gold mine, and by the public at large seeking more varied and interesting programming.

One by one the transition governments had to give up their monopoly position in radio and television. By the end of the transition period considered here, broadcasting was operating under three different systems in the region, with some countries more characterized by one broadcast system than another.

"Public" broadcasting, of the kind typified by the BBC in the United Kingdom or NPR/PBS in the United States, was probably the preferred model by most of the audiences in most of East/Central Europe. That model most nearly fit the people's broadcasting experience with and interest in programs of high culture, in-depth information, and informed debate.

Commercial broadcasting, of the kind typified by U.S. stations and networks, was growing, however, with sitcoms and soap operas gaining audiences, and advertising increasing, in spite of the fact that most East/Central Europeans traditionally eschewed a materialism based on hard-sell marketing. The United States' TV programs and movies were available to these broadcast operators at a much lower price than it would have cost to produce their own indiginous programs, and these U.S. shows gained the wide audience advertisers sought.

Official broadcasting, however, still continued in much of the region. Many governments held onto some channels and frequencies and facilities. In some cases, religion came to be a new kind of official broadcaster, with Poland certainly the best example.

It is doubtful that any one media system will come to dominate East/Central Europe in the near future. If anything withers away, it will probably be the partisan press. As in the United States, television may well serve to shift public attention from political ideologies to pragmatic issues, from ideals to personalities, leaving purely partisan media without an audience. Television may change values as well, as people spend more time with sitcoms than ballet, more time with tabloid news than analysis and commentary, more time being entertained than being informed.

If these developments occur, partisan media and "public" media may give way to commercial media, and the commercial media may pressure official government or religious media out of business for purely economic reasons, and a purely commercial media system would be the end result. But it is still too early to predict that outcome.

MEDIA LAWS

Ideally, press freedom and independence grow out of a system without cumbersome media laws or censorship restrictions. Constitutional protection of freedom of the press expressed in the simplest and most concise terms of the First Amendment has served the United States well since its democratic birth in the 18th century. Laws to govern press action in times of war, or when national security is threatened, may be exceptions to this, but are rarely, sparingly and only reluctantly imposed.

As for press transgressions, a body of libel law has built up incrementally from cases brought into the courts by individuals or organizations who feel they have been unjustly maligned and demand press retractions and monetary damages. On the other side, press freedoms have been better defined by the media's ability to defend their actions successfully in court.

The Central and East European region, by contrast, presents a melange of national media laws, a weed patch that has grown out of a variety of traditions and objectives. The most onerous are those that were designed in a totalitarian atmosphere of control that spread throughout the Communist bloc following World War II and which undermined individual expressions of opinion or reporting by the news media, print, or electronic mediums.

Underlying many of these actions was the overall Leninist philosophy that the news media and most channels of information were to serve the state, and journalists were there to primarily facilitate this objective.

In every country of the Soviet bloc there were elaborate laws that set forth how the news media should function, and the list of banned topics grew and grew. Anything that put the operations of the state in a negative light were generally forbidden, sometimes reaching the point of the ludicrous, more often dangerously infringing on the right of a people to get the information and informed opinion they needed to survive and protect themselves in today's complex society.

News institutions were authorized by law, and those that operated outside this circle were treated harshly. All means of newsgathering, processing, production, and distribution were strictly controlled in favor of the party and the state.

Overt censorship, with censors red pencilling every word, paragraph, and page existed in times of greatest potential rebellion, was not uncommon. But more often, a process of covert selfcensorship evolved in which the news practitioners themselves did the censoring, picking up on the nuances of what the regime wanted.

A process of reward and punishment was often "de facto" rather than "de jure". Editors were carefully selected and trained in universities designed as propaganda training centers rather than in independent journalism education programs founded on principles of press freedom, objectivity, balance, and robust reporting of news, regardless of who might be offended, as long as it was accurate and true.

Licensing in various forms was often an underpinning for the controlled media. In order to practice as journalists, individuals might be
accredited through a complex system of recruitment, training, and required
membership in journalism associations sanctioned by the state. As a journalist moved up the ladder toward the top editorships or broadcast management positions, Communist party membership or the blessing and title
of "nomenklatura" bestowed on those who were not party members but
considered safe adherents and supporters of the party, received the choice
positions and other perks of the controlled society. Those who fell from
grace were reprimanded, fired from their jobs, or in the most extreme cases
jailed or exiled during periods of martial law or particular tension.

After the democratic changes began in 1989 in the
Central/Eastern European regions, the Berlin Wall tumbled in a vastly
symbolic way that signaled the opening of a closed society that once had
smothered much of the European continent from its central heartland to
its eastern-most regions in a stifling confinement.

Adherents of a free and open society focused on abolishing censorship laws as a primary first target. Press laws that had become second nature in almost every country were also heavily scrutinized and
targets of dismantling or revision, although this proved more difficult.

Former Communist nations, without a recent tradition of press
freedom and responsibility, feared that immediate elimination of press
laws governing journalistic conduct might lead to chaos and unfair
maligning of innocent individuals and their reputations. Even by 1996,
many of these press laws, or large chunks of them, were still on the
books. Often the former Soviet bloc nations were engaged in arduous
rewriting or initial drafting of new constitutions that were a necessary
precursor to press freedoms and a vetting of the press laws.

As a result, some countries after the fall of Communism sought
to introduce stringent rules defining who might use the title of journalists, the level of education required, and even the number of years of
apprenticeship before one could carry the title of "journalist," or the
span of experience required of top editors to hold such titles.

To counterbalance this, Western advisors from the United States
and other countries constantly urged that any such restrictions be avoided. Certification or licensing also carried the double-edged threat of
decertification and forfeiture of the license, it was argued, and was a
grave threat to press freedom.

The interchange has set off lively and beneficial debates that can
resonate on both sides. U.S. advisors, for example, could admirably argue
for unfettered press freedom, but they had to answer well-meaning skeptics
in Central/East Europe, who demanded to know what protections for the
individual or group exist against the raw power and abuse of the press.

Press laws are not uniformly opposed in all democratic nations, and critics of the U.S. news media often argue that extremes of sensationalism, invasion of privacy, failure to fully, promptly, and prominently correct published or broadcasted mistakes cry out for some legal guidelines, not just self-regulation. Then, too, the reporting of criminal investigations, naming of suspects, and all of the requirements of care needed to ensure free press and fair trial present great challenges for dealing with these concerns.

Today, the robust discussions being carried on in the Central and East European nations regarding these issues reflects an inevitable process that will confront any other nation or sector of nations globally who shift from a controlled or totalitarian society to a free and open one. The exercise also confronts the more senior democratic nations seeking to provide guidance and counselling to the newer entrants into the democratic circle with reason to reflect on their own performance and need for improvement.

As these debates ensued, it became clear that press laws would not disappear with light-switch, on–off speed, as much as the advocates of full democracy demanded. It took time to develop a cadre of well-trained and educated journalists who could act responsibly and fairly, giving access to all segments of their society, even their former enemies. It also took time for the courts to find their footing in a democratic setting and for a body of law to develop through adjudication of libel and slander cases.

Finally, gradual and slow was the ability of professional journalists to find their own ethical footing, identify transgressors, and punish their colleagues through public censure and a tradition of apprenticeship, hiring and firing for ethical breaches of journalistic conduct.

BROADCASTING LAWS

Equally complex a problem, are the ways in which to reform broadcasting laws in the Central/Eastern European region against a backdrop of decades of government and party control. In many ways it has been easier to bring fresh air to the once-closed rooms of the print world. Variety and competition, and a minimum of legal requirements beyond registering a print publication for reasons of copyright protection or favorable postal distribution rates, are needed in publishing.

With the Central and Eastern European region confined to a finite and densely populated world region, the precious airwaves for broadcasting radio and television, and today the more technologically advanced wireless voice, video, and data communications require special care to preserve press freedom.

The pattern for the rewriting, even the loosening of stringent broadcast laws, which gave the state monopoly control over the airwaves, has been one of slow and reluctant change. Licensing of independent radio and television stations proceed far more slowly in the several years following the abrupt changes of government after 1989.

Scarce airwave space made the creation of independent stations supported by commercial advertising rather than state subsidy and control far more difficult. Nations were reluctant to give up established state channels. State-controlled radio and television stations, already in place with staff, equipment and established audiences, took a controlling share of the fragile supply of paid advertising in an embryonic market economy.

However, with the infusion of domestic resources and foreign capital and expertise, donated equipment and training programs, the independent broadcast media have established a far more visible presence today. Laws privatizing broadcasting resources have been passed in most countries. Regulatory bodies free of executive or parliamentary interference to grant broadcast licenses and oversee fair and equitable use of the airwaves have appeared, although abuses of independence are still too many.

Laws to transform former state broadcasting into more independent public broadcasting entities of the British, French, Canadian, or U.S. tradition are vigorously being developed in the Central/Eastern European region. But much is still needed to protect the regulatory boards from arbitrary firings or manipulation by the government in power. Subsidized state television must find alternate ways of getting funding at a time when many nations in the region are facing grievous budget deficits, or a population reluctant to pay for broadcasting services through annual receiver set fees voluntarily paid.

The protection of news and documentary production staffs in the state-owned or controlled broadcasting outlets of the Central/Eastern European region is quite problematical. Decades of government control and staffs pliantly submissive to party demands and unyielding government leadership does not easily disappear. The same laws that create firewalls between the broadcast regulators are needed to protect the public or state broadcasters.

The Central/Eastern Europe must also confront the tendency of some of its parliaments to pass laws that seek to protect majority values in a country, even when this might mean imposing the values of one dominant dogma or religion in the nation on the content of broadcasting. Or it might mean openly democratic adherents of government suddenly imposing restraints on opponents who seek access to the airwaves as we saw in the 1996 coverage of the presidential elections in Russia in which Boris Yeltsin benefitted from a compliant broadcast media come to mind.

Finally, as news media become more advanced in their daily operations and sophisticated in their techniques, many print and broadcast professionals in the Central/Eastern European region are devoting, or should devote, more attention to access to information laws. Freedom of information laws that facilitate access to government information, laws that protect journalists and their sources of information are all essential to do investigative and entrepreneurial reporting. In this regard, specialists from the United States and other countries where such laws are well established are helping their journalistic counterparts in the Central and East European region.

MEDIA ECONOMICS

There are many economic engines driving the media changes in Central and Eastern Europe, and the implications for similar transformations in other global sectors undergoing comparable democratization are many. Perhaps the most wrenching changes deal with the need of a command economy similar to the one found in the Soviet bloc countries before 1989 to suddenly survive and flourish in a market-driven economy. Here news and information products, whether print or broadcast, or those encapsulated in newer media such as the Internet, must find an audience willing to pay for them and advertisers ready to underwrite them to sell products.

In the Central/Eastern European region, the initial traumatic economic issue was how to move from a system in which publications and broadcast programs sanctioned and paid for by the Communist Party and its supporting governments could survive on their own. Many newspapers and periodicals that once were assured of their subsidies regardless of their demand by readers, and many broadcast programs that coasted along with or without major audiences, suddenly confronted competition for scarce resources.

The initial period of transition saw many such news and information products disappear. The difficulty of attracting adequate advertising was compounded by a lack of specialists in marketing and advertising. In addition, advertising presupposed a market-driven economy in which there were products to advertise and sell. First empty shelves had to be filled, and then a transition had to be made to an economic structure in which people had more money for goods and services and the ability to pick and choose. It was the equivalent of creating a railroad while the engine and cars were being built at the same time the track was laid and the customers enticed on board.

But with more robust market economies taking hold in the region, and a cadre of experts in advertising and marketing being trained in house or with the help of Western expertise, a source of steady funding for free and commercially supported media is gradually evolving.

State radio and television, gradually being transformed into a public television model of more independent and self-sustaining media, have taken a lion's share of commercial advertising. They are in place with staff, equipment, and broadcasting licenses. In addition, they usually have a base of guaranteed support from revenues derived from annual license fees paid by the public using television and radio.

In the Central/Eastern European region, there is concern that with state broadcasting siphoning off such advertising revenues, private commercial media find it even harder to get a foothold. In addition, print media must confront dangerous competition, in which scarce advertising revenue is being channeled away from them while broadcast audiences increase.

Although surviving the drubbing from decreased or totally eliminated public subsidies, the publications must often face a shrinking audience. Whereas before 1989 readers might buy two even three papers a day, they now may buy one or none, depending instead on television. Stagnant wages make it more difficult to buy multiple newspapers, and the costs of the papers per copy have also risen significantly without the former government subsidies.

As a matter of public policy, Central/Eastern European governments must face these concerns and decide whether some form of tax breaks or subsidy must be initiated to assist the print press. With broadcasting, legislation is needed to restrain the state-supported broadcasting while allowing an independent commercial broadcasting structure to survive and compete on a more level playing field.

The entire structure in the world of daily and weekly newspapers and periodicals, aside from outright cash subsidies, also benefitted from a Communist Party-supported infrastructure in which newsprint or magazine paper, inks, printing presses, wire services, the editorial buildings, the means of distribution, the kiosks, and other distribution avenues were provided as subsidy, and today are rapidly disappearing, or already gone. This economic vacuum must be filled with market-driven resources—not an easy task.

The Central/Eastern European nations also have experienced widely different levels of foreign investment in the media. Some countries such as Hungary and the Czech Republic received early infusions of foreign investment. Other countries such as Poland welcomed such investments, but also instituted more stringent controls and approached such investments more warily, even blocking sales of privatized papers if they threatened the ethnic information balance in the region confronting outside foreign investment.

Not surprisingly, media investors from Germany, France, Italy, and Scandinavia showed the greatest initial interest in investing in their neighbors, whereas to a lesser extent Great Britain and the United States did likewise. Where the United States did excel was in providing significant philanthropic grant funds for equipment and to encourage democratization of the news media through assistance to universities and media training centers in key and capital cities of the region.

Individual media launched joint ventures with their counterparts in the Central/Eastern European region, ranging from joint publications to translated insert material. Such ventures will continue as the shakeout continues to occur and the more prosperous media of the West join with counterparts from the Central and Eastern European regions.

With broadcasting, much more stringent laws in the Central/Eastern European region countries, reflecting similar caution in the West, put greater restrictions on economic investments and foreign ownership of television and radio properties in the C/BE. Direct broadcast satellites and other technologies that easily jump national boundaries, however, make such economic media protectionism more difficult. The emergence of the Internet as a global spiderwork of communication, news and information will also have a growing impact on such economic issues.

As the Central/Eastern European countries seek to build market-supported media they must confront massive attitudinal changes in their readership and audiences. Too often, the populace associated advertising as needless material clutter—Western evils that ought to be avoided in their socialized cultures. Now this is gradually changing as goods are more plentiful, services more competitive, and advertising commonplace.

Another potential roadblock is a population that often associated advertisements and public pronouncements with the hard sell of discredited governmental regimes. The leap of faith from distrusted governments using the media to manipulate public opinion to advertisers promising love, success, and sex in their toiletries or deodorants is not an easy one to make. But a skeptical population is suddenly forced to deal with such advertising promises nonetheless.

JOURNALISTS

The popular U.S. view was that the Communist system, all of its institutions, and the application of the Marxist-Leninist philosophy were relatively monolithic. Of course, although basic similarities in approach and even end results existed, there were significant differences from one Communist country to another. The preparation of those who ended up working for the Communist media in the various countries under consideration is a case in point.

In pre-1989 days, the minimum requirements were that the journalist be a party member or at least be willing to tow the line at the most elementary level. Beyond these minimum "qualifications," in some countries like the Soviet Union, the completion of a degree in journalism at one of the universities was one requirement, but not one altogether essential as long as one had earned a university degree in some discipline germane to the media work to be done. In other countries such as Hungary or Romania, a degree in journalism was only obtainable from the Communist Party school, at which the emphasis was far more ideological than professional. Most of their journalists did not hold journalism degrees.

The end result of this varied way of preparing those who would be reporters and editors was that the corps of journalists from East Berlin to the Sakhalin Islands varied in their professionalism to the same degree the Yugo may be different from a Mercedes. However, in either case, professionalism was defined within the parameters set by the definition of media roles in a Marxist-Leninist socialist society—whether of the Communist totalitarian type or the post-Communist authoritarian one.

For instance, some journalists in the Soviet Union were competent and professional investigative reporters. The same may have been true in other nations within the communist family. But their professionalism, even when present, stopped when the politico-ideological requirements demanded its deprofessionalization. Not to report something that was discovered, to put a twist to it, to lie about it outright, or to actively dissimulate on the subject was part and parcel of the requisites of "professionalism" in the journalism practiced east of the Elba.

Post-1989 journalists who continued their work, now for a media that was quickly multiplying in numbers, in originating points and in sociocultural and politico-ideological intent, were joined by new journalists who entered media work coming from a range of work and educational backgrounds. Few had any formal journalism training, and those who did received this training from the Communist-era journalism schools, with the old curricula, textbooks, and instructors. The majority by 1996 either had no formal training at all or were (a) products of the Communist-era journalism schools, with the old curricula, textbooks, and instructors; or (b) the newly established programs whose curricula, textbooks, and instructors were also questionable in regard to their ability to produced bona-fide journalists for a media whose role(s) are consonant with an open and democratizing society. Most of the new journalists who stepped into the profession after 1989 were in their 20s and 30s, and had earned a university degree already, many of them in the engineering fields.

Whatever their background, educational and professional preparation, the post-1989 journalists share a work pattern and a professional existence:

1. The personal and politicized approach is present in the service of a now diversified media
2. Factual reporting is minimally practiced with some exceptions, on some occasions and subjects, for some media by some journalists.
3. Some solid investigative reporting is being carried out.
4. The economic factors (low pay scales, the death and birth of new media outlets) has journalists (a) playing musical chairs and moving from one media outlet to another, (b) working more than one job and sometimes crossing from one medium to another, and (c) at times crossing that not-always thick line between journalism and public relations.
5. The absence of defined media roles does not allow for the definition of a universally accepted ethic or an accepted process by which journalism is to be practiced.
6. Professional solidarity is relatively limited with journalists having the opportunity of joining a variety of professional organizations whose activities are often limited, particularly in regard to the defining and enforcing of professional standards and behavior.
7. The journalists' loyalties are with (a) their own interests and ambitions, (b) the media outlet they work for, (c) the politico-ideological interests held by the journalists and/or the party that also supports the media outlet, and (d) the audience. The question of how to instill democratic tendencies and responsibilities in a profession whose goals, parameters, training/education, and very raison d'etre have not been defined by still-reforming societies has not been answered.

The mix of older, Communist-era trained and bred journalists with the new, post-1989 introduced journalists often makes for a murky concoction that is difficult to distill into a new journalistic corps more apt to serve a transition to an open, democratic society. In most countries under consideration there is not yet a media outlet that can be considered an elite one from the standpoint of professionalism or the highest standards to be achieved and, therefore, to be emulated. Journalists have not yet put their own house in order, a not very surprising state of affairs given the disorder found all around them.

MEDIA CONTENT

Media content in pre-1989 East/Central Europe and the Soviet-republics ranged from the limited, ideological, and cult-of-personality-driven materials in Romanian and Albanian newspapers and broadcasts to the more varied one found in Soviet, Czechoslovak, and Hungarian media. On subjects of importance to the communist regimes, that is, domestic political matters, ideology, foreign affairs, the military, and the Communist leadership itself, media content was less a journalistic production than a careful public relations presentation. In some instances it was simply not included in the day's newspapers or broadcasts.

Also on subjects important to the Communist regimes and their leaders, the presentation was often couched in ambiguous terms and/or in the Orwellian language that required readers, listeners, and viewers to read between the lines to try and get to the real meaning of the messages disseminated. Long interviews and un-edited speeches by Communist leaders took up an inordinate amount of media time and space.

To one degree or another, and varying from country to country, all topics covered by the media had to pass a regime-outlined test to cull out anything that might suggest anti-socialism or anti-regime messages. In the majority of countries, the seal of approval was stamped on by official censors.

The fall of the Communist regimes opened the door for a completely uninhibited journalism. Media contents in East/Central European and former Soviet republics began resembling a grab bag whose contributors might have included the likes of grocery stores, K-Marts, toy stores, and Texas bordellos.

The pattern was almost uniform across the board: Contents remained highly politicized with the added ingredient of a multipartisanship to reflect the multiparty systems established after 1989. No subjects were taboo. No limits or few limits existed/exist on the nature of journalism practiced, the language used, and/or the targets of what became very personal journalism, vituperative, sometimes libelous and irresponsible.

The range of topics covered by the new post-1989 media increased sharply, testimony to growing civil societies, an array of political parties and politicians, privatizing economies, the figurative and literal opening of borders, the changing nature of domestic and foreign policy and its establishments and the opportunities to express a myriad of opinions and views. Contributions from foreign journalists and Westerners business people, academics, and others were also included after 1989, foreign television shows and films increased in number and variety, and lively television discussions on an array of topics filled the small screen.

Pictures of nude women became a regular staple in many newspapers and magazine, signaling a change in the media as well as in the former regimes' official puritanism.

There was no particular order to the media contents in the first few post-1989 years. As each media outlet began to define itself better, an order to their contents was established, but that too will change as the redefinition and reorientation continues.

MEDIA AUDIENCES AND TECHNOLOGIES

Audiences for mass media in East/Central Europe are changing, largely as a result of technology. Prior to Communism, the market for print media was fairly homogenius and monocultural. Most books, magazines, and even newspapers were aimed largely at uniform readers of educated, adult males. Only a few media were targeted for women and children, and even fewer for ethnic, religious, or political minorities.

Under Communism, religious and political communication was obviously even more marked by a single message for a single audience. Indeed, the Communists developed the most massive media system and largest audience in human history. The major Soviet newspapers had daily print runs in the millions, and the leading Soviet broadcast programs reached audiences in the hundreds of millions. Under the Soviets, some specialization was encouraged, especially magazines aimed at women and at children, but most messages were meant for the masses.

The end of Communist domination came at a time in human history marked by explosive changes in technologies. In fact, there was no doubt a connection, a cause-and-effect relationship, between changing communication technologies and the demise of a one-party totalitarian system. It was not too difficult for the Communists to bring total control to the print media, which required large expensive printing presses and complex distribution systems, both of which could easily be centralized and monopolized. It was also easy to dominate the early technologies of radio and television, again requiring enormously expensive equipment and a distribution system in which frequencies and channels could be easily controlled. (Radio and television sets, for example, could be manufactured so they would only receive the set government frequencies.)

However, the new communication technologies that began to proliferate in the 1960s, 1970s, and 1980s were much harder to centralize or control. The computer, an essential new technology, was seen as such a threat by the Communists that they sought to outlaw its use by average citizens, and as a result large parts of the communist world remained computer illiterate for a much longer period than did the West. (This in itself had disasterous economic consequences for the old Soviet Union, and instead of burying capitalism, as Kruschev had promised, the Soviets with their heads in the computer sand buried themselves.)

Other new technologies also came to East/Central Europe in spite of the Communist Party. Photo-offset lithography and xerography made printing inexpensive and impossible to centralize. Microchips made broadcast equipment easy to handle and cheap to acquire. Audio- and videotape recorders and players made inexpensive and amateur production possible. These new technologies created samizdat, the underground media that helped bring Communism down.

These new technologies also changed the audiences of mass media. Most important, they made *mass* media less relevant and *specialized* media more important. Samizdat themselves were highly personalized and specialized communications media, aimed at small, sometimes very small, audiences. Photocopy machines were outlawed in the Soviet Union to curb their use as printers of small subversive publications. VCRs were regarded as instruments of subversion, and, in fact, that is what they became as more people acquired hand-held cameras and recorders to make videos that were then bicycled around to small audiences, giving viewers another version of the news.

With the demise of Communism, and the end of measures to suppress the new media made possible by the new technologies, specialized media proliferated, especially print media. For the first time in this region, whole new audiences were created. The old had been large captive audiences, held to mass media by authoritarian and totalitarian systems. The new were small groups of individuals, free to seek out the specialized information or entertainment they wanted.

Under Communism, the old audiences had been forced to read daily newspapers, sometimes three or four a day. People were encouraged by the party to read the papers because they were the party's instrument of indoctrination and influence. The newspapers were heavily subsidized so they could be printed and delivered to each household for a fraction of their real costs. People could afford to read three or four newspapers a day, and by reading three or four they could glean glimpses of the truth "between the lines," as the common expression went.

With the end of government subsidies and the drastic increase in the cost of production and distribution, newspapers and other print media had to raise their prices. People could no longer afford to subscribe to three or four national newspapers. Readership of print media declined across the board. Instead of three or four, readers kept one newspaper subscription, perhaps bought a street-sales tabloid from time to time, and found new publications that provided them with the specialized information of their chosen interests. The newspaper they chose to keep was usually the one that now appealed to their political interests.

In sum, the audiences of print media were fragmented into various political groups and dozens, then hundreds, and ultimately thousands of special interest groups. In fact, these new audiences may be less well informed about the large picture of the world, better informed about their special interests, and perhaps more narrowly informed about political ideologies.

Audiences for broadcast media evolved in the same direction, although more slowly. By the time the transition from communism was in full bloom, most people in East/Central Europe had access to a dozen or more different radio stations—some local, some national, some international—and even more different television programming, through cable systems, satellite dishes, and direct broadcast satellites. Probably the largest media market of all was the proliferation of video stores where tapes could be rented for home viewing, a media use behavior pattern more fragmented and specialized than anything that had happened before.

In the future, if newspapers become more commercial and less political, if only a few major newspapers survive, and if they then strive to serve a large general audience with more general news and information, mass newspaper audiences may reappear. It seems unlikely that magazines will not continue to find specialized niche audiences as their best markets. It also seems likely that radio and television will find market success by programming for audiences who want less to be informed and influenced and more to be entertained.

Changes in Mass Media in East/Central Europe, 1900-1996

	Systems	Laws	Audience	Content	Economics	Journalists
Pre-Communist	Authoritarian	Royal Decrees	Homogeneous, reached with low technologies print only	Literary, analytical	Small business, private ownership	Politicians, literary writers, poets, university trained, high status
Communist	Totalitarian	Constitution with rules and regulations, specifying controls	Homogeneous, reached with print, radio, TV	Propagandistic	Large business, state ownership, centralized budget, government subsidy	Bureaucrats, party trained, low status
Transitional	Mixed	Drafting new constitutions and laws	Heterogeneous, reached with new technologies print, radio, TV, cable, VCR, satellite	Dissident, partisan, commercial, informational	Small & large business, private, state & party ownership, some free market, some subsidy	Mixture of old, new bureaucrats, literary/political journalists, entrepreneurs, some university, some untrained, some high status, some low status
Future	Libertarian, social responsibility, or mixed	Restrictive laws, or new constitution with guaranteed access and free expression	Heterogeneous or fragmented, reached with high technologies, including computers and world wide web	Partisan, commercial, informational	Small & large business, private ownership, free market	Mixture of journalists and entrepreneurs, university trained, professional, high status

Author Index

Subject Index

A

AB Konyvkiado, Hungarian publishing house, 66
"Adevarul", Romanian newspaper 60
Adrounas, Elena, 52, 53, 80, 88
Advertising, 96-97, 115, 119
Aksakova, Olga, 135
Albania, 12, 64, 65, 71, 87
  and journalism education/ training, 149, 159, 173
  media content, 198
  media progress in transition, 119, 136
Albanian communists, 31
Albanian journalists, 132
Albanian media
  Modeste, 87
Albanian television, 31-32
Antall, Josef, 83
Askar, Akaev, 132

Asyov, Ivan, 134n
Atheneum, Hungarian printing house, 69
Aumente, Jerome, 80, 82, 176
Austria, 68
Austrian
  media laws, 88
  overlords, 45
Azerbaijani Radio, 132

B

Baltic
  church assistance, 70
  independence, 57
  journalism education/training, 148, 150-51, 167
  media, general, 11, 25, 26
  news censorship, 54
  protests, 56, 72
  publications, 53
  states, 57